# SMOKE

## THE ROMANCE AND LORE
## OF CUBAN BASEBALL

# SMOKE

## THE ROMANCE AND LORE OF CUBAN BASEBALL

### MARK RUCKER AND PETER C. BJARKMAN

#### FOREWORD BY HANK AARON

DESIGN BY MARK RUCKER AND TODD RADOM

KINGSTON, NEW YORK     NEW YORK, NEW YORK

THIS BOOK IS FOR PEDRO URQUÍA, "OUR MAN IN HAVANA,"
AND THE BASEBALL FANS IN CUBA.

Peter C. Bjarkman:  p. 156 bottom-right, p. 202 top, p. 211 top, p. 215 all.

Bohemia Magazine, Havana:  p. 83.

Cubadeportes, S.A., Garcia Photo, Ltd.:  p. 20 right, p. 222 bottom, p. 224 bottom, p. 225 bottom-left,
p. 228 bottom-both, p. 229 top, p. 230 top-both, p. 231 top, p. 232 top-left & middle-left, p. 238 top-all.

Collection of Marshall Fogel:  p. 45 bottom.

I.N.D.E.R, Havana :  Title Page, p. 204, p. 221, p. 222 top, p. 224 bottom,
pp. 230-231, p. 232, p. 234 top-both, pp. 236-237 all.

National Baseball Library, Cooperstown:  p. 37 top, p. 45 top, p. 66, p. 84, p. 158 bottom, p. 159 right.

New York State Library:  p. 36 top.

Ralph Maya, Cuban Baseball Hall of Fame, Miami:  p. 116 middle-right, p. 208 top-right.

Récord Magazine,  I.N.D.E.R., Havana:  p. 219.

Osvaldo Salas. Roberto Salas:  pp. 182-183.

Transcendental Graphics:  all others.

Total/SPORTS ILLUSTRATED is a trademark of Time Inc. Used under license.

For information about permission to reproduce selections from this book,
please write to:
Permissions
Total/SPORTS ILLUSTRATED
105 Abeel Street
Kingston, New York, 12401

DESIGN: MARK RUCKER AND TODD RADOM

ISBN: 1-892129-32-9
Library of Congress Catalog Card Number: 99-63228

Printed in United States of America by World Color Book Services.
10 9 8 7 6 5 4 3 2 1

# ACKNOWLEDGEMENTS

What started as a vacation adventure soon became a publishing project during the first trip to Cuba, made with Mark's son Kriston Rucker, whose work as translator was invaluable. We were introduced to Havana by Robert Henry Walz, who first suggested the trip, and who provided critical information and presentations that helped prepare us for the venture. His introductions in Havana got everything started. Right off the bat, the man who got us where we needed to go, to meet who we needed to meet, was Ramón Leonardo Soto Morán. As Chairman of the Department of Nuclear Physics at the University of Havana, he knows more about quarks than curveballs. But utilizing his knowledge of his city and his society was critical to our very good start. And he has maintained his indispensability throughout the project. We had not been there for three days before we were in the offices of the then Secretario of the Federación Cubana de Beisbol, Lic. Domingo Zabala Más, who set the official process in motion for us. The next day we first met with Dr. Pedro Urquía Montano, Director of Development and Public Relations for Cubadeportes, the promotions division of INDER, Instituto Nacional de Deportes Educación Fisica y Recreación.

Dr. Urquía became our champion. Initially he worked to secure the approvals we needed to proceed. With the love of baseball as our bond, we began an extensive program of travel and research. In a number of carefully planned trips, we visited sites from one end of the island to the other, thanks much to the driving expertise of Cubadeportes' right-hand man, Eduardo. These ballpark tours provided many of the images for the book, and also brought insights into the game today, the game yesterday, and the pervasiveness of baseball in Cuban culture. The memories of our cross-country ventures are particularly special for us both. Pedro Urquía's contacts brought us to historical sites and provided photo opportunities unavailable otherwise. Along the way, he has given us suggestions, information, and extensive help. He truly has been "Our Man in Havana."

The Director of the Ligua Nacional de Béisbol, Carlos B. Rodríguez Acosta, has been most helpful in providing ballpark access and informational assistance. He has provided institutional help that was essential to the success of the project. We also greatly appreciate the help of Pedro Cabrera Isidrón, Director of Press and Advertising Projects for INDER, and of the photographer for *Récord* magazine, the official Cubadeportes publication, Armando Hernández López, who provided important photos from the 1960s through the 1990s. Ismael Sené was always willing to share his vast baseball knowledge, Cuban and American, along with his good humor and insight. He gave Mark a grand tour of Havana's historical baseball sites, visiting the Sabourín Monument, Tropical Stadium, and the sites of the lost stadia where so much diamond history was made. Jorge Chacón Alfonso, sports editor for *Bohemia* magazine, allowed his wonderful photo collection to be copied for use in the book. Jesús Suárez Valmaña, sports correspondent for Cubavision Internacional, provided further insights into the relationship of the game's past and present. His family is typical of many in Cuba, keeping history alive in words and pictures. He shared a number of journeys with us, as well as his expertise. Roberto Salas was generous with historical insights, connecting two generations of premier Cuban photographers, and visions of life in Cuba before and after the Revolution. Sigfredo Barros, sports writer for *Granma*, the nation's newspaper, was a constant companion at Havana's Estadio Latinoamericano, providing up-to-the-minute Cuban League statistics. His perceptions and analyses of the games in action were both entertaining and informative. Almost from the beginning Dr. Leonardo Soto Morán and his wife Olguita Chumpitaz Rivera helped us with the essentials of coordinating our information and obligations, showing us how to get around in Havana, helping with living arrangements, and always offering encouragement.

Others in Havana and in the U.S. who gave a helping hand or valuable information were Marcelo Sánchez R., President of the Peña Deportivo "Parque Central;" John S. Kavulich II, President of the U.S.-Cuba Trade and Economic Council; José Fuentes Ochoa; Rolando Sánchez of the Asociación Vitofílica Cubana. Peter is especially indebted to the historical and contemporary Cuban baseball expertise lent by Marcelo Sánchez in Havana and Milton Jamail in Austin, Texas. Ralph Maya helped make contacts with ballplayers from the 1950s Cuban Professional League who are now living in Florida. And members of the South Florida chapter of the Society for American Baseball Research graciously offered comments and advice.

And our gratitude goes especially to John Thorn and George Schlukbier of Total Sports, who had faith in this project long before the name Omar Linares was widely heard in the U.S. They have given us all possible assistance in making the book what we envisioned. The book was enhanced manyfold by Todd Radom's immediate understanding of the look we wanted and by his expert design work. And there were also the other folks at Total Sports, Kingston, especially Donna Harris. Larry Burke and Jed Thorn were copy editors, keeping us verbally and pictorially on target. There are many others who have helped along the way, and we heartily thank them, too, if not by name. The entire process has been a great adventure, and one we hope to recreate in the near future.

# CONTENTS

# FOREWORD
## HANK AARON

This book brings back a lot of fond memories for me. I've been to Cuba several times, and have always admired the strength of baseball's tradition there. You can see the island's love of baseball everywhere you go — on the playgrounds, at the packed stadiums, and in its leader, Fidel Castro.

I interviewed Fidel for a CNN documentary on Cuban baseball in 1996. Even though we came from different cultures, the spirit of baseball had a strong enough hold on each of us that we felt a bond from the start. One thing I found out very quickly was that Fidel's love of the game has nothing to do with politics or ideology. It is a genuine passion for the game, a passion he shares with his country and ours.

*Smoke* displays what Cuba's passion is all about, better than any book I've seen. The first baseball game ever played on the island took place 125 years ago, and the game has been woven into Cuba's heritage ever since. A lot has changed over those 125 years — on the island and in the world — but America's game has become the game of the Americas, and nowhere has it been played with more fervor and skill than in Cuba. This book tells the story of Cuban baseball in a way that makes 1900 seem not all that long ago, and makes 2000 glow with promise.

The heroes of Cuban baseball almost step out of the pages. The book doesn't just record what Esteban Bellán and Dolf Luque and Martín Dihigo accomplished during their careers; you could look that up in the encyclopedia. *Smoke* sends us back in time to stand alongside them on the field, to see how they went about their craft, to hear how they were revered in their country. Whether it's the early years of the game, or the Cold War era, or baseball in Cuba today, *Smoke* puts you right *there*. You can feel the heat.

Baseball is thriving. In the U.S., Mark McGwire, Sammy Sosa, and Ken Griffey Jr. showed us that anything is possible. In Cuba, the visit of the Baltimore Orioles opened up a door of diplomacy that had been closed for more than 40 years. Omar Linares and the Cuban team beat the O's in Baltimore, and proved that the stream of Cuban baseball talent runs as strong as ever.

The United States and Cuba are separated by a hundred miles of ocean, and many differences. But maybe one day soon baseball games between our countries will be ordinary events, with no special political or diplomatic considerations. And when baseball brings people together, nations may follow.

HANK AARON
July 1999

# SMOKE

## THE ROMANCE AND LORE OF CUBAN BASEBALL
## PETER C. BJARKMAN

*"I had heard that Cubans are a deeply religious people. In two days here [in Cuba] I have learned that baseball is their religion."* — **Sam Lacy, Baltimore Afro-American**

In balmy Cuba the baseball countryside is still a landscape of endless charms. For those tradition-minded North American fans altogether fed up with pro baseball's noisome commercialism, a trip around the Cuban ballpark circuit in midwinter — perhaps during the National Series championships which comprise the Cuban postseason — provides a truly refreshing escape into baseball's pristine past.

Here is an island ballpark world utterly devoid of treacly big-league fare: ear-piercing and even soul-numbing electronic Diamond Vision pre-game concerts, cavorting cartoon-style mascots, cookie-cutter shopping-mall stadia featuring intrusive luxury-box opulence and runaway beer and parking prices, plastic-grass outfields with synthetic warning tracks, and (most thoroughly distasteful of all) spoiled-rotten and poorly motivated million-dollar ballplayers. In Havana or Ciego de Avila or Cienfuegos — or perhaps Pinar del Río or Santiago de Cuba — the diamond action remains surprisingly pure, the off-the-field distractions are altogether minimal, and the game itself continues to thrive — as it also still does in our own fading childhood memories — at its own natural pace and rhythms.

One has to love a country where baseball is still played on real grass; where all the game-day entertainment is strictly confined to heaved and batted horsehide missiles, classy glovework, and mad dashes around the basepaths; where the only ballpark sounds are the ping of the aluminum bat (one sole distasteful Cuban compromise to modernism) and the slap of the leather and the lusty cheers of the hometown grandstand faithful; and where the naïve ballplayers themselves seem to compete more out of raw passion for the game than any acquired love of the lucre. There are no 10-story Diamond Vision scoreboards on Fidel Castro's island to overwhelm the senses and drown out the game's age-old endemic music. Cheering in Cuban ballparks is still innocently spontaneous and never orchestrated by garish electronic cues. For *aficionados* with traditionalist bents, the secretive island nation of sugarcane and salsa rhythms and Santería religious cults is thus also a rare fantasy trip straight back into baseball's seemingly lost innocence of a near-forgotten pre-television epoch.

All contentious politics aside, it is only in Fidel's modern-day socialist Cuba where one still finds the nineteenth-century Panamerican pastime anachronistically existing in its unadulterated and most pristine forms. Cuba may no longer provide much of a pipeline for island-bred major-league recruits, as it once did before Castro's 1959 communist revolution and before the Supreme Leader's decision to supplant professional ballplaying with a more patriotic amateur version, but it does nonetheless still promise an unparalleled fast-track escape to baseball's universally revered past.

Havana's mammoth 55,000-seat Estadio Latinoamericano (it was called "El Gran Estadio del Cerro" before the revolution) is itself a genuine throwback to earlier diamond fare. The ancient ballpark's electronic center field scoreboard features only dimly lit postings of lineups and linescores and is entirely devoid of video displays or between-inning commercial messages. Cuban ballplayers' uniforms are equally archaic, closely suggesting the modern-day industrial league or softball togs worn on sandlots here in the States. Havana fans remain intently focused on the unfolding game alone for nine full innings — or sometimes less, since Cuban baseball until recently featured aluminum bats and the Olympic 10-run rule after seven innings — and these local "fanaticos" seemingly commune joyfully with baseball's timeless rhythms, the ebb and flow of hits and outs and the mesmerizing regularity of heaves and tosses between pitcher and catcher. In a nation experiencing severe material shortages, baseball still serves as a most welcome and also fully indulged national panacea.

Of course, there are stark differences from old-time North American baseball that one visiting an island ballpark cannot fail to notice. The outfield wall decorations of Cuban parks — often crudely painted slogans in stark white or yellow — urge spectators to remain loyal to the four-decade-long peoples' revolution and thus to the still-reigning spirit of institutionalized socialism. A nationwide paper shortage throughout the 1990s has meant no printed scorecards or glossy team yearbooks for fan consumption and thus also no concourse souvenir stands or grandstand vendors patrolling bleacher aisles. Bleacher beer and soft drink sales are also unheard of, though in some parks beer (in flimsy waxed paper cups) can be purchased behind the grandstands and coffee vendors (with Thermos bottles of mud-thick espresso) do regularly roam among the box seats.

On the field itself, team rosters in the Cuban League represent geographical regions and players are therefore never traded among league teams. In Havana or Camaguey or Matanzas the ballplayers actually can be recognized without a scorecard even from one season to the next. And a final distinctive sight entirely foreign to North American ballparks — glowing electric-light foul poles — always reminds any Yankee visitor to Estadio Latinoamericano or Pinar del Río's Estadio Capitan San Luís that this indeed is not the Bronx or Philadelphia.

To visit a modern-day Cuban ballpark is thus to experience a mindbending timewarp. It is hard to imagine from one's grandstand seat in Havana's stately half-century old Estadio Latinoamericano or Holguin's quaint single-decked Estadio Calixto García that one has not somehow been magically transported all the way back to the richly revered baseball "golden age" of the 1950s. While all of Havana is itself something of a giant decaying museum piece, where time seems to have stood absolutely still for nearly four decades, nowhere is this feeling more pronounced than within the big-city or small-town Cuban ballpark.

And it is more than just the overly simplistic present-day trappings of Cuban baseball — stark, streamlined scoreboards rather than video billboards, crude grandstands rather than air-conditioned luxury boxes, ballplayers with the infectious spirit of schoolboys rather than the haughty attitude of spoiled rock stars — that is so thoroughly backward-looking. Cuba itself almost everywhere oozes with diamond history — its own amateur-league variety as well as that left over from bygone epochs of Negro league, winter-league, and even mid-century big-league action. In the busy streets and teeming public parks of Havana, legions of dedicated Cuban fans talk as endlessly and animatedly of Martín Dihigo and Adolfo Luque and Orestes Miñoso and the revered outfielder Pedro Formental as they do of contemporary heroes such as Cuban league icons Omar Linares and Orestes Kindelán, or big-league refugees Livan Hernández and Rolando Arrojo.

At the heart of Cuba's rich century-long baseball history reside the great blackball stars of a bygone era, only recently resurrected to mainstream popularity in the States. Between two world wars Cuba was a delightful garden spot for blackball diamond action played out in a shadowy world long hidden from the mainstream North American baseball press. Today Cuba's greatest blackball heroes of the '10s, '20s, '30s and '40s remain legends who only barely emerge from those age-old shadows. Names such as José Méndez (a short-lived pitching phenom once judged by John McGraw to be the equal of the great Christy Mathewson in New York) and Cristóbal Torriente (a .300 hitter against major-league barnstormers who once outshown none other than Babe Ruth head-to-head) and Martín Dihigo (a star at eight different positions and acknowledged in many blackball quarters as baseball's greatest all-around talent) stand among mid-century black baseball's most gigantic individual monuments.

Equally memorable are a handful of Cuban big-league pioneers who once stood squarely in the vanguard of the first waves of a Caribbean big-league invasion. Dolf Luque was the first great Cuban star light-skinned enough to make his way onto big-league diamonds. Luque was first among his countrymen to appear in a World Series and also first to win 20 games in a season and amass 100 victories in a career. But men such as Miguel ("Mike") González, Armando Marsans, Rafael Almeida, Orestes ("Minnie") Miñoso, and dozens of others also made their lasting mark as daring big-league pioneers. Marsans and Almeida were first among their countrymen to crack a big-league roster when they debuted in Chicago for Clark Griffith's Cincinnati Reds on July 4, 1911. Mike González joined Luque in the shadows of World War I as a Cuban trailblazer and later also earned a lasting niche by coining one of baseball's most cliched phrases. It was the long-time catcher turned coach, manager, and eventually scout (while filing a report on light-sticking Jewish prospect Moe Berg) who first uttered the well-worn phrase "good field, no hit" — a laconic condemnation which ironically later became an inescapable tag for so many hopeful Latino youngsters, themselves bent on big-league glory. And finally, a fleet-footed and irrepressible "Minnie" Miñoso was by almost any standard of measure the Latin American version of Jackie Robinson when it came to knocking down baseball's odious racial barriers on major-league diamonds of the early 1950s.

There is also the romance of Caribbean winterball, especially in the heyday seasons of the '40s and the '50s when Havana was the acknowledged off-season baseball capital of the universe. This was the Golden Age for Cuban League play, when four entrenched teams with colorful traditions ruled the Havana sporting scene during the century's middle decades. In Cuba one grew up a lifelong fan of either Havana (the "Reds") or Almendares (the "Blues") — less frequently of Cienfuegos or Marianao — and the loyalties were seemingly fixed by birthright. Yale historian Roberto González Echevarría — himself a Havana youngster of the period — observes that the rivalry (especially that between Almendares and Club Havana) would often "define or divide families" and inspired such uncontrollable passions that the most intimate friendships were regularly put to test.

Many of the mid-century Cuban League stars also became colorful cult figures on the big-league scene in the '40s and especially the '50s. Few if any stateside fans of that era are unaware of the Washington Senators and their unbreakable Cuban connection in the final years of Clark Griffith's penurious reign. Camilo Pascual, "Pistol Pete" Ramos, Connie Marrero, Sandy Consuegra, Mike Fornieles, Willie Miranda, and the colorful Carlos Paula (who regularly endangered himself trying to fend off fly balls in center field but could hit like a hall of famer) are among the inventory of Cuban stars and journeymen which lent such a flashy Caribbean flavor to Washington rosters of the era. And few have not heard of legendary talent scout "Papa Joe" Cambria who mined Cuban soil for cost-effective (cheap!) big-league imports. The image built by Griffith and Cambria in Washington was only enhanced by the daring Minnie Miñoso in Cleveland and Chicago in the late '50s, by sweet-swinging Tony Oliva in Minnesota in the '60s, and by the incomparable and charismatic Luis Tiant in Cleveland and Boston throughout the '70s.

Cambria's legend would itself eventually become almost larger than life. Over three decades he inked hundreds of Cuban prospects to pro contracts. Washington baseball writer Morris Bealle once praised Cambria's effort as a scout yet moaned in print that the flamboyant bird dog "would do even better if he could get over his predilection for Cubanolas" (lame praise indeed for the Baltimore laundryman turned superscout). With his ever-present Havana stogie, broken Spanish, wide-brimmed Panama, and unfailing bird dog's nose for raw talent, Cambria became his own version of a living baseball folk legend. Papa Joe would even be credited with attempting to recruit and sign Cuba's most famous ballplaying citizen — Fidel Castro himself. The legend of Fidel as legitimate pitching prospect and sure-fire big-league recruit has over the years taken on a rather fantastic life of its own. Rare is the fan who has not heard the familiar Castro ballplaying legend: if scouts had only been more persistent in getting Castro's fastball under contract, the entire second half of 20th-century Western Hemisphere politics would have taken a different turn. In truth it is all a phantasma, of course. Fidel was admittedly a crack student-athlete in high school, but never a promising or even marginal future big leaguer. He attended several tryout camps on his own but never turned Joe Cambria's astute eye. That the story of Castro as a ballplaying prospect is entirely apocryphal again only seemingly enriches the Cuban baseball saga.

Even when the doors on Cuba's big-league pipeline slammed closed, Cuban baseball was not about to disappear from the scene. Nor would it fade very far from the realm of enduring myth and legend. Soon there would be a new Cuban League emerging as part of Fidel's grand revolutionary plans, and thus also a new bevy of Cuban diamond heroes — ones that would miss the majors but nonetheless impact impressively on world amateur baseball play. Few north of Miami have heard much of genuine stars like Augustín Marquetti (long the island's muscular home run champion) or Antonio Muñoz (a southpaw Tony Pérez by most accounts) or Aquino Abreu (who matched Johnny Vander Meer's feat of consecutive no-hitters). But in Cuba itself these new stars replaced old legends just as readily as Mays inherited the mantle of Musial, Spahn replaced Hubbell and Dean, or Williams gave way to Yastrzemski. The elements of mystery and romance have in recent decades only fleshed out the enticements of the Cuban baseball story.

That story has its roots deep in the game's nineteenth-century past. The favored legend about baseball's origins on the island is one that has U.S. sailors tantalizing longshoremen in Matanzas with the novel North American bat and ball game. A more patriotic and even jingoistic tale contends that native inhabitants actually invented their own version of the bat and ball sport hundreds of years before Doubleday, Chadwick, or North American versions of British rounders. Legend has it that Cuban Indians (Taínos, who were the island's original inhabitants) once played a version of bat and ball which they called *batos* in their own tongue (conveniently suggestive of the Spanish word *bate*, which means "bat") and which may lend an aura of legitimacy to the island's claim as a baseball birthplace. The legend is not lost on post-revolution Cuban baseball authorities who have appropriated "Batos" as the brand-name for Cuban-made sporting goods. But authorities on Taínos culture such as Irving Rouse assure us that the indigenous game was far more like tennis than baseball.

The real credit goes to a pair of enterprising teenagers from Havana who, like pioneering big leaguer Steve Bellán, had learned their baseball as visiting North American students. Brothers Nemesio and Ernesto Guillot first picked up bats and balls on a prep school campus in rural Alabama (Spring Hill College in Mobile) and then stowed their equipment for the trip home in 1864. It was these youngsters who first brought Alexander Cartwright's rules to the city of Havana when they organized pickup games with their strange-looking equipment in a Vedado section then known as "Baños de San Miguel" and today overlooked as the actual birth site for Cuban baseball.

Two other names nonetheless vie equally for the mythical title of "Father of Cuban Baseball" and each seemingly has legitimate claims to stake. The baseball-playing career of at least one begins (as with Nemesio Guillot) in the United States. This ex-patriot student of the same post-Civil War decade was of course Esteban Enrique Bellán, Latin America's first representative in U.S. organized baseball. Dark-skinned Steve Bellán was the most accomplished athlete of the dozen or more original Cuban converts who received both their school-book education and their ballplaying education deep in Yankee territory. Bellán was thus destined to become the first Latin American big leaguer, signing on with the National Association's Troy Haymakers fresh off the campus of Fordham University in 1871, and later also playing a handful of games with the same league's New York Mutuals. His professional career was hardly distinguished: parts of three seasons, 59 games with 288 official at-bats, 68 hits, a lame "dead-ball"-era batting average of but .236. Little is known of Bellán's life beyond the fact that he was born in Havana (sometime in 1850) and also died there on August 8, 1932.

But Cuban fanaticos remember Bellán for a much more significant pioneering role as organizer of the first formal game — between his own hastily assembled Havana club and a team from Matanzas — played late in the year of 1874. Bellán also earned additional distinction as the first-ever player to connect for three home runs in a single Cuban game when he accomplished this rare dead-ball feat in that very first one-sided contest (Havana was victorious by a score of 51-9) on December 27, 1874. As one anonymous commentator puts it, if Nemesio Guillot introduced the American sport to island culture, then Bellán performed the marriage between baseball and the Cuban people.

The celebrated first game underscores a delightful mixing of myth and lore with authentic history. Like their North American neighbors, Cubans apparently also needed their own "immaculate conception" origins myth for their fledgling national pastime. There is clearly an element of Doubleday and Cooperstown in the popular accounts of the first Matanzas ballgame. For one thing, this was certainly not the first afternoon of ballplaying on the island and likely not even a first organized game. Play had been in progress for nearly a decade since U.S. Marines had first arrived toting balls and bats into Matanzas harbor, and since the Guillot brothers had introduced Cartwright's rules in Havana's Vedado neighborhood. For another thing, the Havana team was only one of several clubs formed during the first decade of ballplaying in the capital city. And finally, the very name of the historic ballfield in Matanzas also sports its own elements of large-scale mythmaking.

One Cuban ballpark historian has already peeled away layers of legend and distortion surrounding the historic Matanzas ballgame. Again it is Roberto González Echevarría who has provided valuable insights into the symbolic trappings attached to the name of the historic playing grounds. As González recounts in his own book *The Pride of Havana*, Palmar de Junco is indeed Cuba's parallel to the myth-laden pastures of Cooperstown village. Reigning legend labels the historic Matanzas grounds as Palmar *del* Junco ("the palm grove with the reed") — a poetic treatment which evokes nationalism (the royal palm is a longstanding emblem of Cuban nationality) and even biblical overtones. The actual name is the more prosaic Palmer *de* Junco (Junco's Palm Grove), a simple tribute to the man who once owned the pasture. The latter-day revered ballpark built on the spot to commemorate the historic occasion has — in González's view — the same historical illegitimacy as the similar structure found in Cooperstown.

Bellán's rival in the early years of Cuban baseball was a fellow Habanero, Emilio Sabourín. Like Bellán, Sabourín contributed early as a player yet made his far greater mark as a league organizer and a ballclub manager during the pioneering years of Cuban organized baseball. It was Emilio Sabourín (Rob Ruck calls him the A.G. Spalding of Cuban baseball) who reputedly played a fundamental role in establishing the *Liga de Béisbol Profesional Cubana* and organizing a first league tournament (1878) which was launching pad for eight decades of pre-Castro Cuban pro baseball. (Cuban baseball authority Angel Torres nonetheless believes that Sabourín's pioneering role here has been falsely inflated and points to weighty evidence that Sabourín had little role in directing the Havana club until a decade after the inaugural tournament.) And Sabourín also took the field for the first historic game in Matanzas in December 1874. Bellán caught, reportedly hitting his three homers and scoring seven runs for the winners. Sabourín played in Havana's outfield and scored eight markers himself. Emilio Sabourín would eventually manage, with nearly the same success as Bellán, at least when it came to collecting coveted tournament trophies. Like Bellán (who managed the Havana club to championships during the first three seasons of league play), Sabourín also claimed three titles (1889, 1890, 1892) as bench leader for the same invincible Havana ballclub.

Bellán's ballplaying and managerial rival was also a colorful character whose life away from the baseball diamond was immersed deeply in island politics and in the ongoing military struggle against Spain. A ten-year war for independence waged against Spanish overlords brought continued chaos to the Cuban island between 1868 and 1878, but ceased temporarily in the very winter when Sabourín reputedly launched his first professional league tournament. Evidence that baseball and politics were already as inseparable in Cuba in the late 19th century as they have remained in the late 20th century is found in the fact that revenues from this tourney were apparently surreptitiously funneled directly into the hands of those carrying on guerrilla rebellions against the hated Spanish overseers.

Eventually this mixture of baseball with anti-Spanish politics led to Sabourín's arrest in 1895 and lifelong sentence to a dingy Moroccan prison, where the erstwhile baseball manager died of pneumonia a mere two years later. In the end Sabourín's contributions of baseball-ticket revenues to the anti-Spanish independence movement headed by José Marti not only cost the ballplaying patriot his personal freedom but also resulted in a short-lived Spanish ban on the game across much of the island colony. Throughout three final decades (1870s through 1890s) of European control over Cuba, Spanish colonial authorities had always deeply distrusted rebellious Cuban students and likely assumed that bats and balls used in the popular pastime of "pelota americana" were merely cleverly disguised implements of rebel warfare. Sabourín himself was easy enough to eliminate with imprisonment, but the new sporting passion of the masses in the end proved far more difficult to eradicate.

Sabourín's rival claim to the parentage of Cuban baseball may indeed lie to a great extent in his adjunct status as Cuban revolutionary hero — especially during the fervent patriotic days that followed Fidel's ascension to power. Although a documented player and successful manager in his own country, Sabourín never played in any professional, collegiate, or amateur leagues in the United States and was thus more a popularizer than an importer of the North American pastime. Sabourín's position as legitimate baseball inventor is hardly as tenuous as that of Abner Doubleday, but if Bellán is more rightfully the Cuban version of Alexander Cartwright, Sabourín may be more justly set down as a Cuban Henry Chadwick.

Down through the years numerous noteworthy Cuban stars earned a bulk of their reputations in a league that was as old and proud in tradition as the venerable National League of North America. The professional league of Cuban baseball was founded in the spring of 1878 and would open play with a short round-robin season that same winter. The team known as Club Havana would dominate most of the first two decades of league play by owning nine of the first dozen championships contested. Bellán and Sabourín would remain in the forefront as managers and captains of that famed red-clad team. Another legendary outfit, Almendares, became the legitimate rival to Club Havana in the first two decades of the 20th century. Almendares would not capture its own first Cuban League title until 1894, but over the next half-century it would compile 25 trophies, compared to 30 for Havana. What Cuban baseball fanatics and even casual fans would most cherish, however, would be the bitter and always heated 20th-century rivalry between these clubs, most especially in seasons immediately before and after a second world war.

The '20s and '30s brought new clubs, new stars, and the biggest Cuban blackball legend of any era - the incomparable Martín Dihigo (DEE-go). Here was the grandest Negro leaguer of them all, standing taller in legend and achievement than all the other shadowy legends who slugged, shagged flies, and hurled fastballs on Cuban soil — Oscar Charleston, Judy Johnson, Mule Suttles, Buck Leonard, James "Cool Papa" Bell, Terris McDuffie, or even John Henry Lloyd, "the Black Honus Wagner" by reputation and deed. Dihigo, for one thing, played every defensive position regularly except catcher and he excelled at them all by every account. When Negro league alumni voted their all-time best team they placed Dihigo at second base, but also voted for him at several other spots in the lineup. "El Inmortal" pitched the first-ever no-hitter in the Mexican League and won a league batting title the very same year. Yet Dihigo also remained so unknown to a wider white baseball audience that in the very year of his posthumous Cooperstown election, celebrated author Ron Fimrite, writing on Cuban baseball for *Sports Illustrated*, spelled his name DIHIJO and not DIHIGO.

While Dihigo and other blacks (from Méndez in 1908 to Ramón Bragaña in the '40s) were heroes back home in Cuba and also performed in blackball obscurity in the U.S. and Mexico, Adolfo Luque carried the Cuban banner in the big leagues. And he carried it with considerable if also sometimes damaging flair and flamboyance. Luque was by all accounts a dominating pitcher in the big leagues, especially at the peak (1923, when he won 27 in Cincinnati) and crest (1933, when he saved the deciding World Series contest for the New York Giants) of his lengthy career. But the times in which he played unfortunately fit him more for the role of a harmful stereotype. An incident in the early '20s, when Luque, then with the Cincinnati Reds, charged the Giants bench to kayo Casey Stengel, and other such tempermental outbursts solidified a popular hot-blooded image that rapidly became a standby with all Caribbean ballplayers. Nonetheless there were two sterling World Series outings for Luque that would surely have been quite enough to override such damning tales for any non-Latin player. Long before "Little Looie" in Boston and Livan in Miami emerged as Cuban World Series wonders, there was already an unforgettable Dolf Luque.

During the pair of decades between two world wars a rich Cuban amateur baseball tradition was also thriving. While world amateur play remained in the baseball shadows back in the States, it was always center stage in tropical Havana. The Cuban team would come to dominate the world amateur arena after Fidel's arrival in a way that it has not been dominated in any other sport, certainly not so completely nor nearly for so long — not even by the Russians in hockey, Scandinavians in alpine events, or Americans in basketball. Yet it all began many decades and many nationalistic showdowns earlier. Almost from the first International Amateur Baseball Federation tournaments at the end of the 1930s (the first was staged in London in 1938 and the next five in Havana) Cuba was an unparalleled powerhouse and relentless trophy winner. Conrado Marrero's greatest fame came not in American League parks as a charismatic Washington Senators junkballer in the '50s but as an amateur performer on the world stage a full decade earlier. Marrero reached heroic status on his native island especially during 1941 and 1942 epic battles between the Cubans and Venezuelans, losing a gold medal match in the first showdown, then gaining sweet revenge with a brilliant shutout of the defending champions the following October. And Havana was a natural locale to host many world tournaments (six between 1939 and 1952) showcasing its own native national game.

The true glory epoch for Cuban baseball, nonetheless, would emerge with the years immediately following World War II. The Cuban League would rise to its grandest heights of talent and prestige by housing such local and imported stars as Pedro Formental, Orestes Miñoso, Cocaína and Silvio García, Adrián Zabala, Andres Fleitas, Max Lanier, Agapito Mayor, Ray Noble, Danny Gardella, Hank Thompson, Roger Craig, Lou Klein, Camilo Pascual, Monte Irvin, Julio Moreno, Rocky Nelson, and dozens more. The heated rivalries of the four great teams — Havana's Lions, Marianao's Tigers, the Almendares Alacranes (Scorpions), and the Cienfuegos Elephants — would annually simmer and sometimes boil to a fever pitch. And for a brief while (1947-48) there were even two Cuban pro leagues, so deep was the available local and imported talent.

Cuba's rank as prized jewel of the winter-league scene was most thoroughly demonstrated with the decade of Caribbean Series competitions that spanned the same dozen years between 1948 and dictator Bastista's 1959 ouster. Cuba was the dominant team during most years

of the event, winning seven of 12 tourneys. And the Cubans enjoyed some grand individual performances from the Almendares (1949, 1959), Club Habana (1952), Marianao (1957, 1958), and Cienfuegos (1956, 1960) rosters that copped individual trophies against all-star rivals from the Venezuelan, Puerto Rican, and Panamanean winter circuits. Agapito Mayor made pitching history in the very first Series (1949) with a still unduplicated three mound victories. Jesús "Chiquitín" Cabrera would match southpaw hurler Mayor with his hitting prowess (13 for 21) two winters later, and Pedro Formental (a record 14 hits) nearly duplicated Cabrera's slugging feats in 1953. Washington Senators ace Camilo Pascual would also post a half-dozen victories without defeat across three tournaments, claiming a stellar 1.90 ERA for the same stretch.

Cuba had first rocketed into our North American consciousness, of course, at the time of the first dead-ball-era tours across the island by big-league teams. While the very first such grand ballplaying tours were those that encountered embarrassment at the hands of such swarthy island pitching phenoms as José Méndez ("El Diamante Negro") and Eustaquio "Bombín" Pedroso during the winter seasons of 1908 and 1909, other such tours (especially in 1910 and 1911) were to follow and each would create bulky legends of its own. With each new visit to the "gem of the Caribbean" it seems that an eloquent John McGraw or Frankie Frisch or some other big-league manager would return home with covetous praise for talented black Cuban baseballers he lusted after for his own roster but yet could not hope to sign in a league still cursed by a reigning "gentleman's agreement" to shun blacks.

A generation later Cuba would also receive further headline-grabbing attention as spring training base of operations for the 1947 Brooklyn Dodgers featuring a pioneering Jackie Robinson. It was quite ironic, indeed, that while Cuban stars perhaps suffered more injustices than any single group under the exclusionary "gentleman's agreement" during the century's first half (for no place were there any more talented blacks clearly capable of immediate stardom in the big time than in the environs of Havana), it would be the very nation of Cuba that would eventually provide the ideal stage for the prologue and opening act of Branch Rickey and Jackie Robinson's bold integration drama during the 1946 and 1947 seasons.

Robinson was first sheltered in Montreal during the 1946 minor league campaign, since Canada provided a largely colorblind city likely to accept the pioneering Negro on ballplaying talent alone. If Montreal was nearly free from the bigotry of big-league cities to the south, Havana was an even more ideal location for Robinson's final spring tuneups prior to the precedent-shattering 1947 campaign. Cuba was a winter diamond paradise that had been freely and peacefully showcasing black and white ballplayers on the same field of play throughout the entire first half of the century. Rickey even briefly considered a flashy but perhaps uncontrollable Cuban star of the early '40s named Silvio García (a rifle-armed fielder who hit to the opposite pasture with power and like Dihigo before him was often as comfortable on the mound as in the infield or outfield positions) as his integration martyr. And Cuba also meant a distant escape as well from the pernicious New York media glare that would have been relentless and unavoidable stateside, say in the more normal spring training venues of Florida, California, or Arizona.

In the decade following World War II North American baseball would become a more regular visitor to Fulgencio Batista's Cuba, suddenly offering far more than brief spring training tuneups or occasional barnstorming junkets by vacationing big-league outfits. For in 1946 the North American minor leagues also arrived on the scene, first with the Class C (and later Class B) Havana Cubans housed in the Tampa-Miami-Key West-based Florida International League. A proud final chapter of the Cuban baseball saga is that surrounding the next installment, the beleaguered International League Havana Sugar Kings (1954-60) franchise which soon authored some of organized baseball's most colorful moments during the years immediately preceding the sudden outbreak of Fidel's perhaps inevitable revolution. Havana promotions mogul and one-time amateur star with the Vedado Tennis Club ballclub, Bobby Maduro (later also assistant to Major League Baseball commissioner Bowie Kuhn and inspiration for a ballpark of the same name located in Miami) owned and operated the new Havana franchise and hoped (as did perhaps all Cubans) that this major-scale entry into organized baseball would be a true first step toward eventually landing a National League or American League franchise for baseball-crazy Havana. Unfortunately, however, the most famous incident surrounding the short-lived Havana International League ballclub is itself now forever linked with the history-making Castro-led revolution which all but ended the Cuban professional baseball story.

Fidel took great pride in the presence of the short-lived Havana Sugar Kings in International League play. Always a rabid fan of the game which he himself had played with some limited successes in high school, the new Cuban leader at first saw professional baseball on the island as an important form of both public morale-building at home and much-needed public relations abroad. But the political realities of the revolution which Fidel had created would soon stack the cards against any hopes for maintaining a minor-league or major-league presence for Fidel's Caribbean capital of Havana. The new president and inspirational leader nonetheless became a regular spectator at Sugar Kings games in the months following his rise to power. The Havana high school hurler now turned political figurehead would early and often use the public arena of the local ballpark as his own personal promotional stage.

Such was the case when the fastballing "presidente" took the mound at El Cerro Stadium on July 24, 1959, for an exhibition contest staged to show off his reportedly considerable pitching talents. Fidel hurled two scoreless innings to lead his Cuban Army Team — "Los Barbudos" ("The Bearded Ones") — to victory over a local Military Police ballclub during the tune-up to an official International League matchup featuring the local Sugar Kings and Rochester Red Wings. An action photo of the celebrity righthander warming up — replete with sunglasses, the familiar inches-long beard, and a uniform emblazoned with the team name, "Barbudos" — was even featured in the next day's edition of the Rochester (New York) *Democrat and Chronicle*. A half-dozen more photos also capturing Fidel batting, hurling and autograph-signing also appeared in the Havana editions. A *Democrat and Chronicle* story detailing the Maximum Leader's famous rookie mound appearance (with a bold headline reading "Castro Scores Smash Hit as Baseball Player" and subtitled "Fidel Whiffs 2 in Mound Stint as 25,000 Fanaticos Applaud") also appeared, set in prominent center-page position above the smaller game account of that night's Red Wings-Sugar Kings league contest.

It was to be a final loud hurrah before disaster ironically struck Fidel's baseball fantasy a mere one night later. On the evening of July 25, 1959, gunfire — reportedly an aimless discharge of rifles and pistols both inside and outside the stadium from a band of loyalists celebrating patriotic fervor on the first post-revolutionary anniversary of Fidel's 1953 storming of the Santiago Moncada military barracks — followed a dimming of ballpark lights and mass singing of the nation's anthem at the stroke of midnight. Crowd exuberance then disrupted play when stray pellets struck both Red Wings third base coach Frank Verdi (nicking his batting helmet and knocking him unconscious) and Sugar Kings shortstop Leo Cárdenas (tearing a uniform sleeve). The night's play was immediately suspended with the game tied at 4-4 in the 12th frame and the panicky visiting ballclub hastily took the first available plane out of the country.

While play did return to Havana in time for that fall's "Little World Series," in which the surprising Sugar Kings bested the American Association champion Minneapolis Millers, the days of pro baseball in Cuba were now indeed severely numbered. Before the middle of the next season (July 8, 1960) the International League board of governors (perhaps under some political pressure from Washington officials who sought every available avenue to embarrass Presidente Castro) voted to immediately relocate the Cuban Sugar Kings franchise to Jersey City in New Jersey. Transfer took place on July 13, 1960, with the team at that time on the road in Miami. Manager and Cuban native Tony Castaño decided to return immediately to his homeland and was replaced by coach Nap Reyes, already a popular figure in Jersey City, where he once played minor-league ball. But eleven Cuban players (including future big leaguers Raúl Sánchez, Orlando Peña, Mike Cuéllar, Leo Cárdenas, and Cookie Rojas) decided to abandon their native land for the lure of continuing a "professional" ballplaying career. With this overnight departure of Havana's proud minor-league franchise, the curtain was thus suddenly rung down on nearly three quarters of a century of Cuban baseball glory.

Baseball did not die in Cuba after the doors to the island were yanked shut by spatting between Fidel and his Washington rivals. It might better be said that the sport on Cuban soil underwent a peculiar and — for the outside world — largely secretive rebirth and transformation in the form of unprecedented dominance within amateur-league play. On the international level Cuba has now won 25 of the 34 senior level world amateur baseball tournaments held since 1961, in the process establishing the same iron grip on international amateur competitions that the island once exerted on Caribbean World Series professional play. If junior world champions are added into the mix the victory skein is more one-sided still. The constantly replenished Cuban National Team would in fact lose only one of the 73 "official" tournament games (tour-

ing exhibition contests excluded) it played against international competition (throughout the U.S., Europe, Latin America, and Asia) over a five-year span that separated the 1987 Pan American Games in Indianapolis from the 1992 Barcelona Olympics. Most prominent among the roster lists of the powerhouse Cuban team of this era were pitcher Rene Arocha, the first Cuban player to leave Cuba during the Castro era and briefly a regular with the St. Louis Cardinals, and third baseman Omar Linares, a 32-year-old veteran in 1998 who is still considered by most to be a can't-miss big leaguer and by far the best amateur ballplayer in the world.

Behind an iron wall of secrecy the exciting spectacle of Cuban amateur play has continued equally unabated on the island's home front. From November through February (now October to March with recent expansion of the regular season and dropping of the Select Series second season) nearly 450 ballplayers with an average age of about 23 compete on 16 teams in an action-filled 90-game national tournament designed to select Eastern sector and Western sector divisional representatives to meet in a final national championship showdown. Each of the ballclubs in this ruthlessly competitive amateur league represents a different Cuban province (Havana Province alone has three different teams) and thus regional pride and socialist ideals of sportsmanship have replaced professional salaries as the driving force of championship play.

For two decades, from the mid-'70s to mid-'90s, a more complex arrangement featured two separate Cuban seasons. When the regular-season playoffs closed down in late winter, a second league with its full schedule of games rapidly filled the void. The 63-game Selective Series constituted a formalized tryout period which once ran from February through late summer. The circuit boasted only eight ballclubs (again representing provinces but with several provinces collapsed into each ballclub) and featured 225 of the island's best young athletes. The prize was not so much a team championship but cherished spots for the two dozen or so best players on the nation's showcase national team, which would compete during prestigious summertime Pan American Games, world tournament, or Olympic Games competitions.

Cuban baseball has again been an exceedingly hot topic of late. Furor in the press surrounding the Baltimore Orioles' visit to Havana in March 1999 — the first sojourn to the island by a major-league team in four decades — only fanned flames already crackling. The exploits of Livan Hernández with the Florida Marlins (1997 World Series MVP) and Orlando "El Duque" Hernández with the New York Yankees (also a top Series performer a season later) have emboldened the image of the modern-era Cuban League and fueled the rumors of a great untapped source of diamond talent. Each new departure to the United States by Cuban Leaguers (there have been a couple dozen such escapes in the past half-decade) brings speculations about eventual floods of Cuban hurlers, sluggers, and acrobatic infielders. And the ongoing exploits of the Cuban crack national team against mediocre world amateur rivals (including Team USA rosters filled with inexperienced collegians) further fuels such speculation.

Livan Hernández awakened Cuban baseball fans across the island and around the United States with his memorable postseason performances, which also stirred a Miami Cuban-exile community to fever pitch. Half-brother Orlando (bearing the name of his father, another "El Duque" Hernández, who pitched in the Cuban League in the '70s) seems already to promise big-league mastery which will rival his own Cuban League exploits (where he recorded the best-ever lifetime won-lost percentage). And other Cuban defectors have enlivened the big-league scene and also spurred debate about the role of baseball in Cuban-American politics. Rolando Arrojo has recently been a rookie pitching sensation with the expansion American League franchise in Tampa Bay. Rey Ordoñez (who left Cuba in 1993 when it appeared he would never overhaul entrenched Germán Mesa or promising Eduardo Paret as the National Team shortstop) in turn has for several seasons thrilled New York Mets faithful and baseball fans everywhere with incomparable middle-infield defensive wizardry.

Such "defectors" are considered traitors by perhaps the bulk of fans and fellow ballplayers back home. They stand justly accused of abandoning a system of sports training that honed their athletic skills and gave them a first opportunity to shine. But in North American cities they have found renewed respect for their ballplaying talents and they have also reaped personal riches in the form of lucrative big-league contracts that island denizens can hardly imagine. The question may well remain open whether or not they have also lost an admirable sporting innocence in the bargain. What is beyond debate is the demonstration by Arrojo, Ordoñez, and the rubbery-armed Hernández brothers of the impeccable quality of a Cuban baseball training which spawned them.

The small army of Cuban "defectors" have also somewhat overshadowed the considerable glories of the thriving Cuban league itself. Through much of the 1990s baseball struggled in Cuba, due largely to economic squeezing brought on by a reprehensible ongoing U.S. blockade of the island. Attendance had been on the wane for several campaigns before a sudden revival of baseball interest near the end of the recently concluded 1998 season. For the first time in as much as a full century baseball seemed to lose some of its luster for Cuban sports fans, and also some of its grip on the national attention. Basketball tournaments were occasionally outdrawing Cuban League games in Havana during the past two winters. And the nation's few sports pages in *Granma* and *Trabajadores* have devoted increasing coverage to the island's crack women's volleyball program, as well as to soccer and the perennial favorite sport of amateur boxing. But despite the ills which have gone hand and glove with the nation's recent severe economic woes, baseball is nonetheless still very much king of the Cuban sports scene.

Yet in the most recent two seasons there has been a remarkable revival. The fans have come back in droves to Havana's majestic Estadio Latinoamericano, captivated by old team rivalries (Industriales versus Havana, Metros versus Matanzas, Industriales versus Pinar del Río) and exciting new stars such as Pinar's adriot second baseman Yobal Dueñas (1999 batting champion) and Club Havana junkballing righthander José Ibar (the league's biggest winner two years running). The longer season and revised National Series format have stimulated renewed excitement as well. There was a most gripping pennant chase, especially in the postseason tournament, between Pinar and Havana teams last spring, and a surprise playoff finals appearance by capital-city favorite Industriales in most recent months. Ibar emerged in 1998 as a newly minted model of an old Cuban prototype — the tantalizing junkball specialist. His pursuit of 20 victories in two consecutive campaigns has been a lightning rod for fan enthusiasm which was less than a year earlier focussed primarily on Livan Hernández in the distant major leagues. And old names such as Linares and Pedro Luís Lazo have again shown bright during a pair of recent postseason runs by Pinar del Río, the New York Yankees of Cuba. Further rekindling of enthusiasms around the Cuban circuit came with the 1999 reinstatement of temporarily suspended stars Germán Mesa and Eduardo Paret; Mesa was the biggest story of the 1999 winter season when his transfer to the Industriales roster piqued a flood of interest in Havana and his fielding magic drew renewed comparisons with Cooperstown-bound Ozzie Smith.

The spark of Cuban baseball has also been fanned in both Havana and stateside by relentless Cuban triumphs on the international scene. Most attention-grabbing for U.S. fans was a pitifully easy gold medal victory by red-clad Cuban forces at the 1996 Olympic games in Atlanta, while U.S. collegians slugged it out with Nicaragua for a bronze. And a decade earlier there was the dramatic Pan American Games U.S.-Cuba showdown in Indianapolis which introduced Omar Linares to the world and culminated in a late-inning Cuban comeback against U.S. mound ace Cris Carpenter. And elsewhere Cuba dominated as it had for decades in the past, racking up a seemingly endless string of IBA world tournament and Intercontinental Cup titles. In Barcelona in 1992 there was the savory plum of a first-ever Olympic gold medal for baseball. In Italy a half-decade later Cuba was still on top of the heap with yet another IBA world championship trophy and another unbeaten sweep past Japan, Korea, Team USA, and the rest of the international field.

Yet the future of Cuban baseball nonetheless raises numerous questions that do not have easy answers. Are the recent escapes to the major leagues by star Cuban ballplayers a reliable signal for a groundswell of new island talent, or perhaps a mere temporary abberation? Will Fidel's socialist government seize eventually upon a long-distateful tactic and begin peddling the front-line Cuban players — the nation's most valued natural export — to an equally distateful capitalist big-league enterprise? Are the top Cuban players truly of major-league caliber, and if they are, how many might actually be future Miñosos, Pascuals, Luques, or Olivas? Or will the current crop of Cuban stars prove to be less than promising big-league prospects due to the lack of first-rate competition in their own amateur league back home?

And from another perspective, how will major-league general managers divide up Cuban talent if it becomes part of baseball's biggest-ever fire sale? Will the present lottery system for international free agents prevent secret signings and other skullduggery, and how will a suddenly available flood of first-rate Cuban ballplayers affect current pro recruiting from the remaining Caribbean nations? More centrally — at least in the eyes of international amateur baseball watchers — what will happen to baseball in Cuba itself once the island's best players again have access to high-paying major-league careers?

Only time holds the answers to what may indeed be some of the most exciting baseball questions of the final decade of the 20th century.

Much of the interest in current Cuban ballplayers is fueled by a persisting aura of legend that surrounds and sustains the full century and a quarter of baseball fanaticism on the magical island. If contemporary ballpark legends (a notion, for example, that Omar Linares is the finest third basemen on the planet) are today seemingly a bit bigger than life, such has always been the case for Cuban baseball and the lively myths it irrepressibly engenders. First arose the mythic quality of Méndez and Torriente, shadowy black warriors who were true Giant killers (or Tiger slayers or Phillies bedazzlers) invincible against visiting big-league talent. There was Torriente going mano-a-mano with Babe Ruth in Havana in 1920 and embarrassing the Babe at his own slugging game; and the fastballing Méndez dominating and frustrating John McGraw's patchwork big-league barnstormers a decade earlier. Dihigo carved out a still more lasting image in the decades that stretched from Méndez and Torriente on one end to the shadows of the Second World War on the other.

Fidel himself became subject of an undying baseball legend which had him once trading in a chance to hand-cuff Yankees batters in New York for an opportunity to harass Yankee politicos in Washington, D.C. Since Fidel's rise to political power with an improbable mid-century revolution (itself the seeming stuff of storybook romance) reported heroic deeds by mysterious players with names such as Braudilio Vinent (a masterful moundsman) or Wifredo Sánchez, Augustín Marquetti, and Lázaro Junco (potent sluggers all) have only occasionally escaped from behind the disinformation wall that long surrounded Cuban baseball. Such reports — now attached to Omar Linares, Germán Mesa, Victor Mesa, and Pedro Luís Lazo — continue to circulate each time a recently arrived Livan Hernández or Rey Ordoñez sparks a bidding war among eager big-league teams. The surprising showing (here in the U.S., perhaps, if not also on the island itself) of Cuba's vaunted national team in its recent exhibition series with the big-league Baltimore Orioles only turned up the volume on widespread speculation about a latent talent pool buried away in Cuban League enclaves.

Where, then, does recorded Cuban baseball history separate itself from fanciful Cuban baseball lore? Perhaps nowhere, since Cuban baseball has always been mostly the raw stuff of romance and of folklore. The island, to a surprising degree, has lived and flourished at home and abroad through its generations of baseball heroes and continues to do so in the final decade of the century. Nowhere is the game more revered in the teeming stadiums or dusty sandlots. There is no single baseball location on earth where everyday fans are more passionate or more knowledgeable. And nowhere is the game long apocryphally credited to Doubleday more reflective of a culture which supports it. (This, of course, includes the United States, where basketball today captures the public imagination as the single sport most reflective of a space-age, technological, and urban-oriented new millennium.) In brief, nowhere is baseball so much more than just a frivolous game or luxurious leisure pastime.

The pages which follow are far more than a mere chronicle or celebratory tour of Cuban diamond exploits. They represent instead a rare visual passageway into baseball's forgotten past. The economic circumstances within Cuba during recent decades have regrettably meant the wholesale destruction of much of the island's printed record of its past, and baseball here has been no exception. Collectors of memorabilia (with an eye on bottom-line dollar value) have ransacked much of the material treasures (tobacco cards, felt pennants, glossy photos, uniforms and caps, ceramic statues and emblems, medals, scorecards, magazine and newspaper accounts) to be found on the island. Tropical climate and the sagging economy have sabotaged much more as acid-based paper has readily succumbed to Caribbean humidity in a land with little air-conditioning and less attention to scientific archiving.

Many of the images reproduced here will not survive another half-decade in pristine condition; others already are lost in their original published forms. This volume thus preserves the rare and even irreplaceable images of an all-too-rapidly disappearing legacy from a proud nation and its cherished native game. The narrative text (written by Bjarkman) which accompanies the painstakingly compiled photographic record (collected and designed by Rucker) also retells an incomparable story of the heroes and events that have been one of baseball's richest and yet least-exposed chapters. The reader is thus invited to enter into the nearly lost world of one of baseball's most beguiling sagas. Like most visits to the exotic island which is today's isolated and anachronistic Cuba, this brief journey of the imagination will hopefully inspire one's dormant baseball enthusiasms and also whet one's appetite for recapturing baseball's tragically lost promised land.

# CUBAN BASEBALL HISTORICAL TIMELINE

## JUNE 1866

Caribbean baseball apparently born when sailors from American naval ship, anchored at port in Matanzas Bay, demonstrate diamond play for crowd of Cuban dock hands employed loading sugar cane onto North American vessels. Cubans reportedly joke that American instructors seemed highly motivated by desire to sell baseball equipment to their raw diamond recruits. One competing account of baseball's Cuban origins suggests it was actually Nemesio Guillot, an upperclass youth educated in the United States, who first introduced equipment and demonstrations of this popular Yankee sport upon his return in 1864 to his native Havana.

## APRIL 1871

Cuban Esteban "Steve" Bellán mans third base, second base, and outfield for Troy Haymakers during inaugural season of National Association, baseball's first recognized big-league circuit. Bellán, who acquired his diamond skills while studying at Fordham University and was a fancy fielder if light hitter over three professional seasons, thus becomes first official Latin American major-league ballplayer.

## DECEMBER 27, 1874

Only eight years after game's reported introduction in Matanzas, city known as "Athens of Cuba" hosts Havana in first recorded organized ballgame between native Cuban teams. Playing for Club Havana are two early giants of Cuban baseball, ex-big-leaguer Steve Bellán and patriot Emilio Sabourín, later the organizing genius behind Cuba's own professional league. Bellán plays third base and Sabourín scores eight runs for Havana during 51-9 rout of talent-thin Matanzas ballclub.

## DECEMBER 29, 1878

Professional Baseball League of Cuba begins play in Havana, making Cuban League world's second oldest professional baseball organization, trailing North America's National League in seniority by only two seasons. Havana wins first game 21-20 over Almendares in contest featuring ten men to a side (extra position was "right short"). Inaugural Cuban championship consists of only three clubs — Havana, Matanzas, Almendares — and Havana wins trophy with 4-0-1 record behind leadership of manager and captain Steve Bellán.

## NOVEMBER 23, 1879

American George McCullar, catcher for Colón, hits first Cuban League home run in 13-8 victory over Havana.

## DECEMBER 25, 1879

Pitcher Carlos Maciá of Almendares is credited with first attempt to bunt not for sacrifice but for base hit. Maciá's unique play comes full dozen seasons before same strategy introduced in U.S. with John McGraw and Baltimore Orioles.

## JANUARY 21, 1882

First switch-hitter recorded in Cuban baseball is José María Teuma of Club Fé, who played all nine positions, posting 4-3 pitching record and .225 batting mark over seven (then brief) seasons. Same winter witnesses apparent single-game world record of sixty errors committed in Cuban semi-pro contest between Club Caridad (39 miscues) and Club Ultimatum (21). It seems safe to assume ballplayers at this sloppy Havana spectacle wore no fielding gloves during their crude rag-tag match.

## FEBRUARY 2, 1886

Carlos Maciá, Almendares pitcher, blanks Club Fé 16-0 in first recorded Cuban League shutout. Maciá allowed three base hits.

## 1886

Official statistics kept for first time in Cuban League and Wenceslao Gálvez is first batting champion (.345). Gálvez three years later publishes *El Baseball en Cuba*, Cuban baseball's first known history.

## 1886-1887

Cuban Giants appear as first salaried all-Negro team, but popular touring ballclub ironically contains on its roster not a single native-born Cuban. Club is formed by Frank P. Thompson, head waiter at Hotel Argyle in Babylon, New York, who recruited pro players from Philadelphia Keystones to work as waiters and entertain guests with ballplaying. More ballplayers were added from Philadelphia Orions and Washington Manhattens to form famed touring team at end of hotel tourist season.

## FEBRUARY 13, 1887

First professional league no-hitter pitched in Cuba by Carlos Maciá, as Almendares defeats Carmelita by one-sided 38-0 margin. This perhaps was first no-hit, no-run game anywhere in Latin America, though historical records remain cloudy on such matters.

## JULY 14, 1889

Second professional no-hit, no-run game is pitched in Cuba by Eugenio de Rosas (Club Progreso) during 8-0 victory over Cárdenas. Game's highly unusual line score shows Cárdenas with no runs or hits yet astronomical total of 14 errors. This would be final Cuban no-hitter for 47 seasons and only four more masterpieces would be tossed by Cuban hurlers during six pre-Castro decades of 20th century.

## 1890-1891

Cubans introduce baseball in Mexico and Puerto Rico, as well as in Dominican Republic. For efforts in spreading game Cubans deserve designation as "the apostles of baseball."

## OCTOBER 1891

First touring big leaguers visit Cuba for winter exhibitions (October 25-November 8). John McGraw is among group of barnstormers called All-Americans, who post a 5-0 record, but only with help of Cuban reinforcements provided by local promoter Eduardo Laborde to fill out Americans' short roster.

## JANUARY 1892

Havana continues early domination of Cuban League with ninth championship trophy in 14 years. Emilio Sabourín is now manager and captain of Havana ballclub. Sabourín's roles in organizing both league and champion Havana ballclub solidify his claim as true patriarch of Cuban baseball. Antonio Ma. García ("El Inglés") captures second of three individual batting championships (1890, 1892, 1893), each with different club (Havana, Almendares, Aguila de Oro).

## 1893

Ricardo Cabaleiro posts first three-homer game in Cuba while playing for Colombian amateur team versus Cuba's Océano ballclub. Negro leaguer "Cool Papa" Bell would much later (1929) match feat during Cuban professional game.

## 1894

Almendares, under manager Ramón Gutiérrez, wins its first league championship with 17-7-1 record. With arrival of Almendares as legitimate challenger to Club Havana, greatest rivalry in Cuban baseball is born. Over succeeding three quarters of a century Club Havana will gain upper hand, but only barely with 30 championships (including 12 of first 14) to 25 for Almendares.

## 1900

Luís ("Mulo") Padrón leads Cuban League in both pitching victories (13) and also base hits (31). Lefty-throwing Padrón is first but not last to pull off this rare double, also accomplished by Martín Dihigo in 1936. Padrón later pitched two-plus decades in U.S. Negro leagues (1904-26) with Cuban Stars, All Cubans, and Cuban Star of Havana.

## 1902

Famed catcher and Cuban hall of famer Gervasio ("Strike") González makes debut with stellar season for San Francisco of Cuban League. González achieves sterling two-decade record (1902-19) as one of best Cuban defensive backstops of all time, earning special fame as personal favorite catcher of José ("El Diamante Negro") Méndez de la Caridad.

## NOVEMBER 1908

Matanzas-born black Cuban hurler José Méndez — later immortalized by New York Giant manager John McGraw as "Cuba's Black Diamond" — records string of impressive performances against touring Cincinnati Reds. Wiry 20-year-old phenom first posts 1-0 one-hit victory over stunned National Leaguers; two weeks later Méndez throws seven innings of shutout relief plus second nine-inning scoreless performance as starter — a total of 25 scoreless innings against befuddled big-league visitors. Competing against Negro league stars during U.S. tour the following fall, Méndez again distinguishes himself with outstanding 44-2 mound record.

## NOVEMBER 18, 1909

Eustaquio "Bombín" Pedroso (Almendares) no-hits visiting AL champion Detroit Tigers, playing without stars Ty Cobb and Sam Crawford. Detroit wins only four of twelve games versus Almendares and Club Havana during Cuban barnstorming tour, yet twice defeats Cuban ace José Méndez.

## NOVEMBER 1910

Philadelphia's world champion Athletics (4 wins, 4 losses) and Detroit Tigers (7 wins, 4 defeats) again visit Cuba for winter exhibitions in Havana's Almendares Park. Big leaguers once again find Cubans to be challenging opponents with José Méndez twice besting Philadelphia's hall of famer Eddie Plank. One highlight is three straight cutdowns of Ty Cobb in steal attempts against crack Negro league catcher Bruce Petway and Cuban receiver "Strike" González.

## JULY 4, 1911

Outfielders Armando Marsans and Rafael Almeida debut with Cincinnati Reds, becoming first 20th-century Cubans and modern-day Latin Americans to appear in major leagues. Complaints about dark skin color of both ballplayers are met by official club press release that these were "two of the purest bars of Castillian soap ever floated to these shores."

## AUGUST 20, 1911

Mario Castañeda (Vedado Tennis Club) pitches first no-hit, no-run game in Cuban amateur baseball, defeating Atlético de Cuba, 1-0.

## NOVEMBER 1911

New York Giants with John McGraw are one of three professional North American teams which renew wintertime ballplaying visits to Cuba. New Britain of Connecticut League (4 wins, 14 defeats) and National League Philadelphia Phillies (5 wins, 4 losses) join New Yorkers, who fare best with nine straight wins after three straight losses. Cuban ace José Méndez beats Philadelphia twice but also loses once to Phillies and twice to Giants (including head-to-head battle with Christy Mathewson).

## DECEMBER 2, 1918

Baldomero "Merito" Acosta of Club Habana performs rare outfield unassisted triple play, something done by an outfielder on only two other recorded occasions. Others were major leaguer Paul Hines (Providence, National League, 1878) and minor leaguer Harry O'Hagen (Rochester, 1902).

## DECEMBER 22, 1918

Bienvenido Jiménez (Cuban Stars) steals eight bases in same game versus Almendares. Jiménez records three steals each of second and third and two of home, yet his team loses 7-6.

## OCTOBER 3, 1919

Cuban Adolfo "Dolf" Luque becomes first Latin American to appear in World Series, pitching one inning of relief for Cincinnati Reds in Game 3 against Charlie Comiskey's infamous "Black Sox" ballclub in Chicago. Luque, who would later win 27 games for Cincinnati during the 1923 season, also pitched four relief innings in Game Seven, at Redland Field, on October 8.

## OCTOBER 1923

At season's end, Cincinnati hurler Dolf Luque owns major-league-leading won-lost record of 27-8 and ERA mark of 1.93, still top single-season record ever posted by Latin American big-league pitcher.

## OCTOBER 11, 1924

Oscar Levis of Club Havana no-hits Almendares, 1-0. This is first 20th-century no-hitter pitched in Cuban professional-league play.

## MAY 23, 1925

Cuban Miguel González traded from St. Louis Cardinals to Chicago Cubs, thus becoming first Latin player to appear with three major-league teams. Catcher González debuted with Boston Braves in 1912 and joined Cardinals in 1915.

## JANUARY 2, 1929

Outfielder James "Cool Papa" Bell, U.S. Negro leaguer playing for Cienfuegos, becomes first slugger to connect for three homers in single game during Cuban professional play. Bell's feat occurs at Aida Park in 15-11 slugfest victory over Havana. Bell's three homers are struck against Oscar Levis,

"Campanita" Bell, and hall of famer Martín Dihigo, although Bell himself later erroneously claimed all three came off blackball ace Johnny Allen.

## OCTOBER 10, 1930

Visiting all-star teams of U.S. major leaguers play first game at Havana's La Tropical Stadium, with Bill Terry, Al Lopez, Rabbit Maranville, Paul Waner, Sam Rice, Chuck Klein, and Carl Hubbell (losing pitcher) among the most notable big leaguers appearing.

## MARCH 1931

Brooklyn Dodgers make brief spring training exhibition appearance in Havana, playing five games in La Tropical Stadium. Dolf Luque is on Brooklyn roster and hurls all three Dodgers victories.

## OCTOBER 7, 1933

Dolf Luque provides 4.1 innings of stellar relief to gain championship-clinching victory in Game Five of 1933 World Series. In notching Fall Classic title for New York Giants against Washington Senators, Luque becomes first Latin American to post World Series pitching victory.

## NOVEMBER 7, 1936

Raymond "Jabao" Brown of Santa Clara hurls second 20th century no-hitter in Cuba, a 7-0 victory over Club Havana. Five weeks later Brown pitched two games against Havana on same day, losing 1-0 to Luís Tiant, Sr., in 12-inning opener and blanking "Los Rojos" 2-0 in nightcap.

## SEPTEMBER 16, 1937

Black Cuban Hall of Famer Martín Dihigo (only player enshrined in halls of fame in four different countries — U.S., Mexico, Cuba, and Venezuela) pitches first professional no-hit, no-run game on Mexican soil, a 4-0 victory over Nogales in Veracruz.

## DECEMBER 21, 1937

First Cuban League night game played in La Tropical Stadium as Marianao defeats Almendares 6-5. Martín Dihigo is winning pitcher of historic game.

## SEPTEMBER 18, 1938

Cuban star Martín Dihigo, author of first Mexican League no-hitter, also becomes first Mexican League batter to register six hits in six at-bats while playing for Veracruz against Agrario.

## AUGUST 1939

Havana hosts second-ever world amateur championships and defeats Nicaraguan and U.S. teams for country's first world title. Cuba also hosts three of next four events and captures three of those championships, with future big leaguer Conrado Marrero pitching for Cubans in 1941 (loss to Venezuela) and 1942 (victory over Venezuela) title games.

## SEPTEMBER 14, 1940

United States, Hawaii Territory (not yet a State), Cuba, Mexico, Puerto Rico, Nicaragua, and Venezuela meet in Third World Amateur Baseball Championship, the first championship series to feature more than three participants and second held on Latin American soil. Host Cuba is easy victor for second consecutive year. An initial tournament was held in England in 1938 and was also won by the host nation, Great Britain.

## DECEMBER 11, 1943

Manuel "Cocaína" García of Club Havana pitches fifth no-hit, no-run game in Cuban League history, besting Marianao 5-0.

## SEPTEMBER 6, 1944

Tommy de la Cruz, Cuban righthander, tosses first one-hitter by Latin American pitcher in big leagues. De la Cruz pitches just one wartime season for Cincinnati, recording 9-9 won-lost record and 3.25 ERA. De la Cruz was exceedingly dark in complexion, a fact (along with his age of 33) which may have speeded his departure from Cincinnati immediately after 1944's wartime campaign.

## JANUARY 3, 1945

Cuban professional baseball witnesses its sixth no-hit, no-run game, pitched by former big leaguer Tommy de la Cruz of Almendares against rival Club Havana, 7-0.

## JANUARY 7, 1945

In most violent incident of Cuban baseball history, Cuban outfielder Roberto Ortiz of Almendares attacks umpire Bernardino Rodríguez in dispute at home plate and knocks stunned arbiter unconscious.

## OCTOBER 9, 1946

Team of National League All-Stars begins a seven-game exhibition schedule against the Cuban National All-Star

team in Havana. NL team, featuring Buddy Kerr and Sid Gordon of New York Giants and Brooklyn Dodgers Eddie Stanky and Ralph Branca, wins opening game of tour, 3-2.

## OCTOBER 26, 1946

Record 31,000 fans (estimated) attend inaugural game at new Gran Estadio del Cerro in Havana, watching Almendares defeat Cienfuegos 9-1. At the time, this was largest crowd ever to witness a professional baseball game in Cuba.

## AUGUST 21, 1948

Representatives of Cuba, Panama, Puerto Rico, and Venezuela, meeting in Havana, agree to stage four-country round-robin twelve-game tournament to be known as "Serie del Caribe" (Caribbean Series) and launched in Cuba during February 1949. This series, the highlight of winter-league play, will continue uninterrupted through 1960 (Series XII), later be reinstituted (1970), and survive to the present. In addition to the four founding countries, the Dominican Republic (replacing Cuba) and Mexico (replacing Panama) also later participate on regular basis.

## FEBRUARY 25, 1949

Agapito Mayor wins his third game during inaugural Caribbean Series pitching for Almendares (Cuba) against Spur Cola (Panama), thus becoming first and only pitcher to win three games in single year during 40 seasons of Caribbean Series play. Al Gionfriddo, 1947 Brooklyn Dodgers World Series hero with his miraculous catch of Joe DiMaggio's near home run in Game Six, completes three-game eight-for-fifteen batting rampage (.533) which makes him first Caribbean Series batting champion. Gionfriddo also plays for Almendares (Cuba) in this first Caribbean Series, staged in Havana's El Gran Estadio del Cerro.

## FEBRUARY 6, 1950

Seventh no-hitter of Cuban baseball history is pitched by Rogelio "Limonar" Martínez in 3-0 Marianao victory over Almendares.

## DECEMBER 6, 1950

Cuban catcher Carlos Colás provides one of greatest single-game batting displays ever witnessed in winter-league play. Colás registers five hits in five at-bats for Team Venezuela during 10-9 loss to Venezuelan League rival Vargas. Colás also performs rare feat of three triples in single contest.

## OCTOBER 1951

Minnie Miñoso of Chicago White Sox wins *The Sporting News* American League Rookie of the Year award. Miñoso trails New York Yankees' Gil McDougald by two votes for baseball writers' (BBWAA) rookie award, despite 50 more hits, 13 more RBI, and 20-point higher batting average.

## FEBRUARY 21, 1952

Tommy Fine, diminutive U.S. righthander who posted only four major-league decisions with Boston Red Sox and St. Louis Browns, achieves immortality by pitching only no-hit, no-run game in four-decade history of Caribbean Series. Fine hurls for Cuba's Club Havana against Venezuela's Cervecería Caracas, striking out three and walking three in 1-0 victory at Caribbean Series IV in Panama.

## SEPTEMBER 2, 1952

Mike Fornieles, Cuban righthander with Washington Senators, makes sensational major-league debut tossing one-hitter, thus becoming first Latin pitcher and second American Leaguer to toss one-hitter in debut big-league outing. Only AL pitcher preceding Fornieles with this feat was Addie Joss (with Cleveland in 1902) and the achievement has been duplicated only once since, by William Rohr (with Boston in 1967). Only National League hurlers duplicating Fornieles' debut were ironically also Latin Americans, Juan Marichal with the Giants in 1960 and Silvio Martínez of the Cardinals in 1978.

## SEPTEMBER 1954

Cuban Sandy Consuegra (Chicago White Sox) becomes second Latin American pitcher to lead his league in winning percentage, completing year with sparkling 16-3 mark (.842). Cuban Dolf Luque, 27-8 with Cincinnati Reds in 1923, was first to gain such memorable distinction.

## FEBRUARY 11, 1955

Perhaps most emotional and memorable game in history of Caribbean Series is played in University Stadium at Caracas. Emilio Cueche, legendary Venezuelan pitcher, throws brilliant two-hitter for Magallanes (Venezuela) yet loses 1-0 to Club Almendares (Cuba). Near riot in grandstand, in dispute of close call on the basepaths, delays game for more than 45 minutes as spectators throw objects onto field. Major leaguers Vern Rapp, Román Mejías, Rocky Nelson,

Gus Triandos, and Willie Miranda are featured in Cuban starting lineup.

## OCTOBER 4, 1955

Brooklyn defeats New York Yankees 2-0 in Game Seven to capture Dodgers' first World Series championship. Cuban journeyman outfielder Edmundo "Sandy" Amoros is ultimate Dodgers hero with miraculous left field catch of Yogi Berra's sixth-inning line drive, a one-handed grab at fence which launched game-saving double play.

## JULY 25, 1959

Fidel Castro supporters, enjoying raucous "July 26th Celebration" in Havana's El Gran Estadio del Cerro (El Cerro Stadium), halt International League contest between Rochester Red Wings and Havana Sugar Kings with several random gunshots from grandstands. Rochester third base coach Frank Verdi and Havana shortstop Leo Cárdenas both suffer minor flesh wounds during infamous incident, causing Red Wings manager Cot Deal to pull his team from field and retreat to downtown hotel. International League officials promptly cancel remainder of Sugar Kings' homestand and will eventually relocate franchise to Jersey City during middle of 1960 season. But first Havana wins International League playoffs (Shaughnessy Cup) and also defeats Minneapolis Millers to capture Triple-A Little World Series.

## JULY 13, 1960

Havana Sugar Kings franchise is shifted by International League to new home as Jersey City Reds, ending professional organized baseball in Cuba. Ballclub is playing in Miami at time and all 11 native Cuban players (Raúl Sánchez, Orlando Peña, Andrés Ayón, Mike Cuéllar, Borrego Alvarez, Leo Cárdenas, Joaquín Azcue, Daniel Morejón, Cookie Rojas, Orlando Tanner, and Enrique Izquierdo) decide to remain with team in its new home. Manager Tony Castaños returns to Cuba and is replaced by fellow Cuban Nap Reyes.

## JULY 23, 1960

Kansas City outfielder Whitey Herzog hits into only all-Cuban triple play in major-league history. The round-the-horn putout action is from Washington Senators pitcher Pedro Ramos to first baseman Julio Becquer to shortstop José Valdivielso.

## 1962

First season of new Cuban League (amateur) is held with Occidentales (18-9) as champion. Erwin Walter (.367) wins first batting title and Rolando Valdés (3) is home run leader.

## JULY 10, 1962

Juan Marichal (Dominican Republic) becomes first Latin American pitcher to win major-league All-Star Game with 3-1 National League victory during 1962's first All-Star Game (of two) in Washington. Ironically, Washington Senators ace Camilio Pascual (Cuba) is loser, thus simultaneously becoming first Latin-born pitcher to lose All-Star Game in the majors.

## AUGUST 13, 1962

Cuban native Bert Campaneris pitches two relief innings for Daytona Beach in Florida State League against Ft. Lauderdale, throwing both as righthander and lefthander and allowing only one run during this stunt while striking out four. Normally an infielder, Campaneris was later to make big-league history (September 1965) by appearing at all nine positions for Kansas City in single nine-inning game.

## MAY 2, 1964

Cuban rookie sensation Tony Oliva blasts first of big-league record-tying four consecutive Minnesota Twins homers in 11th inning, pacing 7-4 victory at Kansas City. Following Oliva with roundtrippers were Bob Allison, Jimmie Hall, and Harmon Killebrew, thus equalling feat performed by Milwaukee in 1961 and repeated by Cleveland in 1963. Oliva, in first full big-league campaign, leads junior circuit in hitting at .332, becoming first rookie to gain AL batting title.

## MAY 20, 1964

Cuban pitcher José Ramón López (Monterrey) records 16 strikeouts, nine in succession, in 5-2 victory over Mexico City Red Devils, tying short-lived Mexican League record set in 1959 by Dominican Diomedes "Guayubín" Olivo (Poza Rica).

## JULY 23, 1964

Cuban rookie Bert Campaneris of Kansas City Athletics becomes second man in big-league history to hit two homers in debut game, his first roundtripper coming on

17

first pitch served by Twins hurler Jim Kaat. Bob Nieman of St. Louis Browns earlier homered in first two big-league at-bats (1951) while Campaneris accomplishes feat with first and fourth trips to plate.

## OCTOBER 1964

Minnesota Twins slugger Tony Oliva becomes first black ballplayer to win both batting title and Rookie of the Year honors in same season. By pacing American League with .323 average, Cuban standout becomes only third Latin to win league batting championship.

## FEBRUARY 21, 1965

Cuban Leaguer Inocente Miranda (Azucareros) plays entire game at first base without touching ball, an event that has occurred only five times in major-league history.

## SEPTEMBER 8, 1965

Infielder Bert Campaneris (Kansas City Athletics) becomes first player in big-league history to play all nine positions in single contest. Versatile Cuban mans one position per inning versus Los Angeles Angels, recording single error (in right field), allowing one run and two hits while on the mound, and catching final inning during which he is injured in home plate collision with Ed Kirkpatrick and forced to leave game. Campaneris would later be first batter to face Venezuelan utilityman César Tóvar during first inning of September 22, 1968, game in which Tóvar would duplicate Campaneris's feat.

## OCTOBER 1965

Cuban infielder Zoilo Versalles of AL champion Minnesota Twins blazes new trails as first Latin American ballplayer to earn MVP honors, being named junior circuit's most valued performer.

## JANUARY 16 AND JANUARY 25, 1966

Most overlooked performance in international baseball history occurs in Cuban League when righthander Aquino Abreu (Azucareros) hurls back-to-back no-hitters (versus Occidentales and Industriales) to match Johnny Vander Meer's more famed big-league feat.

## AUGUST 13, 1966

Cuban League strikeout king José Ramón López establishes all-time standard of 309 strikeouts for single season, reaching 309 in game against Reynosa. López, while striking out a dozen batters, loses contest by 2-0 score.

## JULY 11, 1967

Cincinnati Reds third baseman Tony Pérez hits dramatic 15th-inning home run off Jim "Catfish" Hunter to give Nationals 2-1 victory in mid-summer classic at Anaheim. Hitting heroics of Cuban slugger not only ended longest contest in All-Star Game history, but also capped one of most intriguing games of lengthy series: third basemen accounted for all three runs with Dick Allen (Phillies) and Brooks Robinson (Orioles) also homering for game's only other tallies.

## NOVEMBER 1969

Cuba's Mike Cuéllar is first Latin American winner of coveted Cy Young Award, leading powerful Baltimore Orioles staff (2.83 team ERA, plus 20 staff shutouts) with outstanding 23-11 record and 2.38 ERA.

## JANUARY 4, 1976

Executives of International Amateur Baseball Association (IABA) meet in Mexico City to end long-standing feud between delegations, creating new organization named Asociación Internacional de Béisbol Amateur (AINBA). With U.S. returning to IABA fold after several-year absence, first AINBA world championship is scheduled for Cartagena, Colombia, and Cuban Manuel González Guerra is named first AINBA president.

## SEPTEMBER 12, 1976

Minnie Miñoso becomes oldest player to record major-league base hit, singling off Sid Monge in first game of doubleheader with California Angels. Seeing limited duty as DH, Cuban star has only one hit during eight 1976 plate appearances. Miñoso is nine months past 53rd birthday at the time, thus eclipsing mark set in 1929 by Nick Altrock, who collected his own final hit for Washington Senators only days after turning 53.

## AUGUST 8, 1977

Black Cuban star Martín Dihigo, considered by most as greatest all-around Negro leagues performer, is voted into Cooperstown by BWAA Veterans Committee. Dihigo thus becomes second Latin hall of famer and first player ever enshrined in three different national halls (Cuba, Mexico, U.S.). Dihigo was a top pitcher and also a standout at every other position except catcher, was a batting and home run champion several times in Negro league play, and is credited with pitching first Mexican League no-hitter.

## APRIL 12, 1980

For only time in Cuban League history, two players from same team smack grand slams in same inning. Rey Vicente Anglada and Jorge Beltrán (Habana) accomplish feat on same day that Don Money and Cecil Cooper (Milwaukee Brewers) also pull it off in major leagues.

## OCTOBER 4, 1980

After nearly four seasons as coach and ballclub public relations executive, Minnie Miñoso makes token pinch-hitting appearance for Chicago White Sox. Miñoso thus becomes second player in big-league history to appear in official league play during five different decades. Ever-popular Minoso enjoyed four earlier stints with Chicago (1951-57, 1960-61, 1964, 1976) and is 57 at time of final pinch-hitting appearance, a promotional stunt orchestrated by Sox owner and ultimate baseball show-man Bill Veeck.

## JANUARY 31, 1984

Cuban League enjoys game with fewest-ever hits when southpaw Jorge Luís Valdés (Henequeneros) throws no-hitter against Villa Clara, while opposing moundsman Reynaldo Santana allows only two safeties in 1-0 loss.

## AUGUST 1984

Cuba hosts 28th IBA World Championships in Havana, defeating Chinese Taipei for gold medal and also beginning still-current string (as of 1998) of six straight world titles. Subsequent victories will follow in 1986 (Holland), 1988 (Italy), 1990 (Canada), 1994 (Nicaragua), and 1998 (again Italy).

## 1985

Lázaro Vargas (Industriales) sets Cuban League consecutive-game hitting streak standard with base hits in 31 straight games.

## DECEMBER 9, 1986

Batters for Las Villas in Cuban League bash ten consecutive singles against pitchers from Agropecuarios, matching feat not performed in major leagues since June 2, 1901.

## FEBRUARY 11, 1987

Outfielder Luís Ulacia (Camagueyanos) becomes first and only Cuban League player to smack home runs from both side of plate in same game.

## AUGUST 22, 1987

Cuba rebounds from early-round loss to USA to defeat Americans 13-9 in dramatic come-from-behind championship match of Pan American Games at Indianapolis. Cuba rallied against future big-league pitcher Cris Carpenter for two runs in eighth and three more in ninth. Victory runs Cuba's Pan American Games gold medal streak to five straight (with two more to follow in 1991 and 1995). Opening-round defeat will be Cuba's final loss of any single game in international senior-level tournament play for next ten years (until Intercontinental Cup finals of 1997).

## MARCH 3, 1988

Rare event occurs in Cuban League when Camaguey defeats Las Villas three times in same day. First loss for Las Villas results from previous night's contest which extends past midnight, while other two come in afternoon doubleheader.

## 1988

José Canseco, Cuba-born star with Oakland Athletics, becomes first player in major-league history to record season with 40-plus home runs and 40-plus stolen bases. American League leader in both homers and RBIs, Canseco is second Cuban to win MVP honors (Zoilo Versalles, 1965). Two seasons earlier he was also second Cuban to win rookie-of-the-year honors (Tony Oliva, 1964).

## AUGUST 22, 1989

Righthander Lázaro Valle hurls eight-inning perfect game (11-0) against South Korea while striking out 13 of 24 batters. Masterpiece comes in Intercontinental Cup tournament in Puerto Rico, where Cuba grabs fourth straight gold medal by beating Japan 8-2 in finals. Tourney MVP is Cuban leftfielder Lourdes Gourriel, who bats .435 in eight games.

## 1990

Omar Linares bats better than .400 for third time in Cuban League play to win his third batting title. Linares

is already widely considered in amateur baseball circles and among professional scouts as "the best third baseman on the planet."

## JULY 1991

Catcher José Delgado smacks dramatic tenth-inning single to salvage 5-4 win over Japan in finals of 10th Intercontinental Cup in Barcelona, clinching Cuba's fifth straight IC championship. Lefty Omar Ajete is also tournament hero with 0.00 ERA in preliminary round, ninth-inning save in 2-1 semifinal victory over Chinese Taipei, and starting role in gold medal game.

## AUGUST 31, 1992

Texas Rangers and Oakland Athletics swap Latin American sluggers José Canseco (Cuba) and Rubén Sierra (Puerto Rico) in most sensational trade ever involving Hispanic superstars. Canseco joins Texas in exchange for switch-hitting Sierra, as well as relief ace Jeff Russell and starting hurler Bobby Witt. With Canseco on same roster with AL home run leader Juan González (Puerto Rico), slugger Rafael Palmeiro (Cuba), and former batting champ Julio Franco (Dominican Republic), Rangers boast most potent Latin slugging lineup ever.

## SEPTEMBER 1992

Cuba captures first-ever Olympic baseball gold medal competition with undefeated record (8-0) and 11-1 triumph over Chinese Taipei in finals. Pitchers Omar Ajete and Giorge Diaz and slugger Omar Linares are Cuban gold medal heroes. Closest games for Cubans are 9-6 (opening round) and 4-1 (semifinals) victories over Team USA.

## APRIL 1993

Tony Pérez debuts as Cincinnati Reds manager, but debut is anything but successful as Pérez is fired only 44 games into season. Hopes are high in Cincinnati for pennant challenge, and when Reds flounder early (20-24 on May 24th date of Pérez's firing), even stature as revered star of 1970s Big Red Machine teams was insufficient to save Pérez's slow-starting managerial career.

## APRIL 9, 1993

José Canseco with Texas Rangers becomes first player since Ted Williams (1947) and 17th in baseball history to reach the 750 career-RBI plateau in 1,000 games or less. Canseco's milestone RBI comes in game against Royals at Kansas City (his 999th career contest).

## JUNE 7, 1993

MVP Omar Linares smacks homer, double, and sacrifice fly in three at-bats as Cuba defeats IBA World All-Star squad 8-2 in Tokyo Dome. IBA World All-Star Game III is first such match between defending Olympic champion and all-stars representing all other nations.

## MARCH 1994

Lázaro Junco, Cuba's all-time longball slugger, wins eighth Cuban League home run crown. Junco retires with Cuba's career longball record of 405 (later surpassed by Orestes Kindelán).

## OCTOBER 1994

José Canseco tabbed American League Comeback Player of the Year after stellar season (his last with Texas Rangers) in which he slugged 31 homers, drove in 90 runs, and batted respectable .282.

## AUGUST 31, 1995

Pedro Luís Lazo tosses no-hitter and strikes out 17 as Cuba defeats USA 5-0 in semifinals of World University Games at Fukuoka, Japan. Lazo pitched six-inning 12-1 one-hit victory earlier in same tournament versus Taiwan, striking out 11.

## OCTOBER 1995

José Canseco of Boston Red Sox finishes season with 300 career roundtrippers, becoming only third Latin player to reach 300-homer plateau. Canseco now stands only 79 circuit blasts behind Tony Pérez and Orlando Cepeda for all-time top spot among Latin sluggers.

## JULY 1996

Cuba (9-0 for tournament) once again dominates international amateur scene by breezing to victory in Summer Olympics at Atlanta's Fulton County Stadium. Cuba defeats Japan 13-9 in gold medal game and Omar Linares (8) and Orestes Kindelán (9) perform awesome two-week display of aluminum-bat home run slugging. Kindelán blasts longest four-bagger ever witnessed in Fulton County Stadium.

## APRIL 8, 1997

Omar Linares of Pinar del Río slugs four homers in one

game at Captain San Luís Stadium, becoming only third player ever to accomplish feat at any level in Cuban amateur or professional baseball. Linares matches Leonel Moa (Camaguey, December 10, 1989) and Alberto Díaz (Matanzas, December 17, 1995) with his four roundtrippers. Umpire Nelson Díaz ironically works all three of these historic games.

# AUGUST 10, 1997

Japan surprises Cuba 11-2 in finals of Intercontinental Cup at Barcelona, ending ten-year Cuban domination in international senior tournaments plus string of seven straight Cuban titles in Intercontinental Cup competition. Loss on heels of 1996 Olympic victory shocks Cuban fans and INDER officials and leads to changes in both the format of the Cuban League and leadership of the Cuban national team.

# OCTOBER 1997

Livan Hernández stars in World Series for Florida Marlins and refocuses attention of U.S. fans on proud legacy of Cuban baseball. World Series MVP performance by Hernández also creates considerable stir among fans back in Cuba.

# APRIL 1998

José Ibar wins 20 games on mound for Club Havana and becomes first pitcher in modern-era Cuban League with 20 victories in single season. Pinar del Río behind slugger Omar Linares and mound ace Pedro Luís Lazo captures Cuban League championship for second straight year.

# JUNE 1998

Orlando "El Duque" Hernández makes major-league debut with New York Yankees. Half-brother of Livan Hernández, "El Duque" left Cuba in December 1997 and signed with New York in February after tryout session at Caribbean Series in Venezuela.

# JULY 1998

José Canseco surpasses Tony Pérez and Orlando Cepeda (379 each) to become Latin American career leader in big-league home runs. Canseco approaches 400 career homers before season's end.

# AUGUST 1998

Cuba recaptures long-standing reputation for international domination by winning IBA World Championships in Italy, posting unbeaten 9-0 record in tournament and defeating South Korea 7-1 in finals. Cuba's stars are ageless Omar Linares, slugger Orestes Kindelán, and pitcher José Contreras, who hurled title game five-hitter. Cuba also beats Nicaragua (14-2) in semifinals and Netherlands (12-1) in quarterfinals to capture 25th senior-level world title in 27 outings since 1952 (including IBA World Championships and Intercontinental Cup Tournaments).

# MARCH 28, 1999

Major leaguers appear in Cuba for the first time in 40 years for historic meeting between the Baltimore Orioles and Cuban National Team before 55,000-plus frenzied fans in Estadio Latinoamericano. Omar Linares singles home the tying run in the eighth but the major leaguers finally prevail 3-2 after 11 thrill-packed innings.

# MAY 3, 1999

Two triples by shortstop Danel Castro, a ninth-inning round-tripper and joyous dance around the basepaths by DH Andy Morales, and 6 2/3 innings of hitless relief hurling by Norge Vera highlight a stunning 12-6 romp by the Cuban national team in their rematch with the Baltimore Orioles in Camden Yards. The game — the first-ever meeting on U.S. soil between a Castro-era Cuban team and a major-league ballclub — establishes Cuban League credibility and sets off wild celebrations throughout the streets of Havana.

# BASEBALL'S PAN-AMERICAN ORIGINS

Mystery has always been the true byword of Cuban baseball history. The origins of the game in this "Cradle of the Caribbean" are shrouded in hopeless confusion and enmeshed in a tangled web of contradictory accounts. But there can be little doubt that Cuba was somewhere in the vanguard of baseball's earliest 19th-century Caribbean explosion. At least from the time of the North American Civil War, baseball was already being played on the island of Cuba, and in the third quarter of the past century the Cubans were the energetic disciples and apostles of the new "American" sport, spreading it almost everywhere throughout the rest of the Caribbean Basin.

These first Cuban emissaries of bat-and-ball playing were, granted, mostly North American-trained college boys who had mastered diamond play on their trips to the United States (usually for their university education, and often to New York and its environs), then carried their new-found passion for bats and balls back to their homeland. The earliest among these enthusiastic Cuban "baseball importers" to be formally recorded by history was Nemesio Guillot, a Havana-born student who first introduced equipment and rules to his friends on the island as early as 1864.

Caribbean baseball took root — according to still another popular legend — when sailors from an American naval ship, anchored at port in Matanzas Bay, demonstrated diamond play for a crowd of curious Cuban dockhands employed in loading sugar cane onto North American vessels. The Cuban hosts were later reported to joke that their American instructors seemed largely motivated by a desire to sell baseball equipment to these raw diamond recruits. (This economic interest was, of course, an impure motivation which also moved another of the game's pioneering fathers, Albert Spalding, and even goes a long way toward explaining Spalding's own proselytizing for the new national game.

Spalding — himself a sporting goods dealer — also saw baseball's spread as a source of expanded commerce.)

But the competing and perhaps less apocryphal account of baseball's Cuban origins suggests that it was actually Nemesio Guillot and not the sailors who first unveiled the pioneering equipment and offered the first crude demonstrations of the Yankee sport upon his own 1864 return to his native Havana. Both versions may strike somewhere near the truth and thus neither has exclusive claim on the first reports of cracking bats and flung balls along the northern Cuban coastline.

What can be more safely documented is the first widely reported organized ballgame between native Cuban teams. This occurred in December 1874 — a mere eight years after the reported invasion of U.S. Navy baseballers — and again involved Matanzas. The dreamy coastal town known as the Athens of Cuba hosted a club from nearby Havana. A challenge match took place on a field known then and still preserved today as Palmar del (de) Junco and located near the port city's central square.

Playing for *El Club Havana* that day were two early giants of Cuban baseball, former big-leaguer Steve Bellán and patriot Emilio Sabourín, reputed organizing genius behind Cuba's soon-to-be-born professional league. Bellán played third base while Sabourín scored eight runs for Club Havana during its 51-9 rout of the talent-thin host nine. Guillot, or perhaps the U.S. Marines, may well have introduced the first bats, balls, and gloves to the verdant Caribbean island, but it was Bellán and Sabourín who performed the true marriage between baseball and the Cuban people. And across the century and a quarter that has followed it has proved to be a vibrant and prosperous marriage.

While it is not altogether clear who best deserves the prestigious title of Father of Cuban Baseball it is certainly well-documented that — unlike the shadowy Abner Doubleday of Cooperstown — names such as Nemesio Guillot (also often spelled Guillo), Esteban Bellán, and Emilio Sabourín (insert) all have legitimate connections with the Cuban game's inaugural events.

Guillot was perhaps only one of a number of sons of wealthy Havana families who enjoyed the advantages of a U.S. university education in the 1860s and thus returned with enthusiasms for the new Yankee national game. Guillot was merely fortunate among that number in having his name most often mentioned in earliest printed records of Cuban ballplaying.

Bellán, the first Cuban to appear in U.S. organized baseball, was indisputably an organizer of the first recorded game at Matanzas in December 1874, as well as the first manager of the famed Havana club when Cuban League play was launched in 1878. Sabourín has always received a large sympathy vote among flag-waving Cuban baseball historians, though he was not the first Havana manager as sometimes has been claimed. He apparently served a more minor role than is usually reported in formation of the Havana team, and enjoyed his considerable managerial success with that same club (1888-92) only after Bellán had given up the post.

Sabourín has undoubtedly benefited in his eventual associations with baseball's foundations in Cuba from his simultaneous role as an inspired patriot in his country's ongoing guerrilla warfare for independence from Spain. The ballplayer-turned-political agitator contributed baseball gate receipts to the José Marti-led revolutionary cause in the years immediately before his arrest and fatal imprisonment at the hands of the Spanish colonial government. (He died in a Moroccan detention center in 1897.) A Sabourín monument in Havana (shown at right) carries in part the following inscription: "Illustrious Havana native, fervent patriot, and revolutionary baseball pioneer. Founder of Club Havana who organized the first official championship season and also labored for national independence." The stone memorial was erected in September 1953 to mark the one hundredth anniversary of Sabourín's birth. The indistinct background image on these two pages is the earliest known Cuban baseball photograph, showing action on a field in Matanzas (perhaps it is the Palmar de Junco site of Cuba's first known official game). It apparently dates from the 1870s.

E. SABOURI.

Nineteenth-century Almendares stalwarts included Moises Quintana (top left) and José Muñoz (top right). Hall-of-famer Quintana was acclaimed one of the top catchers of the past century and also managed Almendares during the early 1900s. Muñoz was a top-flight moundsman, serving all of his 15 seasons (1900-14) with Almendares save one, and also leading the league in winning percentage in 1906 (8-1, .889) and in both victories and games started on several other occasions. Ricardo Martínez (lower left) played in seasons spanning three different decades (1879-91) with Matanzas, Colón, Fé, Havana, and Almendares. Martínez enjoyed the high water season of his hall-of-fame career with Los Azules in 1887, when his league-leading batting mark (.439) was the first .400-plus season in Cuba.

Club Havana was the champion in the first dozen seasons of Cuban League play, winning the first six round robins and losing only three banners (two to Fé and one to Matanzas) of the first twelve contested. By the end of the first decade in the new century, however, such one-sidedness would be a thing of the distant past. By 1905 Almendares had finally emerged with a strengthened lineup and future decades would witness an on-going intense Almendares-Havana rivalry which would eventually conclude only with the league's demise in 1961. Ultimately the Reds of Havana would hold only a slight 30-25 championship advantage over the Blues from Almendares.

Almendares first entered the championship fray in 1894 with its first coveted tournament victory, one based on a 17-7 record which had left it two games better than Matanzas and four on top of usual winner Havana. It was only the start of serious annual battles between teams and fans of the Havana club, based in the downtown Vedado section of the capital city, and the Almendares forces representing a nearby neighborhood known as El Cerro. And it would be a close rivalry over the nearly three-quarters of a century. In total Almendares would post 25 firsts, 24 seconds, 14 thirds and eight fourths during the 71 championships competed, winning 1,522 games and losing 1,304 for an overall .539 percentage. For Havana the numbers would be 30 firsts, 22 seconds, 16 thirds, and six fourths, with a final ledger of 1,553 victories and 1,338 defeats (.537). In the end it was nearly a dead heat between the two rivals, by almost any measure.

Cabinet card photos (above) of early-century Almendares players include: (1) Pedro Medina, 1903, (2) Miguel Prats, 1904, (3) Abelardo Díaz, 1903, (4) Alfredo Cabrera, 1903, (5) Agustín Molina, 1905, (6) Regino García, 1905, (7) Esteban Prats, 1905, (8) Inocencio Pérez, 1905, (9) Armando Marsans, 1905, and (10) Heliodoro Hidalgo, 1905. While the 1903 Almendares edition posted a lame 6-21 record, and the 1904 team was little improved at 7-14, the 1905 club suddenly rose to championship proportions.

Champion Almendares Base Ball Club of 1905, including Esteban Prats (top row, far left), manager Abel Linares (middle row, center), Angel D'Mesa (front row, far left), Armando Marsans (middle row, far left), and Rafael Almeida (middle row, second from left). This team posted a 19-11-2 mark to capture its second league championship. Prats was the league leader in plate appearances while D'Mesa (10-4) was the circuit's winningest pitcher.

Champion Almendares Base Ball Club of 1907, including Esteban Prats (top row, second from left), Alfredo Cabrera (top row, second from right), Gervasio González (front row, second from right), and Armando Marsans (front row, far right). This third championship edition of Los Azules (the Blues) was managed by Eugenio Santa Cruz (not pictured) and finished with a 17-13 record to outdistance Club Fé (16-14) and Club Havana (12-18).

Champion Almendares Base Ball Club of 1908, including (1) Esteban Prats, (2) Evaristo Pía, trainer, (3) Alfredo Cabrera, (4) Heliodoro Hidalgo, (5) Juan Sánchez, manager, (6) Armando Marsans, (7) Armando Cabañas, (8) Rogelio Valdés, (9) Rafael Almeida, (10) Ortega (first name unavailable), (11) Emilio Palomino, (12) José Muñoz, (13) Gervasio "Strike" González. The Blues took their second straight championship banner and third in only four winters on the strength of a 27-6 record that was three games better than Havana's. Fé (8-24) and Matanzas (5-27) brought up the rear in the obviously unbalanced league. Palomino (.350) was the league's batting leader while hall-of-famer José Méndez (not pictured) had a perfect 9-0 pitching record. It was during this season that Méndez began a marvelous string of 45 scoreless innings, a string which was not broken until 1909 and which included 25 whitewash frames against the touring big-league Cincinnati Reds.

CLORIA AL INVICTO HABANA B.B.C. CHAMPIONSHIP DE 1885 A 1886

Nineteenth-century stars Carlos Royer and Alfredo Arcaño (top insets on opposite page) were among the earliest Cuban hall of famers, Royer inducted with the original 1939 class of 10 and Arcaño elected as the sole inductee the following year. But these were only the cream of the full crop of 19th-century stars laboring for powerful Club Havana. Above is the 1885 Havana Base Ball Club, winner of four of seven matches and the fourth Havana BBC to fly the championship banner. Players pictured are Fernando Santana, Rafael Hernández, Emilio Sabourín, batting champion Pablo Ronquillo (top row); Esteban Bellán, star pitcher Adolfo Luján, manager Francisco Saavedra, Vicente Diaz (middle row); Victor Plana, José Luján, Manuel Landa, Alejandro del Castillo (bottom row).

The team on the opposite page is the 1889 Havana BBC, another league champion and the first managed by Emilio Sabourín. Included are: Fernando Santana (1), José Estrada (2), Antonio Maria García (3), Francisco Delabat (4), Adolfo Luján (5), Moises Quintero (6), Pablo Ronquillo (7), Miguel Prats (8), Gustavo Aróstagui (9), Alfredo Arcaño (10), and Francisco Alday (11). Valentín González, who played with Havana from 1890-1911, is shown (left) after scoring a run against Club Fé on Jan. 23, 1908. This is one of the earliest known candid photos from Cuban League play.

Left is Carlos "Bebe" Royer, who hurled brilliantly for Havana for nearly two decades (1890-1907). Royer led all pitchers in victories or winning percentage on four different occasions and posted a brilliant 17-0 ledger in 1902. Right is Alfredo Arcaño, whose 22-year career with Club Havana (1887-1909) stretched even longer than Royer's. Arcaño captured a single batting title in 1895 (hitting .430 during the unfinished season suspended by the war of independence against Spain) and was one of the first Cubans to post a .400 batting average for an entire championship season.

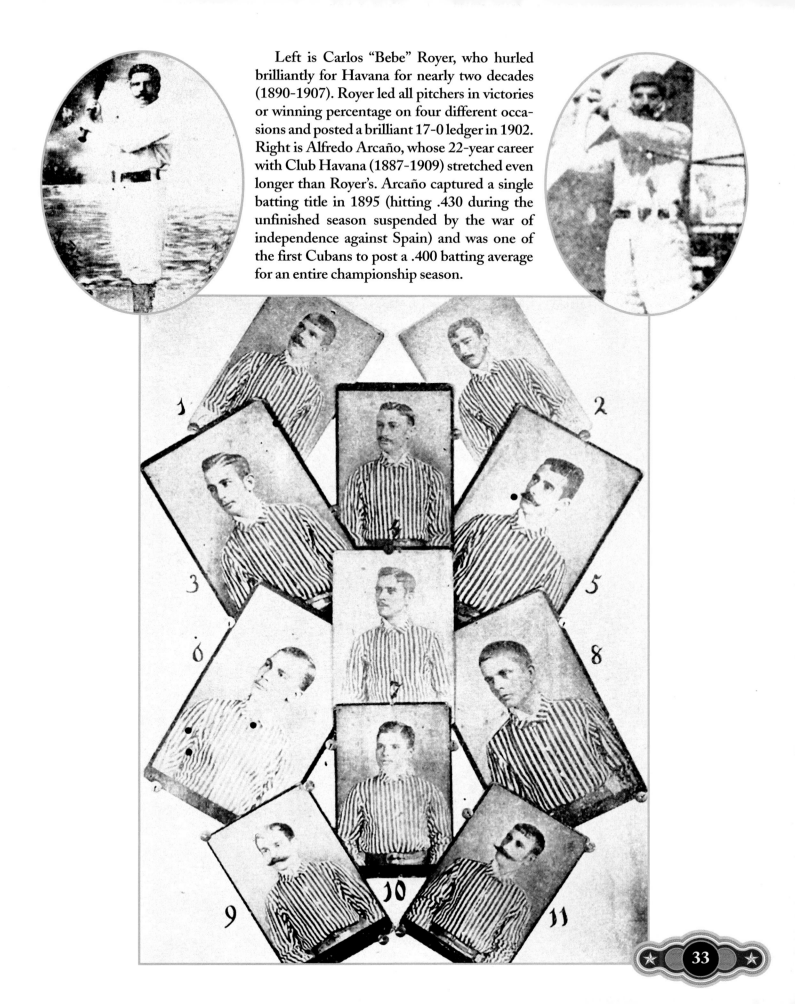

Unlike General Abner Doubleday and the spurious Cooperstown myth, Cuba's handful of sanctioned baseball founding fathers all have easily documentable connections with the actual game. Guillot was already teaching the rules to his friends in Havana late in 1866, the year he returned home from schooling on U.S. soil. Sabourín was a dedicated player, club manager, and league organizer who deserves as much credit as anyone for launching a professional league on the island in 1878. And Bellán was likely the most talented player and enthusiastic proselytizer of the bunch, a veteran of the first U.S. professional league (the National Association of 1871-75), and chief organizer of what remains the earliest documented game between local teams held on Cuban soil.

Bellán's brief big-league career was significant only because he was first among his countrymen to play at the highest professional levels in North America. Only a fair hitter with the Troy Haymakers and two other upstate New York ballclubs (between 1868 and 1873) he did nonetheless post one 5-for-5 game against the pitching of Boston's Al Spalding, a Hall of Famer. Otherwise Bellán displayed little power and a normal .250-range batting average. Playing in the days before fielders' mitts, Bellán was likely a good blocker of grounders, yet threw erratically and committed numerous "boots" from his various infield and occasional outfield positions. He may well have learned the game as a student at Fordham University, but little is known about his life before his sudden emergence as an enthusiastic ballplayer.

*Bellán (circled) with 1868 Unions of Lansingburgh*

Bellán's spot in island baseball history was assured by his center-stage presence at the sanctioned first official game on Cuban soil. The historic game of December 27, 1874, took place on a makeshift Matanzas field already known as Palmar del Junco, with Bellán undoubtedly playing a major role in organizing the match between his own well-established Havana Club and a less-practiced local nine from the host city. The contest was almost certainly not the first ever attempted on Cuban soil, since there were at the time several ballplaying clubs in place in the capital city. But it was a showcase for Bellán himself. He served as the Havana catcher, reportedly smacking three homers and scoring seven runs for the winners, who dominated 51-9. Sabourín also appeared as an outfielder in the Havana lineup and scored eight runs. Bellán's sudden display of power may be the most revealing measure of the primitive level of play that historic day, since the experienced professional had never before belted even a single long ball against National Association pitchers.

Bellán (circled in team photos at left) was also a pioneering figure during the first two decades of the Cuban Professional Baseball League following its founding in 1878, only three years after the birth of the National League in North America. For the seven seasons of actual competitions during the Cuban League's first decade (two seasons were skipped and a third suspended) it was Bellán who was both manager and captain of the powerful Club Havana team. Bellán was a regular catcher for the Havana nine throughout most of the 1880s, with Sabourín — one of the team's founders back in 1868 and later Bellán's replacement as manager — normally manning second base. Havana thoroughly dominated most of the brief winter championships, winning trophies in the first half-dozen seasons that were completed. Bellán was the victorious manager on three of those occasions. Sabourín, who has occasionally and erroneously been credited with being the first Club Havana manager, did not actually receive nomination to that position until late in 1888.

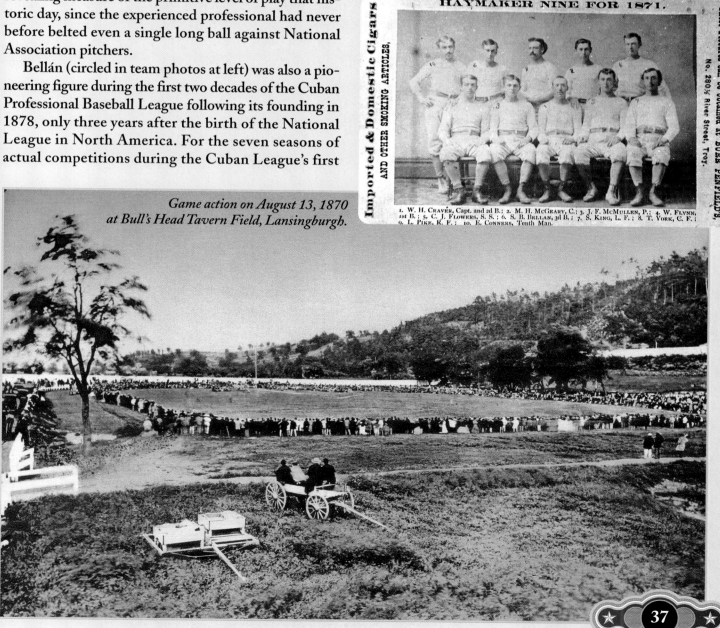

*Game action on August 13, 1870 at Bull's Head Tavern Field, Lansingburgh.*

A short-lived entry in the turn-of-the-century Cuban League was the team known as the Cubanos BBC, which entered the fray on the heels of the Cuban War for Independence (known ironically by North-Americans as the Spanish-American War). The new club debuted in 1899, winning five of its dozen contests to trail both Havana and Almendares in the round robin standings. Pictured above are three members of the 1900 Cubanos ballclub: hall-of-famer Francisco "José" Poyo (top left, and above center), along with teammates J. Vidal (left of Poyo) and D. Miguel (right of Poyo). Cubano's final season came the following winter and left the team with an overall 20-34 three-season record, two third-place finishes, and one lowly fourth. In addition to Poyo the Cubanos ballclub boasted a handful of talents which included Esteban Prats (the 1900 batting champion), pitcher Carlos Royer (the league's best pitcher with Havana in 1901), and Angel D'Meza.

Matanzas BBC was another late-19th-century Cuban outfit with limited history and few bragging rights. Matanzas did manage to pull off a championship season in 1893, among its eight years in the circuit, and also boasted the league's winningest pitcher in Enrique García that season. The 1893 championship Matanzas team (pictured at left) included (1) Ricardo Cabaleiro, (2) Enrique García, (3) Enrique Meléndez, manager (4) Enrique Pividal, (5) Leopoldo Matos, (6) Avelino Cairo, (7) José Castañer, (8) Román Calzadilla, (9) Julio López, (10) Leopoldo Posada, (11) Manuel Podrón, (12) Pedro Matos, (13) Evaristo Piá, trainer and (14) Eduardo Ruíz.

Club Fé boasted a longer and more distinguished history than Matanzas, including four championships between 1888 and 1913, plus a noteworthy pioneering role in signing North American Negro league stars who soon were filling up the Cuban League with fresh and unparalleled talent. The club's importing of blacks began in 1907 (the first year for Negro leaguers in the Cuban League) with Preston Hill, Bill Monroe, and Rube Foster, among others. It reached its zenith in the early teens with powerhouse Fé ballclubs featuring the likes of Spotswood Poles, John Henry Lloyd, Dick Redding, and Smoky Joe Williams. The 1908 Fé BBC (above) included (clockwise from top left) Luís González, Austín Parpetti, Eustaquio Pedroso, José Borges, José Govantes, Conrado Rodríguez, Francisco Morán, Carlos Laguardia, Ricardo Hernández, Miguel Prats, and Juan Quiveiro. The next season "Bombín" Pedroso would turn big-league heads up north by tossing a no-hitter (for Almendares) at the barnstorming Detroit Tigers (without Ty Cobb or Sam Crawford in the lineup).

Juan Manuel Pastoriza (above) of Fé BBC is pictured in 1890, his second season of championship play. The hall-of-fame pitcher later served with the Almendares and Aguila de Oro ballclubs, was the champion pitcher (best winning percentage) in 1894, and also led the circuit in starts, complete games, and losses on several other occasions in the 1890s.

# BARS OF PURE CASTILIAN SOAP

RAFAEL ALMEIDA 3ᴬ. B

MARSANS, ST. LOUIS - FEDERALS

The true origins of baseball on the island of Cuba may well be lost forever in the mists of legend surrounding the importing of the American game to the environs of Havana and Matanzas during the late 1860s. Esteban "Steve" Bellán may also remain a shadowy figure whose pioneering "big-league" credentials are marred by his limited play in the marginally recognized National Association. But there is little question about when Cubans (and thus also Latin Americans) made their first mark on the consciousness of the North American major leagues. The date, ironically, was the star-spangled Yankee holiday of July 4th, 1911, and the location was Chicago's West Side Grounds, home of the National League champion Cubs.

On that afternoon a pair of swarthy-complexioned Spanish-speaking outfielders took the field for the Reds from Cincinnati and thus became the first 20th-century Cubans to taste big-league action. Rafael Almeida and Armando Marsans (both right-handers and neither with much thunder in their bats) were harbingers of a coming Cuban big-league invasion which would begin as a mere trickle over the next few seasons with catcher Mike González (1912) and pitcher Adolfo Luque (1914) in Boston, outfielders Merito Acosta and Jack Calvo in Washington (1913), and middle infielder Angel Aragón (1914) and hurler Emilio Palmero (1915) in New York.

The history of America's national pastime between the closure of the dead-ball era (immediately after World War I) and the demise of an odious "gentlemen's agreement" (shortly after World War II) is replete with more than one incident of big-league management passing off dark-skinned Latinos as "Cubans" or "Castilians" though certainly not as "Negroes." But first came the once-celebrated and now largely forgotten saga of two olive-skinned flychasers discovered in the lost outposts of the Connecticut League by Cincinnati manager (and later Washington Senators owner) Clark Griffith. Armando Marsans (below right) and Rafael Almeida (below left) enjoyed short-lived but historically significant careers with the tailender Cincinnati teams of the immediate pre-World War I period. Almeida would hit but .270 over three short seasons of National League play. Marsans stretched out his own career until 1918, compiling only a .269 lifetime average but bashing the ball at a .317 clip during a stellar 1912 season. Yet both were the center of immediate controversy resulting from their prominent olive-colored skin, and a worried Cincinnati management was soon forced to send off to Cuban officials for documents to certify that the two imports were of Castilian (that is, Spanish) and not African (that is, black) ethnic heritage.

ALMEIDA-CINN:NAT.

Base Ball.

Almeida
C-21.

Hermann   Kling   Johnson

Middle Row: Bescher, Ames, Almeida,
Sitting: Sheckard, Packard, Blackburn,

1913   CINCINNATI

FAT
TUR
CIGA

Popular reports have it that even Griffith experienced mild concern when hearing of club president Garry Herrmann's reservations about signing the Cuban prospects ("We will not pay any Honus Wagner price for a pair of dark-skinned islanders," said Herrmann), and when Herrmann appeared to greet the imports upon their arrival at the Cincinnati railroad station, he suffered near heart seizure when a couple of brown-skinned Pullman porters disembarked moments ahead of the anticipated ballplayers. Soon enough, however, Cincinnati newspapers were boasting that the dark-skinned Cubans were "two of the purest bars of Castilian soap ever floated to these

shores — but only after the needed assurances and documentations had arrived from Havana. The Reds had stumbled upon the duo when Griffith offered a tryout to a touted Cuban (Almeida) playing with the Class B New Britain club in the spring of 1911. Almeida spoke almost no English and thus brought along a teammate as his personal interpreter. That teammate (fellow outfielder and Cuban compatriot Marsans) surprisingly impressed Griffith as much if not more than the original prospect, and soon both Cubans were ensconced in the outfield at Cincinnati's Redland Field.

ARMANDO MARSANS
R. F.—Cincinnati Reds
111

A. MARSANS L. F.

MA

BLEND

ETTES   NATIONALS

© Pictorial News Co.

Marsans and Almeida were not the only swarthy-skinned Cuban big leaguers to walk perilously on a racial tightrope across the American and National leagues during the decades after Ragtime and Shoeless Joe Jackson and before wartime rations and one-armed Pete Gray. Venezuelan hurler Alejandro "Patron" Carrasquel (Washington Senators) passed only tolerably well for a white ballplayer between 1939 and 1945 and was often heckled by opposing fans and players for his extra-dark complexion. Bigger-reputation Cubans like St. Louis backstop Miguel "Mike" González (above) — who debuted with the Boston Braves in the early teens and was still

in the big time in the early '30s — regularly suffered a similar uncomfortable fate.

Mike Gonzáles enjoyed a lengthy playing career of 17 seasons and better than 1,000 games on big-league diamonds before swapping his receiver's gear for brief managing/coaching stints in the big leagues and a more prominent managerial career back home in Cuba. González sailed uncharted waters for Latins when given the chance to manage as an interim skipper for St. Louis (23 games in 1938 and 1940). The steel-faced Cuban also owns two permanent niches in baseball lore, one as coiner of the standby phrase "good field, no hit" (which he supposedly used in a scouting report on Moe Berg), another as the third base coach who waved home a streaking Enos Slaughter with the winning run of the 1946 World Series.

If Marsans (below taking batting practice with the Reds, 1913) and Almeida had once caused something of an uproar in the conservative midwestern "frontier" town of Cincinnati, there was soon to be a similar upheaval on the professional diamond of the nation's capital. Racial questions also greeted the brief major league appearances of two additional Cubans of the same era — outfielder Jacinto "Jack" Calvo (oval inset and shaking hands with teammate Germany Schaefer) and pitcher José Acosta. Calvo appeared briefly with the Washington Senators in 1913 and again in 1920 (33 games, .161 BA, 1 HR) while Acosta hurled for the same ballclub as well as for the Chicago White Sox between 1920 and 1922 (10-10, 4.51 ERA).

Merito Acosta, Marianao B.B

Jacinto Calvo
C-48-

# EL SCORE

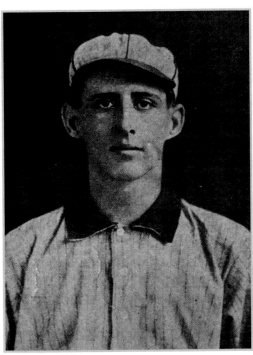

As baseball in Cuba grew in popularity by leaps and bounds during the final decade of the old century and first decade of the new century, the Cuban press naturally increased its reportage on the professional ballplaying circuits both at home and abroad. Publications such as *La Petit Habana* and *El Score* were soon standard reading for Havana's many sporting fanatics. These weeklies carried up-to-date news on Cuban pro and amateur league play, as well as reports on big-league stars and action up north. *El Score* provided game stories, box scores, and detailed individual player stats for both the big-league scene and the Cuban circuit, as well as for island amateur play and for Negro league action that featured native Cubans or teams with island names (such as the All Cubans or Cuban Stars). Today the few existing copies of these early Cuban baseball publications provide rare glimpses of turn-of-the-century stars whose photographic images are seldom seen elsewhere. For example, on this page Tomás Románach (at left), a second baseman on the Almendares Park ballclub, and Mederos (above right, first name unavailable), pitcher for the Havana Park BBC, stare across the decades from a well-preserved 1911 issue of *El Score*.

EMILIO PALOMINO R. F.

A powerful Havana team that featured such notable names as Rube Foster, Preston "Pete" Hill, Luís Padrón, and Luís Bustamente was edged out for the 1908 championship by one of the best Almendares ballclubs ever (one that boasted Rafael Almeida, José Méndez, Strike González, and batting champ Emilio Palomino). This memorable Havana lineup (pictured below) included (clockwise from upper left) Angel D'Mesa, Luís Busta- mente, J.A. Magriña, Agustín Molina (jacket), Luís Padrón, George "Rat" Johnson, Preston Hill, Rube Foster (jacket), Clarence Winston, and Regino García. Busta-

mente (also pictured at top left of this page) was a hall-of-famer who batted .323 in 1908. Hill collected more hits than any player in the league that winter. Padrón had once led the Cuban circuit in both pitching victories and base hits in the same season (1900). Not appearing in the team photo below was Julian Castillo (above right), a hall-of-fame slugger who batted .320 for Havana in 1908 and then captured a batting title with Club Fé one season later. But the Almendares presence of top-flight players like pitcher Carlos "Bebe" Royer would eventually tip the pennant race in the favor of Los Azules.

While pitching giant José Méndez wrote most of the headlines in 1908 and 1909, it was hall-of-fame catcher Strike González, Méndez's regular batterymate, who provided much of the defensive backbone for the champion Almendares contingent. González had debuted in 1902 with San Francisco, then moved to the Havana and Fé teams before signing on with Los Azules in 1907. His notable career would stretch through 1919 and include 10 seasons in Almendares colors. This first great Cuban catcher was most noted for his strong, accurate throwing arm. He was also a clutch hitter and dangerous baserunner, but his lasting reputation was built largely on his fortuitous role as personal favorite receiver of the immortal Méndez.

The winter of 1908 witnessed the season in which Los Azules of Club Almendares first staked their claim as an equal rival to the perennial-champion Havana ballclub that had dominated the early decades of Cuban League play. It was that winter that Almendares gained its first repeat championship. Loaded with front-line players such as ace pitchers Joseito Muñoz, Carlos "Bebe" Royer (acquired that season from Havana), at right, Emilio Palomino (who also doubled as an outfielder), and Andrés Ortega; infielders Armando Marsans, Rafael Almeida, and Esteban Prats; and outfielders Rogelio Valdés, Eugenio Santa Cruz, and Eliodoro "Jabuco" Hidalgo; Los Azules compiled a 37-8 mark, good enough to outdistance Havana by three games. Palomino was the league's leader in batting (.350). The major stars for this first Almendares powerhouse outfit, however, were rookie pitching phenom Méndez, who posted a perfect 9-0 mark on the hill, and sparkplug catcher González, who handled the teams stable of future hall-of-fame moundsmen. It was also in this season that Méndez launched his memorable string of 45 scoreless innings, which would extend into 1909 and included 25 frames against the visiting Cincinnati Reds in November 1908. Reputedly it was the successes of this 1908 season which first give bite to the ballclub motto of "El que gane al Almendares se muere." ("Those that defeat Almendares will perish.") Two ballpark scenes from the 1908 season at the bottom of these pages are set in Almendares Park and feature Almendares BBC doing battle with Club Fé on opening day of the 1908 championship competitions.

C. ROYER P. BEBE

Juan Failde, Manuel Pérez, Agustín Acosta, Máximo Pérez, Abraham Curbelo, Enrique Meléndez, Director, Pío Cárdenas, Tomás Pérez, Juan Lima, Serafín García, Guillermo García, Ezequiel Ramos é Hilario Dobo.

**EL BASE-BALL EN LA HABANA, MATANZAS Y CARDENAS.** Lámina 31

While the two Cuban League juggernauts, Havana and Almendares, were swapping championship banners in the years between the end of the War for Independence (1898) and the outbreak of World War I — with occasional interlopers such as Fé (1906, 1913) and San Francisco (1900) grabbing surprise titles — there were other less memorable ballclubs that attempted to do battle (almost always unsuccessfully) with the two more established nines wearing blue and red. Cuba (1898), Cubano (1900, 1901), Matanzas (1908, 1909), Orientals (1917), Red Sox (1917), White Sox (1917), and Cuban Stars (1919) were the occasional entries that joined San Francisco and Fé in pursuit of the usual leaders. The unusual season of 1917, which witnessed a league of all new teams (Orientals, White Sox, Red Sox), was the only occasion in which a club (Orientals) captured a title in its only season of Cuban League play.

Matanzas BBC was a perennial also-ran during its eight seasons of professional play early in the century. Pictured above is the Matanzas team of 1908. Although there were no celebrities on this team, which won but five games and finished dead last behind Almendares, Havana, and Club Fé, the next season's edition of the Matanzas club would sign four North American Negro leaguers (catcher Phil Bradley, infielders Billy Francis and Al Robinson, and pitcher Jude Gans). It helped little, however, as Matanzas' record in 1909 dipped to only three victories in 39 games.

In the first two decades of the century there were memorable Cuban League stars such as Dolf Luque, José Méndez, Cristóbal Torriente, Bombín Pedroso, Rafael Almeida and Armando Marsans, who made their personal marks — both large and small — in North American ballplaying annals, both in the big leagues and the Negro leagues. There were also less-memorable figures who nonetheless loomed large in their own era. One was catcher Regino García (right), a hefty slugger who set a significant winter league hitting milestone between 1904 and 1907 and also provided one of the heftiest bats of the epoch. When García — also known as "Mamelo" — captured the 1904 league batting crown (.397) while playing for San Francisco, it marked the first of four straight seasons in which the slugger would earn that honor. No other Cuban Leaguer ever matched this feat, and only two others — Antonio García (1888, 1890, 1892, 1893) and Julián Castillo (1901, 1903, 1909, 1910) would ever equal that number over a total career. Suiting up with four different clubs over the course of his dozen professional seasons, García concluded his tenure only a hair's breadth under the magical .300 standard as a batsman, but his quartet of consecutive hitting crowns was sufficient to earn him election into the Cuban Hall of Fame in 1941. The slugging backstop also put in one season (1905) as starting catcher with the All Cubans team, one of the best barnstorming Negro outfits of the era.

R. GARCIA C. MAMELO

A. CABAÑAS 2ª. B.

Another talented Cuban batsman of the era was Armando Cabañas (left), a sure-handed infielder of both Negro league and Cuban League renown. In 1909 Cabañas was refused entrance into the United States at Key West because he was judged by appearance to be an "unwanted Chinaman" ineligible for immigration. A season later, however, he did cross the border successfully to play for one summer with the Negro Stars of Cuba ballclub, a single-season independent barnstorming outfit with many major-league-caliber players in its lineup. While primarily a skinny, glue-fingered infielder with clutch-hitting skills, this versatile Cuban also distinguished himself in the outfield for Almendares during the 1910 winter series in Havana versus the visiting American League Detroit Tigers.

# THE PRIDE OF HAVANA

Tops among early Cuban big leaguers — beyond any serious doubt — was Adolfo Luque, the pioneering and volatile hurler who was both fortunate beneficiary and yet also ill-starred victim of the racial and ethnic prejudices that ruled professional baseball of his era. While dark-skinned Cuban legend Martín Dihigo was barred from the North American majors, a light-skinned Luque was welcomed by management, if not always warmly accepted by bigoted fans in National League cities. Yet while Luque labored, at times brilliantly, in the big-time during the second, third, and fourth decades of the century, his achievements were always diminished, in large part because he pitched the bulk of his career in the hinterlands of Cincinnati, and also in part because his 194 big-league victories were spread thinly over two decades rather than clustered in a handful of 20-win seasons (Luque

enjoyed only one such year). In the current revisionist age of baseball history — when Negro leaguers have at long last received not only their rightful due, but a huge nostalgic sympathy vote as well — Dihigo is widely revered as a true baseball cult figure and duly enshrined in Cooperstown for his Cuban League and Mexican League heroics. Twenty-season big-league veteran Dolf Luque, by contrast, lies obscured in the dust and chaff of baseball history.

Few big-league hurlers have enjoyed such dominance over a short span of seasons as did Luque in the opening years of the Roaring Twenties. Fewer still have proven as durable (20 National League campaigns with Boston, Cincinnati, Brooklyn, and New York were supplemented with 22 Cuban winterball seasons spread between 1912 and 1946) or maintained their dominance over big-league hitters at so hoary an age (at age 43 Luque provided eight crucial wins for the Giants in 1933, including the World Series clincher). Almost none have contributed so richly even after the door slammed shut on an active playing career. Perhaps Luque's most significant gift to the North American version of the national pastime was his proven talent for developing big-league potential in the players he coached over several decades of winterball. While managing Puebla in the Mexican League in 1946 and 1947, one of Luque's brightest and most accomplished students was future American League batting champion Bobby Avila. Another disciple was the eventual New York and Brooklyn Dodger star hurler Sal "The Barber" Maglie, who reportedly learned his tough style of "shaving" hitters close to the chin from his famed Cuban mentor. First as big-league mound ace and winter-league hero, later as unparalleled coach and teacher, no Cuban diamond star accomplished quite so much with so little fanfare as the man once justly called "the Pride of Havana."

Fresh focus on Latin ballplayers has today brought Luque's name — if not the full memory of his career — back into our collective baseball consciousness. Any proper list of all-time Latin American hurlers reveals Luque to be surpassed in accomplishments only by Dominican Hall-of-Famer Juan Marichal, and perhaps also by his own modern-era alter-ego and fellow Cuban countryman, Luís Tiant, Jr. Even today Luque far outdistances all other Latin mound heroes, including such memorable legends as Mike Cuéllar and Camilo Pascual among Cubans and Juan Pizarro, Dennis Martinez, and Fernando Valenzuela from other quarters of the Caribbean. He was a premier pitcher of both the dead-ball and live-ball eras, a winner of nearly 200 big-league contests, the first notable Latin major leaguer, and the first among Latinos to pitch in a World Series (when he appeared in the infamous "Black Sox" fall classic of 1919), win 20 games in a season or 100 in a career, or lead a major-league circuit in victories, winning percentage, and ERA.

Luque's rare claim on durability and longevity is even further strengthened when one takes into consideration his remarkable winter-ball career played out over an incredible thirty-four summers in Cuba. Debuting with Club Fé of Havana in 1912 at age 22, the indefatigable right-hander registered his final winter-season triumph at age 46 in 1936, then returned a full decade later to pitch several innings of stellar relief work in the 1945-46 season at the almost unimaginable age of 55. Luque's combined records for major-league and winter-league service — stretching over almost 35 years — total 284 wins, a figure still unrivaled among all his Latin countrymen.

Base Ball C-38.          A. Luque

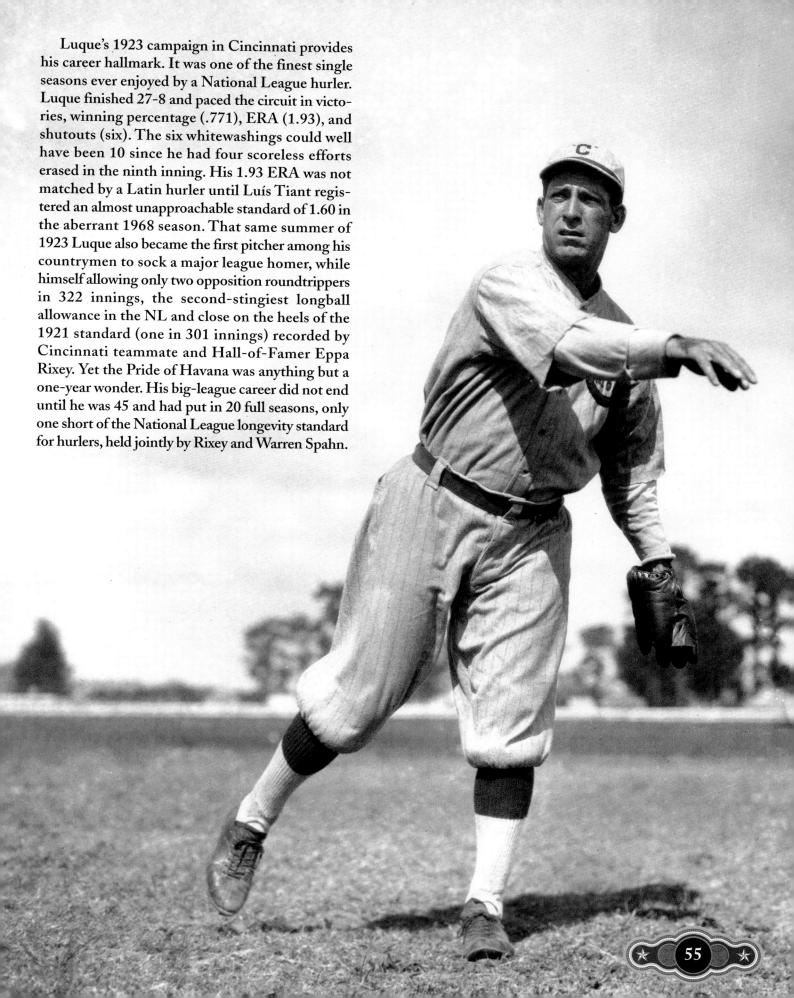

Luque's 1923 campaign in Cincinnati provides his career hallmark. It was one of the finest single seasons ever enjoyed by a National League hurler. Luque finished 27-8 and paced the circuit in victories, winning percentage (.771), ERA (1.93), and shutouts (six). The six whitewashings could well have been 10 since he had four scoreless efforts erased in the ninth inning. His 1.93 ERA was not matched by a Latin hurler until Luís Tiant registered an almost unapproachable standard of 1.60 in the aberrant 1968 season. That same summer of 1923 Luque also became the first pitcher among his countrymen to sock a major league homer, while himself allowing only two opposition roundtrippers in 322 innings, the second-stingiest longball allowance in the NL and close on the heels of the 1921 standard (one in 301 innings) recorded by Cincinnati teammate and Hall-of-Famer Eppa Rixey. Yet the Pride of Havana was anything but a one-year wonder. His big-league career did not end until he was 45 and had put in 20 full seasons, only one short of the National League longevity standard for hurlers, held jointly by Rixey and Warren Spahn.

The much-ballyhooed incident in which Luque reportedly charged the Giants bench to deck heckler Casey Stengel has a basis in fact, but is also distorted by much mythmaking. Like the Marichal-Johnny Roseboro affair four decades later, it appears to have contained events and details infrequently (if ever) properly reported. The setting was Cincinnati's Redland Field (later Crosley Field) on the day of a rare packed house in mid-summer of 1922. The overflow crowd — allowed to stand along the sidelines, thus forcing players of both teams to take up bench seats outside the normal dugout area — added to the tensions of the afternoon. While the Giant bench, as was normal practice, spent the early innings of the afternoon disparaging Cincinnati hurler Luque's Latin heritage, these

taunts where more audible than usual on this particular day, largely because of the close proximity of the visiting team bench, only yards from the third base line. Future Hall-of-Famer Ross Youngs was reportedly at the plate when the Cuban pitcher decided he had heard about enough from offending Giant outfielder Bill Cunningham, a particularly vociferous heckler seated on John McGraw's bench. Luque did, indeed, at this point leave both ball and glove at the center of the playing field while he suddenly charged after Cunningham, unleashing a fierce blow that missed the startled loudmouth and landed squarely on Stengel's jaw instead. The unreported details are that Luque was at least in part a justified aggressor, while Stengel remained a totally accidental and unwitting victim.

Luque's pioneering major league career included an impressive list of landmark achievements:

1. First Cuban and Latin American pitcher to appear in the World Series (1919)
2. First Latin American pitcher to post a 20-victory big-league season (1923)
3. First Latin hurler to top the 100- and 150-career-victory plateaus in the majors
4. First Latin to lead a major-league circuit (National League) in victories (1923)
5. First Latin to lead a major-league circuit in winning percentage and ERA (1923)

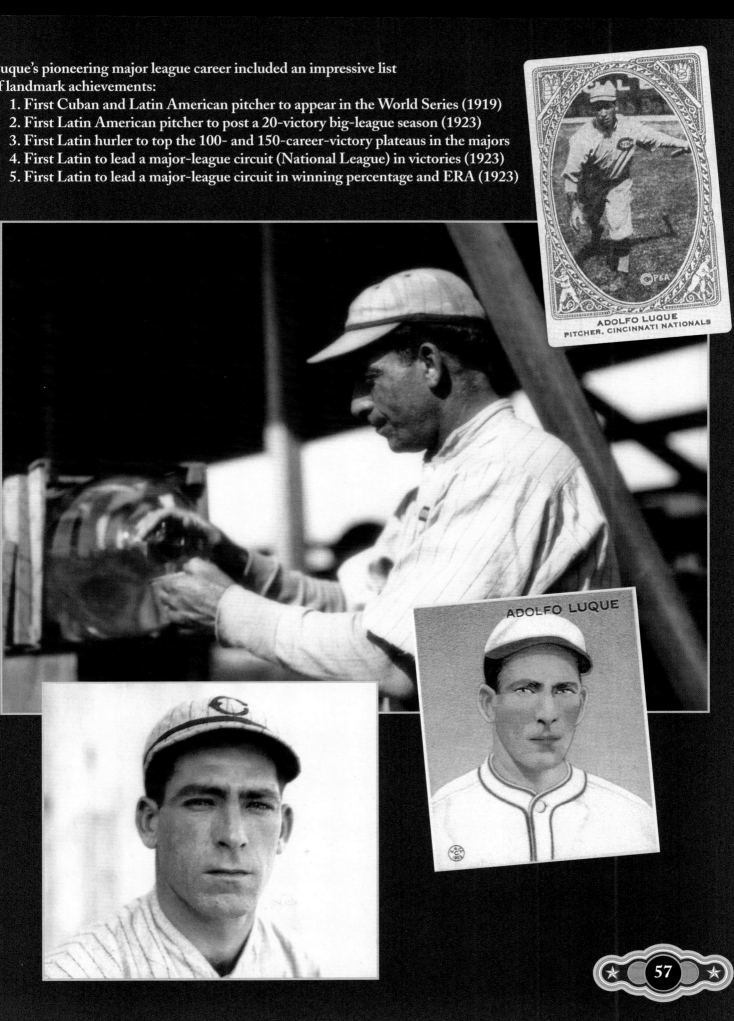

ADOLFO LUQUE
PITCHER, CINCINNATI NATIONALS

ADOLFO LUQUE

New York

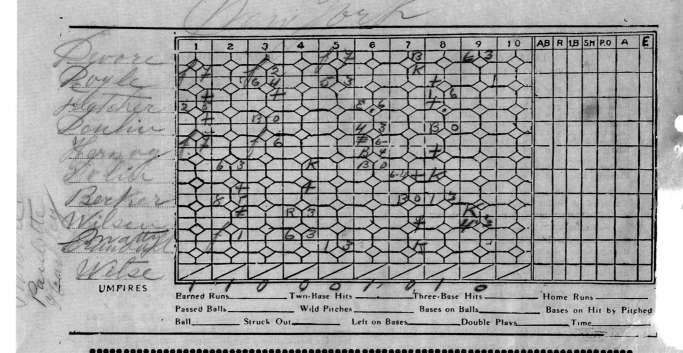

| | 1 | 2 | 3 | 4 | 5 | 6 | 7 | 8 | 9 | 10 | AB | R | 1B | SH | PO | A | E |
|---|---|---|---|---|---|---|---|---|---|---|---|---|---|---|---|---|---|
| Devore | | | | | | | | | | | | | | | | | |
| Doyle | | | | | | | | | | | | | | | | | |
| Fletcher | | | | | | | | | | | | | | | | | |
| Snodin | | | | | | | | | | | | | | | | | |
| Herzog | | | | | | | | | | | | | | | | | |
| Fetch | | | | | | | | | | | | | | | | | |
| Becker | | | | | | | | | | | | | | | | | |
| Wilson | | | | | | | | | | | | | | | | | |
| Crandall | | | | | | | | | | | | | | | | | |
| Wiltse | | | | | | | | | | | | | | | | | |

UMPIRES

Earned Runs_____ Two-Base Hits_____ Three-Base Hits_____ Home Runs_____
Passed Balls_____ Wild Pitches_____ Bases on Balls_____ Bases on Hit by Pitched
Ball_____ Struck Out_____ Left on Bases_____ Double Plays_____ Time_____

---

---

New York

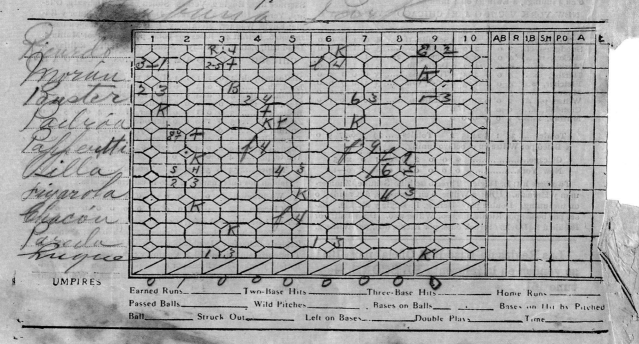

| | 1 | 2 | 3 | 4 | 5 | 6 | 7 | 8 | 9 | 10 | AB | R | 1B | SH | PO | A | E |
|---|---|---|---|---|---|---|---|---|---|---|---|---|---|---|---|---|---|
| Pineda | | | | | | | | | | | | | | | | | |
| Morán | | | | | | | | | | | | | | | | | |
| Baster | | | | | | | | | | | | | | | | | |
| Paulino | | | | | | | | | | | | | | | | | |
| Laffenti | | | | | | | | | | | | | | | | | |
| Villa | | | | | | | | | | | | | | | | | |
| Figarola | | | | | | | | | | | | | | | | | |
| Chacón | | | | | | | | | | | | | | | | | |
| Pareda | | | | | | | | | | | | | | | | | |
| Luque | | | | | | | | | | | | | | | | | |

UMPIRES

Earned Runs_____ Two-Base Hits_____ Three-Base Hits_____ Home Runs_____
Passed Balls_____ Wild Pitches_____ Bases on Balls_____ Bases on Hit by Pitched
Ball_____ Struck Out_____ Left on Bases_____ Double Plays_____ Time_____

Imp. y Linotypo EL SCORE, Neptuno 161, entre Escobar y Gervasio.—Teléf. A-2586.

The immortal Christy Mathewson was one of the earliest big-league stars to taste the rude sting of some surprisingly strong competition from native dark-skinned islanders during barnstorming tours in remote Cuba. The events surrounding Mathewson's debut on Cuban shores came in November 1911, in the wake of a six-game World Series loss to Connie Mack's upstart Philadelphia A's, themselves victims of rude treatment by predominantly black Cuban stars a mere winter earlier. While Matty and the National League champions of John McGraw had set out after some needed R and R for a chance to soothe their egos against backwoods Cuban Leaguers, they would instead suffer further humiliation that again battered McGraw's proud forces and more importantly implanted island legends that would be celebrated back in Havana for decades to come. Upset with their 4-2 drubbing by the Mackmen, the New Yorkers were further shocked with three straight bestings at the hands of a talented Almendares team boasting the young and largely untested arms of José Méndez and Bombín Pedroso. The big leaguers' surprising defeats came at the hands of the two youthful and swarthy Cuban aces, as well as a lighter-skinned unknown named Dolf Luque. Méndez triumphed over Matty 4-3 in 10 innings in the marquee game. The Giants recovered quickly from their slow start, however, and won the next nine straight, kicking off their rejuvenation with a masterful Mathewson 4-0 shutout over Méndez in the much-anticipated rematch of the two legendary aces.

EL BASE BALL EN CUBA Y AMERICA

Herrero,

Mendoza,

Calcines.

1908

CHRISTY MATHEWSON,
CELEBRE PITCHER AMERICANO

Matthewson, p. N. Y. Nat'l

When the New York Giants arrived in Havana in early November 1911, they came with a full contingent of stars which included the likes of (above, left to right) Fred "Bonehead" Merkle (first baseman), Larry Doyle (second baseman), Mathewson, manager John McGraw, and Fred Snodgrass (centerfielder). Snodgrass was only a season away from the infamous dropped World Series flyball which would unfortunately taint his career, but Merkle's equally unjust "boner" of 1908 had already added to the latter's allure. The full contingent of top-flight pitchers which the big leaguers had in tow also included Rube Marquard (24-7 that season), Doc Crandall (15-5), Hooks Wiltse (12-9), and Red Ames (11-10). McGraw was clearly not taking this winter excursion lightly and was thus prepared to throw his best lineup at the upstart Cubans. The "Little Napoleon" had, after all,

visited Havana for ballplaying challenges once before, 20 seasons earlier when he toured as a regular player with the first set of big-league barnstorming visitors to the island. On that occasion the major leaguers won five of five and encountered little resistance from the still-unskilled Cubans. But this time McGraw would be far more impressed with what he saw in the way of loaded opposition. He would later rate Méndez in the same class with the great Mathewson and with Chicago Cubs immortal Mordecai Brown, the two best big-league pitchers of the epoch. The beatings his club suffered at the outset of their 1911 Cuban visit did nothing to lessen the seriousness of the island exhibitions in McGraw's view, likely leading to more than one skull session with his troops like the one in Havana's Almendares Park seen below.

With their pair of visits to Cuba in the second decade of the century (1911, 1920) McGraw's Giants did much to popularize big-league play on the island. (The Giants under Bill Terry, would also return to Havana for a spring training junket in 1937.) Other visiting clubs such as the Tigers of Detroit (1909, 1910), Cincinnati's Reds (1908), and the A's (1910) and Phillies (1911) from Philadelphia also acted as goodwill ambassadors for organized professional baseball. It was thus not rare to find legendary big-league stars pictured on the covers of Cuban baseball publications, especially those New York Giants managed by McGraw. Big leaguers like Giant hurler Art Nehf (right) also appeared regularly on Cuban cigarette cards — this one from a rare Trinidad and Son Cigarette premium. And early-century Cubans also followed big-league action throughout the summer and fall, just as they rooted passionately for their own island-based teams during the winter and spring months. A familiar October scene in Cuba was a scoreboard posting World Series results, like the one here (above) from the 1910 Cubs-A's Series. This scoreboard was sponsored by a popular local beer company.

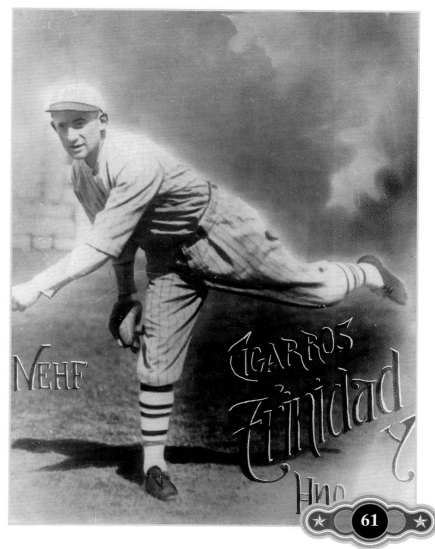

Cuban interest in big-league teams and stars was first fostered by a series of barnstorming exhibitions in Havana during the first decade of the century, games which matched major-league headliners against some of Cuba's finest black stars. Some of the more notable games included:

1908 — Almendares 1, Cincinnati Reds 0. Méndez hurls a one-hitter against the big leaguers and sets a pattern for Cuban successes against island invaders over the next four seasons.

1909 — Almendares 2, Detroit Tigers 1. Eustaquio "Bombín" Pedroso mystifies the Tigers (without either Ty Cobb or Sam Crawford in the lineup) with a no-hit masterpiece.

1909 — Almendares 2, Detroit Tigers 1. Méndez beats another big-league outfit with a five-hitter, making him 2-2 against the barnstormers after a 15-6 Cuban league season.

1909 — Almendares 3, Major League All-Stars 1. Méndez does the honors again for the Cubans, besting Pittsburgh Pirates World Series star Howie Camnitz.

1910 — Almendares 5, Philadelphia A's 2. Méndez wins a pitchers' duel with hall-of-famer Eddie Plank, whom he would beat again (7-5) before the week was out.

1911 — Almendares 3, Philadelphia Phillies 1. This time Méndez also slugs a triple to help his own cause. Later in the week he would again shut down the Phillies, this time 4-0, on a three-hitter.

Throngs of Cuban fans line sidewalks in Havana sometime during the century's second decade to catch a glimpse of posted linescores and game summaries from the major league World Series. These scenes, shown here, pay tribute to the fact that Cuban baseball fanaticism from the earliest years was not restricted to local diamond developments. Barn-storming tours by major-league teams which visited Havana regularly during winter months fired local interest in players such as Ruth, Cobb, Tris Speaker, Sam Crawford, and Mathewson.

The 1911 Cuban winter season was marked by experimental use of lively baseballs embellished with cork centers, but little else seemed to change much around the Havana ballparks as the powerhouse Almendares Blues under manager Juan Sánchez rolled to 20-7-3 record, a second straight championship, and a fourth league banner over the past five seasons. Havana (19-9-2) would trail Los Azules by only a couple of victories, while the circuit's third team, Club Fé (2-25-1), would prove little more than cannon fodder for its two stronger rivals. Despite the new balls there was little evidence of any sudden jump in hitting prowess, and for the only time in a stretch of four seasons (1910-13) the league's best hitter (Preston Hill of Havana) failed to check in with a .400 average.

An interesting footnote to the 1910-11 season was the appearance on the Almendares roster of infielders Marsans (second base) and Almeida (third base), the same pair who would would soon break into the majors later that summer as outfielders with Cincinnati, thus becoming the first 20th-century Cuban big leaguers. The heaviest cannon for Los Azules this particular season, however, was once again ace pitcher Méndez, who started the bulk of the team's games (18), garnered more than half its victories (11), and led the league in complete games (12). It was the fourth and final season that the legendary Méndez would rank as the circuit's top winner, thus establishing another landmark for the memorable 1911 championship season.

The first team to wear the label of Cuban Giants was the famed barnstorming outfit formed by Frank P. Thompson and featuring waiters and other service personnel from the Hotel Argyle of Babylon, New York. Thompson opened up shop with his barnstorming troupe of North American blacks and stayed in the traveling baseball business until the dawn of the 20th century. The name "Cubans" was, of course, strictly a slick marketing device at first, but nonetheless one that spoke volumes about the allure of swarthy Spanish-speaking islanders who could hit and throw a baseball and run the basepaths with entertaining abandon. This earliest team of masquerading "Cubans" wandered the Eastern seaboard of the U.S. for more than a full decade, were recognized in most quarters as the best touring team of the era, and often took up temporary residence in locales such as Trenton, New York City, and Philadelphia. The concept of barnstorming Cuban imports would soon give rise to a long list of teams with similar sounding names, which played both inside and outside of established (but constantly shifting) black circuits during the first three decades of the new century. There would be Cuban Stars West, Cuban Stars East, All Cubans, Cuban X-Giants, Long Branch Cubans, New York Cubans, Jersey City Cubans, Genuine Cuban Stars, Havana Cuban Stars, Famous Cuban Giants, Stars of Cuba, Cuban Stars of Havana, and even a Cuban House of David. All these clubs at one time or another held affiliations with one or more of the many Negro league circuits, and most boasted at least a smattering of genuine Cuban imports. Among native Cubans who played for such outfits can be listed such familiar names (including a smattering of big leaguers with somewhat less swarthy skin tones) as Luque, Marsans, Almeida, Mike González, Merito Acosta, José Acosta, Jacinto "Jack" Calvo, Paíto Herrera, Pedro Dibut, Joseíto Rodríguez, Rogelio Valdés, Antonio María García, Luís "The Elder" Tiant, Martín Dihigo, Cristóbal Torriente, and many, many more.

As the uncontested greatest black star of the dead-ball era, John Henry "Pop" Lloyd was an essential fixture on almost any winning black ballclub of the century's first decades. The remarkable shortstop (who also doubled as a second and first sacker, catcher, and manager) was also a regular Havana winter-season fixture during the same era. If anyone doubts Lloyd's stature they perhaps need only be reminded that no lesser figure than Babe Ruth designated the versatile southpaw swinger as his own greatest ballplayer (any color) of all time.

Two Cuban images of the immortal Henry "Pop" Lloyd reproduced here are a rare portrait from the Aguilitas Tobacco Card set of 1925 (inset circle) and the valuable Billiken cigarette card (right) from the 1923-24 season. Lloyd played regularly in Cuba for more than 20 winters (1908-30) and has been credited by historians with well over 400 island base hits (he topped the league in 1925) and an estimated .330 lifetime batting mark.

Collectible Billiken photo cards from the 1923-24 season capture (clockwise from top left) Edgar Wesley (Havana), Oliver "the Ghost" Marcelle (Santa Clara), Jesse Winters (Almendares), and Frank "the Weasel" Warfield (Santa Clara). Marcelle was the league batting champion and his powerhouse Santa Clara ballclub captured its first championship banner. Second baseman Warfield was the only starter on that juggernaut Leopards club who failed to hit above .300 for the 47-game campaign.

Among the quartet of black stars pictured here in their Cuban uniforms, Marcelle was the most noteworthy. The peer of some outstanding black third basemen in the '20s, he was even selected over Ray Dandridge and Judy Johnson at the hot corner position on the 1952 Pittsburgh *Courier* all-time blackball all-star team. Second sacker Warfield was not the same kind of terrifying slugging batsman, yet he had few rivals in his day when it came to defensive stalwarts at his position.

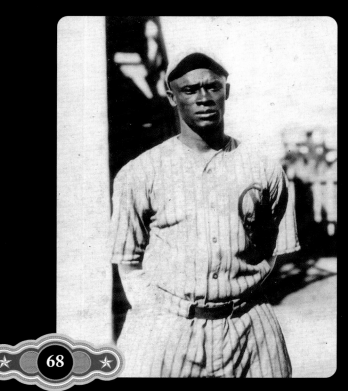

Dick Lundy (left circle, from 1925 Aguili rette card photo) starred with the 1925 league pion Almendares ballclub. Lundy was the circ basestealer that winter and teamed up with a v imported U.S. Negro leaguers on an Almend that captured its first title in five seasons. Als stable for manager Joseíto Rodríguez were Joh "Pop" Lloyd (base hits leader), Oscar Ch (signed away from the Santa Clara team Thomas, Biz Mackey, and Wilbert "Bullet (the league's leading moundsman with 9 victor his part, the switch-hitting Lundy was perhaps blackball shortstop of the '20s and is generall with Lloyd and Willie Wells as the best trio c leaguers ever to man that crucial position.

Additional Billiken tobacco cards feature wise from top left) Clint Thomas (Havana) "Dobie" Moore (Santa Clara), and Mack Eg (Havana). Thomas was a complete player b unparalleled baserunning and throwing sk manned the centerfield pasture and earned t name "Hawk" for both his batting eye and fly agility. Moore was a superb shortstop with or ing defensive range who hit well enough cleanup, while Eggleston was a brainy catche special skills were handling young pitchers on and handling his potent bat on offense.

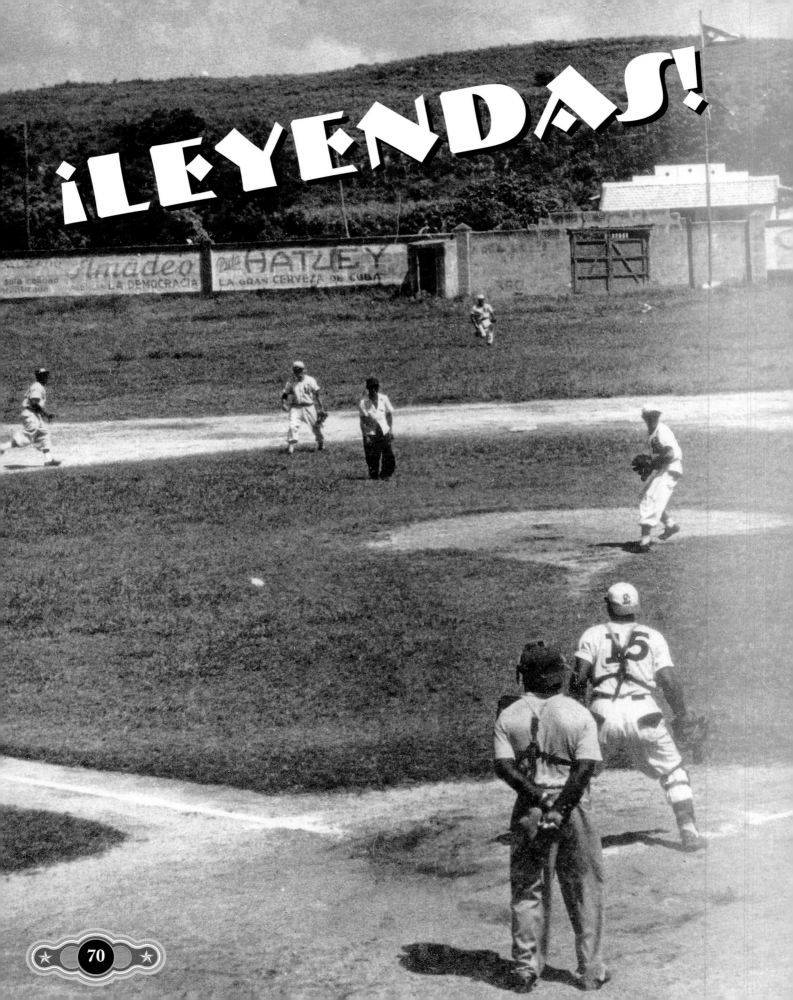

# ¡LEYENDAS!

# THE BIRTH OF LATIN BASEBALL'S LIVING LEGENDS

Dolf Luque and Martín Dihigo remain the great Cuban icons of the first half-century. Despite nearly 200 wins and one dominating National League season, Luque was never a genuine star in the big leagues, but he was the most visible and renowned among Caribbean ballplayers on the major-league scene between the two world wars. Dihigo remained virtually unknown to most North American partisans — as were the bulk of Negro league stars — at least until his name was added decades later to the list of immortals housed in Cooperstown. But back on the island there were other legends that rivaled Luque and Dihigo, even if never quite surpassing them.

There was foremost the brief comet known as the Cuban "Black Diamond" — José Méndez, who turned big-league heads and warmed Cuban pride with his dominations of McGraw's Giants and Cobb's Tigers back in 1908 and 1909. McGraw wanted Méndez for his own roster, despite the Cuban's swarthy skin tone, and even compared him to the immortal Matty. And Luque himself later offered the highest praise for the talents of Méndez. Returning to Havana for a public celebration honoring his own 27-win 1923 campaign, the successful big-leaguer spied Méndez in the grandstand and approached the aging Negro leaguer with a most memorable greeting. "This parade should have been for you," remarked a humble Luque. "You're a far better pitcher than I am."

There was another black baseball star named Cristóbal Torriente, who once outslugged Babe Ruth during a memorable island visit by the Bambino. Much of Torriente's legend is founded not on his stellar decade of blackball play, but upon a brief encounter with McGraw's touring team of big-leaguers (mostly New York Giants) in Cuba during the winter following the 1920 season. And no lesser figure played a key role in this memorable faceoff than Ruth himself, fresh from his miraculous 54-homer debut with the Yankees and enticed to perform in Havana by a then-incredible offer of $1,000 per game from Cuban promoter Abel Linares. With regular Giants third sacker George "Highpockets" Kelly taking the mound for the big leaguers against Club Almendares, Torriente seized the advantage by smashing booming back-to-back opposite field homers. When Ruth (who himself failed at the plate three times) assumed the hill to silence the Cuban slugger, he was greeted rudely by Torriente's third prodigious blow — a ringing double to left that nearly removed the legs of Giants third baseman Frank Frisch. The final count saw Torriente going four-for-five with three roundtrippers and six runs batted in; Ruth stood zero-for-two, having walked twice and reached once on an error. Frisch would later lionize "the Cuban Strongboy" when he remembered the particular blast that nearly amputated his limbs: "In those days Torriente was a hell of a player! Christ, I'd like to whitewash him and bring him up (to the majors)!"

For three decades — between 1910 and 1940 — Cuba was a genuine "Beisbol Paradiso," a true island paradise of winter barnstorming heroics. The big leaguers visited regularly and always returned home with awestruck assessments like the one Torriente had inspired from Frisch. So did the best among blackball stars, who were regulars on the November-January Cuban League scene. And the legends they left behind still vibrate in the island's baseball soul — Cool Papa Bell's three homers (one struck against Dihigo) in a single 1929 game, Ray "Jabao" Brown's first 20th-century Cuban no-hitter, Alejandro Oms' prodigious slugging across two full decades. But as far as most white North American fans of the major-league game were concerned, these tropical barnstormers might just as well have been — in the phrase of historian Douglass Wallop — "playing doubleheaders on the dark side of the moon!"

Of the legendary dark-skinned Caribbean stars, none has greater mythic stature than Dihigo, a resident of both Cooperstown's and Cuba's hallowed halls of immortals (plus those of Mexico and Venezuela for good measure). But Dihigo is far from a lonely star in the Caribbean's rich baseball firmament. Other Cuban stalwarts of the barnstorming era were equally revered at home and respected on blackball and exhibition diamonds stretching far to the north. Perhaps the most mysterious — and thus to baseball historians in some ways the most attractive — of the early Cuban base-ballers was a lithe black pitcher named José Méndez, but soon better known to his big league victims as "El Diamante Negro" ("Black Diamond"). Méndez stood only 5'9" and tipped the scales at a mere 155, yet he hurled a remarkable fastball that seemingly weighed more than he did. John McGraw of the champion National League New York Giants was quick to note the talents of the unhittable Cuban named Méndez. "José Méndez is better than any pitcher except Mordecai Brown and Christy Mathewson," raved the impressionable McGraw, "and sometimes I think he is better than Matty."

Méndez (below and opposite) amazed the sporting press up north almost overnight in the winter of 1908, when he was first discovered by baseball's white establishment, much to the dismay of one set of big-league batsmen who performed for a barnstorming troupe of Cincinnati Reds. When the touring National League ballclub first arrived in Havana that winter for a whirlwind visit, they could hardly have anticipated the rude greeting they and fellow big leaguers would soon receive from an unheralded set of island strikeout artists.

First came Méndez's trio of outings against the bedazzled Cincinnati outfit. The opener was a 1-0 one-hit masterpiece, and to prove that first encounter was no mere fluke, Méndez followed with another seven innings of shutout relief two weeks later. Equally rough on the visitors was another Negro leagues "diamond in the rough," also on the Almendares roster. One winter later Estaquio "Bombín" Pedroso would shock another contingent of big-league tourists wearing Detroit Tigers togs with an 11-inning no-hitter.

Méndez carved out one of the most remarkable legends of Caribbean baseball's wealthy lore. His record against touring North American professional competition (including a number of visiting minor-league clubs) during 1908 and 1909 was a sterling 44 wins and 2 losses. And over the next couple of seasons that record would be anything but diminished. On five different occasions (four in succession) he would pace the Cuban League in winning percentage, five times posting the most shutouts, three times having the most victories, and another three the most complete games. He would stand 25-13 in subsequent seasons against touring U.S. major and minor leaguers. Overall his Cuban and blackball mound record was a marvelous 62-15, an almost unthinkable .805 winning standard.

The Almendares Park ballclub of 1916 (below), which posted a 30-12 season's ledger and walked off with an easy championship, had a near hall-of-fame lineup. The staff pitching ace was Eustaquio Pedroso (number 4 below) who — like legends Dihigo and Cocaína García of later eras — split his time at several fielding positions and simultaneously paced the circuit in both complete games (12) and hitting (with a hefty .413 average). Méndez (#12) also graced the Almendares roster (though he played only the outfield that winter), as did slugger Manuel Cueto (#9) and youthful big leaguer Luque (#3). That winter, Luque led the championship series in victories for the first time with an even dozen.

# EL INMORTAL

There is a special fascination with the truly versatile ballplayer. Baseball is not a game for narrow specialists: the true diamond hero hits with power or at least wields the lumber with precision, possesses a glue-filled glove and a riflelike throwing arm, runs the basepaths with pure abandon, balances strength with speed and agility. It is for this reason more than all others that traditionalists among today's fans abhor the designated hitter rule. Ballplayers who can perform efficiently at multiple positions usually capture fans' hearts and managers' eternal gratitude.

There is but one Latin American ballplayer looming from the lost archives of blackball history who truly stands in a class by himself for defensive versatility. Imagine a ballplayer who manned all positions (actually, all but one — since he avoided the "tools of ignorance"), not as a once-in-a-lifetime stunt like Bert Campaneris or César Tóvar but as an everyday occurrence. And imagine such a ballplayer being praised by famous rivals and teammates alike for his unparalleled mastery at each position. Imagine such

a ballplayer and you have Martín Dihigo (pronounced "*DEE-go*"), baseball's greatest all-around Negro leaguer and in the eyes of many old-timers the best pound-for-pound ballplayer ever. Little wonder that Cubans long called him "the Immortal" or that far and wide — in the Dominican Republic, Mexico, Puerto Rico, Venezuela, and on the Negro-league diamonds of Chicago, New York, Pittsburgh, and Kansas City — he was known simply as "the Maestro," in tribute to his on-field grace, unparalleled star quality, and unrivaled technical knowledge of the game.

It is reported that Dihigo (third from left in back row, with his Cuban League team of 1940) often showed off his all-around skill by taking turns at all nine positions in numerous Negro-league contests (something of an exaggeration, since he rarely if ever caught). In a career that stretched to a quarter-century in Cuba and included at least a dozen Mexican winter seasons and 14 Negro-league campaigns (1923-36), the black Cuban giant was most dominant as a pitcher. His mound credentials would eventually include no-hitters in three countries (Mexico, Venezuela, and Puerto Rico), a documented 119-57 Mexican League record (18-2, 0.90 ERA in 1938), a 93-48 tally across his last dozen Cuban seasons (1935-46), a 218-106 (.673) winter-league and Negro-league ledger in games officially documented, and perhaps dozens of more victories lost to history through shoddy record keeping that typified the barnstorming circuits. As a hitter he was equally devastating on the opposition: a .317 lifetime batting average in Mexico, where he paced the circuit at .387 in 1938 (the same season as his 0.90 ERA on the mound); nine seasons of documented .300 hitting in his native Cuba; more than 130 career homers, with 11-plus seasons for which his longball numbers are entirely missing. The statistics alone earned hall of fame plaques in Cooperstown and in his native Cuba, as well as in Venezuela and in his adopted second winter home, Mexico. Yet his statistics were only half the story.

While Dihigo's hits and pitching victories were never very well recorded, anecdotal evidence for his greatness is often overwhelming. Stories abound of this Cuban's flaming fastball, deadly throwing arm, fence-rattling lumber, and rare grace at virtually every position. Such documented testimonies are legion and make impressive reading. Negro-league great Buck Leonard leads the parade of those who spoke reverently of Dihigo as the game's greatest all-around talent. Leonard was unequivocal: "I'd say he was the best ballplayer of all time, black or white … If he's not the greatest I don't know who is. You take your Ruths, Cobbs, and DiMaggios. Give me Dihigo and I bet I would beat you almost every time." And Leonard's blackball sidekicks agreed almost to the last man. When surviving former Negro leaguers were polled in the early 1980s regarding an all-time black lineup, it was Dihigo who wound up as the second baseman of choice. His selection was all the more impressive for the fact that numerous ballots were also cast for the Maestro at two other positions — outfield and third base.

The legacy of the truly incomparable Martín Dihigo contains these rare distinctions:

1. Only ballplayer elected to halls of fame in four nations: U.S., Cuba, Venezuela, and Mexico
2. Voted all-time best Negro league second baseman while also receiving votes as best at third base and in the outfield
3. Pitched first Mexican league no-hitter, also pacing circuit in batting that same season
4. Served as Fidel Castro's first Minister of Sports and oversaw the transition to amateur Cuban baseball after the 1959 revolution

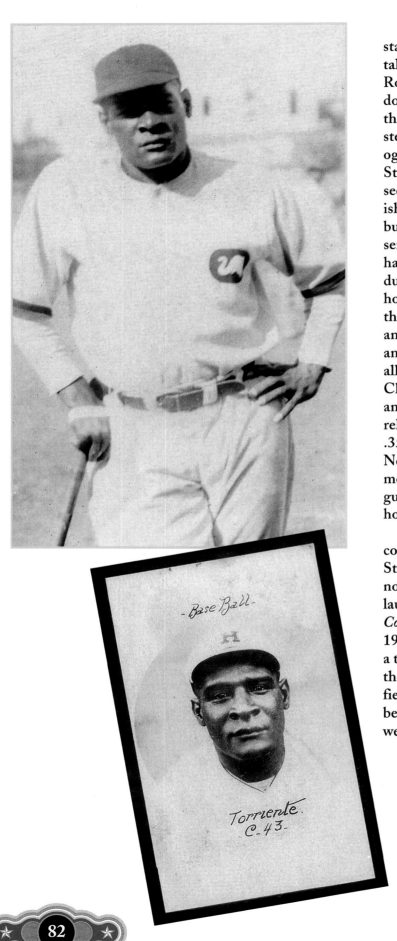

Base Ball.

Torriente.
C. 43.

Méndez and Dihigo were perhaps the brightest stars — one short-lived, the other seemingly immortal — who planted themselves in the pre-Jackie Robinson Cuban baseball firmament. There were dozens of others whose dark skin all but obscured their legends in cities far to the north. Of these, none steps more directly out of the pages of island mythology and folklore than Cristóbal Torriente, the Cuban Strongboy (left). If Méndez fashioned his legend seemingly overnight in Havana against an astonished lineup of touring Cincinnati Reds, Torriente built his day-in and day-out over many seasons of sensational Negro-league play. The huge left-handed-hitting outfielder was the biggest run producer in the potent lineup of Rube Foster's powerhouse Chicago American Giants throughout most of the Roaring 1920s. Experts among blackball historians seem unanimous in placing Torriente squarely among the three greatest Negro-league outfielders of all time (alongside James "Papa" Bell and Oscar Charleston). His reported batting averages in Cuba and the States tell much of the story of Torriente's relentless slugging. His reported lifetime mark of .352 in Cuba is the third-highest recorded; his career Negro-league average stood at .339; he is documented as hitting .311 in exhibitions against big-leaguers (including a .359 clip and several mammoth homers over 11 games in Cuba in 1919).

The raw numbers are supplemented by a lengthy collection of glowing reports concerning the Cuban Strongboy's superhuman blasting of the baseball. But no overall assessment of Torriente's prowess is more laudatory than the one accompanying the *Pittsburgh Courier's* selection of its all-time all-black team in 1952: "A prodigious hitter, a rifle-armed thrower, and a tower of strength on defense … deceptive speed and the ability to cover worlds of territory, from the right-field foul line to deep right center. He was one of the best bad-ball hitters in baseball and could hit equally well to all fields."

Two Cuban legends — Eustaquio "Bombín" Pedroso (above left) and Torriente — posed in 1913 as members of the independent blackball club known as the Cuban Stars. This was Torriente's debut season as a Negro-league center fielder, while Pedroso had already earned considerable fame several years before with his 1909 no-hitter against the island-hopping Detroit Tigers. Torriente's career would stretch until 1932, a full 20 seasons, and he would also play in the Cuban League an additional dozen winters spread over those same two decades.

The trio posing above — from left: Pablo Mesa, Oscar Charleston, Alejandro Oms — is cited almost universally among Negro baseball authorities as the greatest outfield in the history of Cuban baseball. One would also be hard-pressed to find a better tandem anywhere in the annals of Negro league or even major league play. This particular posed image of the Santa Clara trio dates from the 1924 Cuban season and is frequently seen in Negro league history books; in fact, it is likely one of the most famous of all Cuban baseball images.

Charleston is often touted as the purest all-around talent among all Negro leaguers; he might well also rank squarely at the top of any list of non-Cubans who have played extensively in the island's crack winter league. This barrel-chested slugger was so versatile and potent with the lumber that he was often ranked in his own era with none other than Babe Ruth; his slashing baserunning style (especially early in his career) was sufficient to gain additional comparisons with Ty Cobb; as a defender his speed and propensity for playing a shallow center field drew constant analogies with Tris Speaker. Here was three top white hall-of-famers all wrapped in a single package, a package which also added a rare penchant for showboating and crowd-pleasing into the incomparable mix.

Oms was a raw rookie with Santa Clara the winter the team first appeared in league play (1923) and he was already capable of swinging the bat at a .400 clip (.436) — good enough to win the league batting title if he had not fallen a few at-bats short of the necessary number to qualify. Two seasons later he did win the hitting title outright (.393), and he owned it a couple more times down the road as well (.423 in 1929 and .389 in 1930). Like his outfield teammates Mesa and Baró with the Cuban Stars in the early '20s he was more noted defensively for his exceptional speed and range than for his rather average throwing arm. He was also a natural showman who is reported to have delighted crowds at onesided games by catching fly balls behind his back. But it was with his lefthanded slugging that Oms made his biggest mark, hitting consistently better than .300 during six seasons in the Eastern Colored League, once blasting a record 40 roundtrippers.

Mesa drew a lot less attention — especially after his career had ended — than did his pair of more celebrated outfield teammates. Nonetheless he was one of the most complete ballplayers — with longball power, baserunning speed, bunting skills, and outstanding defensive range — ever produced in Cuba, and also an athlete who on occasion rose to his own brief flights of near-stardom. Mesa nearly won his own batting title in

Cuba in 1927 when his average soared to .409, but his plate appearances fell a handful short of qualification (the official crown went to Manuel Cueto at .398). And he actually anchored not one (with Oms and Charleston) but three all-time great outfields while playing on his native soil as well as on the black baseball circuit. In the early '20s he was surrounded in the Cuban Stars outfield (in the Eastern Colored League) by Oms and Dihigo; before Dihigo moved to the outer pastures Mesa also teamed up with Oms and another batting sensation, Bernardo Baró.

The team fielded by Santa Clara in the mid-'20s may well have been the strongest short-span Cuban League outfit ever assembled. Few have dominated a single season as the Santa Clara team did in 1923-24, behind the slugging of Oliver Marcell (the batting champion with a .393 mark), Charleston, Oms, and Dobie Moore (a league leader with 71 hits), plus the pitching of Bill Holland (league pacesetter in winning at 10-2), Méndez (still strong that season at 3-1), Pedroso (a fading veteran who nonetheless won five while dropping eight), and Pedro Dibut (who was just beginning his own brilliant career). It was truly a lineup for the ages. And it was a lineup fielded by a ballclub that was enjoying only its second season on the winter circuit.

BASE-BALL

CHAMPION MESA (R. F.

Charleston, S Clara B B C

Oms, S Clara B.P.C.

FABRICA DE CIGARROS

:·: HABANA :·:

Clark - Catcher · Bischoff - Catcher · Thomas - Outfielder · Westley - Infielder · Cooper - Pitcher · A. Luque - Manager

V. González - (Sirique) · Lloyd - Infielder · Levis - Pitcher · J. Calvo - Outfielder · B. Portuondo - Infielder

Compañía Cigarrera DIAZ
S. A.

Havana Base Ball Club, Cuban Winter League 1923-24 season. Players pictured on these Fabrica de Cigarros tobacco premiums (near right) include (clockwise from upper left): Clarck (first name unknown), John Bischoff, Clint Thomas, Edgar Wesley, Andy Cooper, Adolfo Luque (manager), Bartolo Portuando, Jack Calvo, Oscar Levis, John Henry "Pop" Lloyd, and umpire and former star player Gervasio "Strike" González. Also (far right, top, clockwise from upper left): Busta Quintana, Mack Eggleston, Tatica Campos, Eufemio Abreu, Pelayo Chacón, Merven "Red" Ryan, Buster Ross, Bienvenido "Hooks" Jiménez, Juanelo Mirabal, and Marcelino Guerra. Mirabal was the team's star hurler and the only league pitcher with two shutouts, but Havana, with its 25-23 record, finished a distant second behind Santa Clara. The powerhouse champions dominated most of the individual league categories, including batting (Marcell), runs scored (Charleston), base hits (Moore), stolen bases (Charleston), and pitching wins (Holland).

FABRICA DE CIGARROS

:·: SANTA CLARA :·:

Charleston - Outfielder · Rios - Infielder · Moore - Infielder · Marcelle - Infielder · Tinti Molina - Manager

H. Johnson - Infielder · Holland - Pitcher · Mesa - Outfielder · Oms - Outfielder

Compañía Cigarrera DIAZ
S. A.

TOMAS GUTIERREZ

Quintana - Infielder    Eagglenton - Outfielder    Campos (Manzanillo) Outfielder    Abreu - Catcher    P. Chacón - Infielder

BANDERA

:·:· B. B. C. ·:·:

M. Guerra - Outfielder    Mirabal - Pitcher    B. Jiménez - Infielder    Roos - Pitcher    Ryan - Pitcher

FINLAY 66. - HABANA

Mesa, Bill Holland, and Oscar "Heavy" Johnson. Also (below, clockwise from upper left): Dave Brown, Eustaquio Pedroso, Frank Duncan, Julio Rojo, Pedro Dibut, Rube Currie, Esteban Montalvo, Frank Warfield, and José "the Black Diamond" Méndez. With a mix of star Negro leaguers such as Charleston, Marcelle, Holland, and Johnson, plus aging legendary Cuban pitchers Pedroso and Méndez, this club posted a 36-11 record and outdistanced Havana for the league title. Dibut, in turn, was one of a rare dozen or so Cubans who played both on the Negro circuit and also briefly in the majors.

Santa Clara Base Ball Club, Cuban Winter League 1923-24 season. Players pictured on these Tomás Gutierrez tobacco premium pages (left, bottom) include (clockwise from upper left): Oscar Charleston, Herman Ríos, Walter "Dobie" Moore, Oliver "The Ghost" Marcelle, Agustín "Tinti" Molina (manager), Alejandro Oms, Pablo

TOMAS GUTIERREZ

Brown - Pitcher    Pedroso - Pitcher    Duncan - Catcher    Rojo - Catcher

Méndez - Pitcher

:·:· B. B. C. ·:·:

Wardfield - Infielder    Montalvo (Mayarí) - Infielder    Currie - Pitcher    Dibut - Pitcher

FINLAY 66. - HABANA

Almendares Base Ball Club, Cuban Winter League 1923-24 season. Players pictured on these Tomás Gutierrez tobacco premiums (near right) include (clockwise from upper left): Valentín Dreke, Oscar Fuhr, Isidro Fabre, Armando Marsans, Bernardo Baró, José Rodríguez (manager), José "Cheo" Ramos, Willis "Pud" Flournoy, Oscar Tuero, Rafael Almeida, and Jakie May. Also (bottom left, clockwise from upper left): Kakín González, Jesse Hubbard, Manuel Cueto, "Snake" Henry, Eugenio Morín, José Fernández, Oscar Rodríguez, Lucas Boada, Papo González, and Ramón "Mike" Herrera. Almendares was only the league's third-best team in 1924, with an 18-29 record despite its quartet of former (Marsans, Almeida, Tuero) and future (Herrera) major leaguers. Bienvenido Jiménez (pictured with Havana on the previous page) began the season with Almendares but finished the year as the league's home run champion with Club Havana. Infielder Herrera — like Dibut with Santa Clara — was another of the small handful of players who tasted both Negro-league and big-league action when he joined the Boston Red Sox for the 1925 and 1926 seasons as a rarely used utility man.

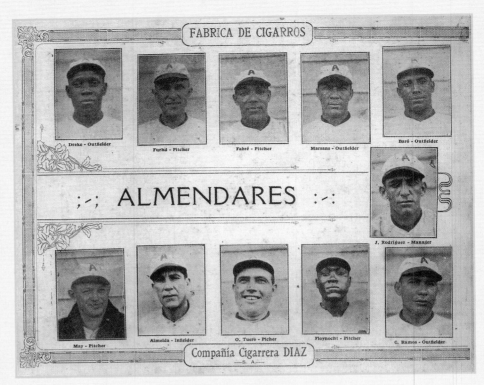

FABRICA DE CIGARROS

Dreke - Outfielder
Furhd - Pitcher
Fabré - Pitcher
Marsans - Outfielder
Baró - Outfielder

:-; ALMENDARES :-:

J. Rodríguez - Manager

May - Pitcher
Almeida - Infielder
O. Tuero - Picher
Floynocht - Pitcher
C. Ramos - Outfielder

Compañía Cigarrera DIAZ
— S. A.—

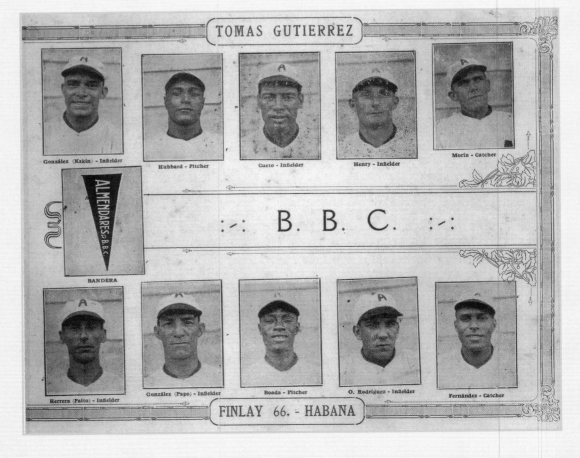

TOMAS GUTIERREZ

González (Kakín) - Infielder
Hubbard - Pitcher
Cueto - Infielder
Henry - Infielder
Morín - Catcher

ALMENDARES B.B.C.

BANDERA

:-: B. B. C. :-:

Herrera (Paíto) - Infielder
González (Papo) - Infielder
Boada - Pitcher
O. Rodríguez - Infielder
Fernández - Catcher

FINLAY 66. - HABANA

FABRICA DE CIGARROS

Petty - Pitcher  |  J. Pérez (Pepín) - Infielder  |  Mc. Curdi - Catcher  |  Dressen - Infielder  |  D - Brown Outfielder

:·: MARIANAO :·:

Merito Acosta - Manager

MAGRIÑAT  |  E. Brown - Outfielder  |  H. Scheiber - Infielder  |  Phelan - Infielder  |  Cooney - Infielder

Compañía Cigarrera DIAZ
S. A.

hall-of-fame umpire Héctor Magrinat. Also (bottom left, clockwise from upper left): Emilio Palmero, Otto Krueger, Rogelio Crespo, Harry Deberry, José Acosta, Ed Morris, Rosy Ryan, Otis Brannan, Slim Love, and Cristóbal Torriente. Torriente (a .346 batter for the season) was, of course, one of the all-time Negro and Cuban League greats and started this particular campaign with Havana before switching to Club Marianao. Outfielder Jack Calvo (another player who doubled in Negro leagues and the majors) made the opposite switch. Yet another player pictured here who crossed the line between Negro-league and big-league play was pitcher Acosta. The Tomás Guiterrez cigarette premiums pictured on these pages are in the form of album pages which were obtained directly from the factory in exchange for complete sets of the now-rare tobacco insert cards.

Marianao Base Ball Club, Cuban Winter League 1923-24 season. Players pictured (above) include (clockwise from upper left): Jesse Petty, José "Pepín" Pérez, Harry McCurdy, Charlie Dressen (the future big league manager), Don Brown, Merito Acosta (manager), Jimmy Cooney, Art Phelan, Hank Schrieber, Eddie Brown, and

TOMAS GUTIERREZ

E. Palmero - Pitcher  |  Krueger - Catcher  |  Crespo - Catcher  |  Deberry - Pitcher  |  Acostica - Pitcher

BANDERA

:·: B. B. C. :·:

Torriente - Outfielder  |  Love - Pitcher  |  Brannon - Infielder  |  Ryan - Pitcher  |  Morris - Pitcher

FINLAY 66. - HABANA

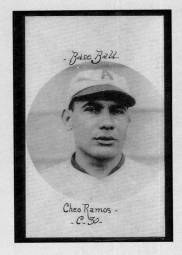

-Base Ball-

Cheo Ramos -
-C-30-

-Base Ball-

Rafael Quintana -
C-55-

-Base Ball-

Fernández -
-C-29-

-Base Ball-

Palmero -
-C-49-

-Base Ball-

-C-24-
Oscar Rodríguez -

-Base Ball-

-Paito-
-C-31-

-Base Ball-

Strike-
C-53-

-Base Ball-

Oscar Lewis-
C-41-

-Base Ball-

Morín-
C-23-

Another set of collectible tobacco cards from the mid-twenties (most likely a promotion for the 1924-25 season) features the following winter league ballplayers: José "Cheo" Ramos, Almendares outfielder; Rafael "Busta" Quintana, Havana infielder; José Fernández, Almendares catcher; Emilio Palmero, Marianao pitcher; Oscar Rodríguez, Almendares infielder; Ramón "Mike" (Paito) Herrera, Almendares infielder; umpire Gervasio "Strike" González, former Almendares star catcher; Oscar Levis, Havana pitcher; Eugenio Morín, Almendares catcher; and Kakín González, Almendares infielder. Palmero (known as "the Blond from Guanabacoa") was a junkball-tossing lefty who broke into the big leagues in 1915 (the eighth Cuban to make the big time) with the New York Giants (0-5) and also had several brief return trips in the 1920s with the St. Louis Browns (4-7), Washington Senators (2-2), and Boston Red Sox (0-1). Back home the Cuban hall of famer was several times a Cuban league pacesetter: in winning percentage (1920), games pitched (1921), complete games (1917), and pitching victories (also 1917).

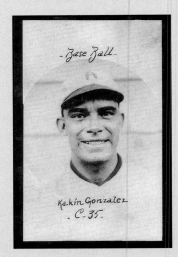

-Base Ball-

Kakín González -
-C-35-

Pictured below are more players from the 1925 Nacionales card set: Valentín Dreke, Almendares outfielder; Isidro Fabre, Almendares pitcher; Oscar Tuero, Almendares pitcher; Rogelio Crespo, Marianao infielder; and Jacinto Calvo, Havana outfielder. Dreke was the most luminous star of this group, enjoying his grandest season with champion Almendares in 1926 when he batted .385 but lost the hitting crown to Negro leaguer Jud Wilson, who clobbered the ball at a .430 clip. Dreke swung a big enough bat to rank near the top of most offensive categories (leading in runs scored) but also impressed long-time fans with his incomparable fielding. The lifetime .307 hitter was a 1945 Cuban hall of fame selection.

Jacinto "Jack" Calvo (1913, Washington Senators) was the fifth 20th-century Cuban big leaguer, preceded only by Almeida (1911, Cincinnati Reds), Marsans (1911, Cincinnati), Miguel González (1912, Boston Braves), and Merito (Baldomero) Acosta (1913, Washington). Calvo's major-league stops would consist of only two partial seasons, a mere 34 games, and a less-than-stellar onfield performance (nine hits, one homer, an anemic .161 BA). Thirteen Cuban winter seasons proved far more productive from the offensive side, with the swift flychaser posting a solid .310 career average across 265 games divided between Club Havana (eight-plus seasons), Almendares (three seasons), Orientales (one season), and Marianao (one partial season). Calvo also joined the list of blackball crossovers when he played briefly (1915) with the New Jersey-based Long Beach Cubans.

TELF. { M-5031
        { A-0004

# La Florida

Obispo & Monserrate Sts.
HABANA - CUBA

## BAR RESTAURANT
### THE CRADLE OF THE DAIQUIRI COCKTAIL

PONCE DE LEON DISCOVERING IN THE "LA FLORIDA BAR"
THE FOUNTAIN OF ETERNAL YOUTH

Baseball was flourishing in Cuba during the "Roaring Twenties" and not only in Havana's Almendares Park, or in Santa Clara, or in Matanzas — sites where professional winter league games were staged — but also on amateur fields everywhere across the island. National amateur championships had been thriving ever since they were first established back in 1914. All-white ballclubs representing Fortuna Sports Club, Havana University, Regla, Hersey, and the Vedado (Havana) Tennis Club fielded the strongest teams during most years and won the bulk of amateur tournaments between 1915 and 1935. While the nation's amateur tournaments in the '10s and early '20s discriminated against black ballplayers, integrated amateur teams began slowly to appear on the scene by the late '20s and early '30s, as witnessed here. By the end of the century's third decade, Havana was rapidly becoming a town renowned for its wild nightlife scenes (above), and the Cuban baseball scene was also transforming itself into a winter paradise for ballplayers of all races, all colors, and all creeds.

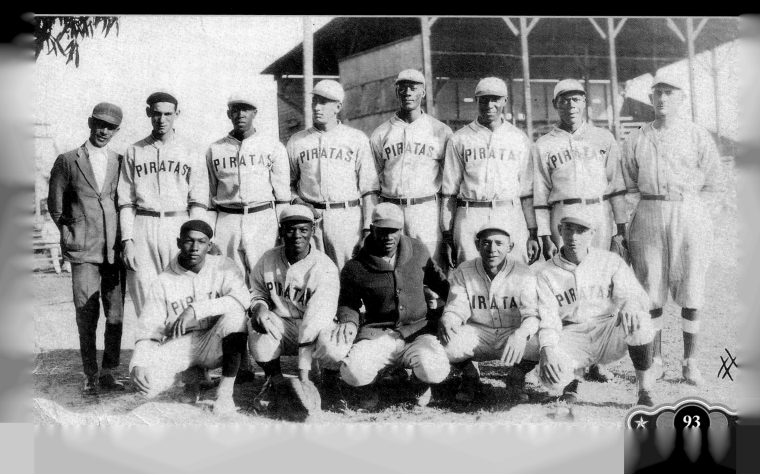

Almendares ("Los Azules") and Havana ("Los Rojos") may well have dominated most of the three-quarters of a century of Cuban professional league competitions, and the Marianao Tigers and Cienfuegos Elephants might still be the other pair of remaining ballclubs today best remembered from the dusty annals of Cuban league history. But no single ballclub dominated the Cuban baseball scene quite so effectively for such a short span as did Santa Clara ("Los Leopardos") during a 19-season span (1923-41). During that period there would be four championships (1924, 1936, 1938, 1939) for the Santa Clara club, along with three seconds, two thirds, and one fourth-place finish. The latter came during Santa Clara's inaugural season, when 27 games were lost via forfeit

(despite a powerhouse lineup that featured Alejandro Oms and Pablo Mesa) when manager Agustín Molina withdrew his ballclub in protest over a controversial game that was lost to Marianao. It would be at the end of the '30s, however, when Santa Clara ultimately peaked with its invincible combination of native Cuban stars (Oms, Mesa, Cocaína García, Lázaro Sálazar, Santos Amaro, Tony Castaño, and Jacinto "Battling Siki" Roque) and blackball legends recruited from up north (Oscar Charleston, Josh Gibson, Sam Bankhead, Johnny Taylor, Ray "Jabao" Brown, and Bob Griffith). Back-to-back championships in 1938 and 1939 included a 1938 record (44-18-4, .710) that proved one of the most dominant in eight decades of Cuban League history.

Santa Clara was the Cuban League's most dominant outfit during the final pair of seasons in the decade of the 1930s. Opposite: Multi-talented Cocaína García (far right, below Amaro) and equally versatile Santos Amaro (far left, with arm on García's shoulder) enjoy an opening day ceremony at the ballpark in Santa Clara, one of the circuit's two ballparks at the time. The occasion here is the inauguration of the 1938-39 campaign in which the Santa Clara forces would again outdistance the league's other four entries for the club's second straight championship banner and fourth league title overall. Below: The stellar 1938-39 Santa Clara outfield was comprised of (left to right) Dominican Juan "Tetelo" Vargas, Manuel "Cocaína" García (also one of the team's top pitchers), Lázaro Sálazar (also the manager), and Santos "Cangaru" (Kangaroo) Amaro. This group dominated a healthy portion of the league's individual statistical categories, with Amaro the pacesetter that year in hits and RBIs and Sálazar outranking all rivals in doubles. García took enough time off from his outfield duties to perform brilliantly on the mound, pacing the circuit in shutouts.

The first of two remarkable late-'30s seasons for the Santa Clara ballclub featured the versatile hitting of Negro leaguer Sam Bankhead. In many respects, however, this was also a season (1938) whose successes could be laid squarely at the feet of manager-outfielder-infielder Lázaro Sálazar. Bankhead dominated the league's individual batting stats with a near-triple-crown performance, outdistancing the field in six categories (.366 BA, 243 ABs, 47 runs, 89 hits, five triples, 34 RBIs) and failing to dominate only in round-trippers and doubles. This was the same capable Sam Bankhead who would eventually be named as utilityman on the 1952 *Pittsburgh Courier* all-time Negro leagues team. Sálazar did his own damage in the Santa Clara lineup, espe-cially at the plate, where he posted the team's third-highest batting average (.318) and tied Bankhead for the league lead in three-baggers, and on the mound, where he captured three victories without defeat. But it was also the leadership role of Sálazar that proved vital to a championship, which he won in his first year of managing by blending a diverse collection of superstars into a cohesive winning unit. One key to the team's unbeatable lineup was certainly a stellar infield, with its even mix of Cuban and Negro-league talent. That sextet is pictured above and includes (left to right) José Delfino (2B), Roberto Ruíz (3B), Sam Bankhead (SS), Antonio "Pollo" (Chicken) Rodríguez (3B), Lázaro Sálazar (1B and manager), and Miguel Solis (utilityman).

Santa Clara, under the continued leadership of Sálazar, would repeat its reign a season later. The hero roles would now be slightly altered, with Bankhead giving way to newly arrived blackball nonpareil Josh Gibson. Catcher Gibson debuted with league-leading numbers in runs scored (50) and longballs (11). While Bankhead slipped (he would rebound atop many of the league hitting categories the following winter) there was nonetheless excellent production from Tony Castaño (league batting champ), Santos Amaro (league base hits and RBI pacesetter), and manager Sálazar (who topped the circuit in doubles). It was hardly a weakening of talent and the mighty Leopards once more finished five games better than runner-up Havana. What sustained the Santa Clara forces, however, was not just heavy hitting. There was brilliant mound work to underpin the slugging, and the durable hurling stars again included both natives and blackball imports. Cocaína García (11-4) enjoyed an early career peak that would be once again matched several seasons later with the Havana team (when he outpitched the

rest of the league in 1943). Ray Brown was also masterful, adding 11 more victories and hurling 16 complete games. The 1939 mound staff is pictured above and includes (left to right) Armando "Indian" Torres, Lázaro Sálazar (who also took up occasional mound duties in his versatile contribution to the squad), Johnny "Colegial" (Schoolboy) Taylor, and Ray "Jabao" Brown. A season earlier (November 7, 1936) Brown had pitched the fourth-ever no-hitter in Cuban League annals, only the second of the century.

If any ballplaying invader from the north ever held his own with the local "peloteros" on Cuban soil it was certainly the great blackball outfielder and slugger Oscar Charleston, who logged nine seasons on the island winter circuit with both Santa Clara (below) and Club Havana (insert). Charleston's career batting average in Cuba was .361 and included a spectacular .405 mark for the shortened season of 1922 and a league-leading .373 during his final visit in 1931.

The wintertime Havana slugging of Oscar Charleston was perhaps only what might have been expected from a Cooperstown hall-of-famer who may have been the greatest all-around player in black baseball history. The phenomenal Negro leaguer peaked on the island with the championship 1924 Santa Clara team, where he provided the heaviest hitting component of a stellar flychasing trio that also included Pablo Mesa and Alejandro Oms. While outhit for average by one teammate (Oliver Marcell) and outpaced in hits by another (Dobie Moore), Charleston still led the circuit in both runs scored and bases stolen.

Rodolfo Fernández (top left) was a big winner on the mound with Almendares in 1932 (tops in the league in victories, complete games, and shutouts), but his successes were equally as grand up north with the Cuban Stars and New York Cubans, and to the west, south, and east with additional winter league teams in Mexico, Venezuela, and the Dominican Republic. Herman "Jabo" Andrews (bottom left) typified the well-traveled Negro leaguer who performed for numerous teams (in this case thirteen) in various blackball circuits while also finding winter employment on Cuban soil. This '30s-era outfielder was never much of a defensive stalwart, but his hefty bat kept him in the lineup of many summer and winter ballclubs, including Club Havana in 1937. A year ear- ~~lier he also appeared with the New York Cubans.~~

While North American Negro leaguers infiltrated Cuban teams, the Cubans also found a comfortable home on U.S. Negro rosters. Cho-Cho (often pro- nounced "Shoo-Shoo") Correa (top right) was a flashy shortstop with a memorable nickname who compiled eleven seasons with Alex Pompez's New York Cubans and Agustín "Tinti" Molina's Cuban Stars in four differ- ent blackball leagues. His career highlight was a .281 bat- ting average and an anchoring infield role for the New York Cubans team which won a NNL second-half pen- nant. Another Cuban Stars mainstay, catcher Eufemio Abreu (bottom right), hammered out a fifteen-year North American blackball career while also playing for Almendares during a celebrated 1920 Havana exhibition series with the touring New York Giants.

Black aces significantly impacted wintertime baseball in Cuba, especially in the 1930s, the same decade in which Satchel Paige and Josh Gibson were rescuing the pennant for dictator Rafael Trujillo in the neighboring Dominican Republic. Negro leaguers filled lineups for all the Cuban teams: Oscar Charleston, Sam Bankhead, Josh Gibson, George "Mulo" (Mule) Suttles, Tom Young, Ray Brown, and Willie Wells with Santa Clara; James "Cool Papa" Bell, Barney Morris, and Frank Duncan with Cienfuegos; Charlie "Chino" Smith, Cliff "Campanita" Bell, John Williams, Frank Crespi, and Ernest Smith for Havana; Rap Dixon, Johnny Allen, Dick Lundy, Harry Kimbro, Ted "Double Duty" Radcliffe, and Theolic Smith on the Almendares roster, and Charleston (once again), Johnny Gill, Barney Brown, and Clyde Spearman with Marianao. Young, Bankhead, and Charleston each won league batting titles; Suttles, Wells, Gibson, Ernest Smith, and pitcher-outfielder Jabao Brown were Cuban League home run champions; and Allen, Griffith, and Brown all won individual pitching titles across the various 1930s-era seasons.

Cubans were, in turn, a major force on the fields of the various Negro leagues, in each and every epoch from the final decades of the past century to the middle decades of the current one. Martín Dihigo, Pablo Mesa, Luís Tiant Sr., Alejandro Oms, Cristóbal Torriente, and even light-skinned Dolf Luque were the most luminous among the various Cuban stars, but there were dozens more who flooded black rosters. These included Pedro Dibut (Long Branch Cubans, left bottom); Busta Quintana (Cuban Stars, Newark Dodgers, left center); Autorio Mirabal (New York Cubans, left top); Oscar Levis (Cuban Stars, Baltimore Black Sox, opposite top left); Armando López (Cuban Stars, opposite top center); and Pelayo Chacón (Cuban Stars, opposite top right). Even the name "Cuban" itself became such a gate attraction on the Negro circuit from the Midwest to the East Coast that it was attached to numerous touring teams (such as the 1913 Cuban Stars ballclub pictured on the opposite page) that often featured only a handful of legitimate Cubanos.

Unlike that 19th-century barnstorming outfit known illegitimately as Cuban Giants and formed not in Havana but on Long Island in 1885, the several black-ball teams which bore the label Cuban Stars during the first three decades of the current century actually contained significant numbers of ballplayers with true Cuban parentage. Most notorious among various Cuban Stars teams was the one (1922-23, pictured below) that boasted a memorable outfield of, first, Pablo Mesa (below, top row, third from right), Bernardo Baró, and Alejandro Oms (below, front row, third from right), and later Mesa with Oms and Dihigo. This team competed in the Eastern Colored League throughout the early twenties. Another stellar Cuba native with various editions of the Cuban Stars was Bienvenido "Hooks" Jiménez, a dazzling infielder known as "the king of Cuban second baseman" and universally ranked among the greatest of the island's base stealers. Jiménez first appeared with the Stars in 1914, while the team was an independent outfit; in later years he played with one Stars team owned by Agustín Molina (which performed in the Negro National League) and an identically named club run by Alexander Pompez (affiliated with the Eastern Colored League). The roster of Cuban headliners on the Cuban Stars payroll would also include skilled pitcher Isidro Fabre (opposite, lower left), who doubled as an outfielder and slugged for a .389 average during the 1927 Eastern Colored League season.

Two distinct teams carried the name Cuban Stars and both flourished in the '10s and '20s. One outfit (owned by Alexander Pompez and known among Negro league historians as Eastern Stars) started as an independent club and later survived as members of both the Eastern Colored League (1923-28) and the American Negro League (1929). The 1928 Pompez team is pictured at the top of the opposite page and the 1923 edition is below. Agustín Molina's rival team (Western Stars) was also first a long-term independent (1907-19) and later a decade-long member of the Negro National League (1920-30). A distinctive feature of both ballclubs was their racially mixed lineups, a condition which introduced several light-skinned Cubans to several seasons of blackball action. One of the number was Cuban hall-of-fame pitcher and infielder Luís "Mulo" Padron (below, top row, far right) whose 18-season Negro-league tenure included stints not only with several Cuban Stars ballclubs but also with an assorted collection of other Negro-league outfits, including the Long Branch Cubans, Chicago American Giants, Birmingham Black Barons, and Indianapolis ABCs. The light-skinned and rangy southpaw outpitched teammate and blackball icon Rube Foster for Club Havana in the 1908 Cuban League, was the first Cuban Leaguer to simultaneously lead the circuit in both pitching and hitting (1900), and by the early '20s was occasionally ranked alongside Méndez and Pedroso as the greatest Cuban pitchers of all time.

Alex Pompez resurrected his earlier Cuban Stars franchise during the mid-'30s, calling his new team the New York Cubans, affiliating it with the Negro National League, and scheduling games in New York's historic Polo Grounds. The memorable team debuted in 1935 and — with only two campaigns (1937-1938) missed along the way — was kept afloat right up to the swan song seasons for Negro-league play, not shutting down operations until 1950. Two absences from the NNL scene resulted when owner Pompez encountered troubles with both New York state authorities and the New York mafia (a result of his gambling activities) and had to flee hastily to Mexico until troubled waters calmed. The strongest team showing came immediately, in 1935, when Pompez's outfit captured the league's second-half banner and battled the Pittsburgh Crawfords for seven playoff games before dropping the year-end championship series. Another second-half championship arrived in 1941, as well as another playoff loss to the Homestead Grays (three games to one) with the league trophy on the line. A postseason championship was finally captured in 1947 with victory over the Negro American League's Cleveland Buckeyes during the Negro league World Series. When the NNL folded operations in 1948 Pompez would keep his team on the field for three final campaigns, now affiliated with the rival western American League.

The partial team portraits on these pages comprise the inaugural New York Cubans roster of 1935, one of the strongest lineups Pompez would ever field. The roll call includes (opposite, top, left to right) outfielders Caudo López, Alejandro Oms, Martín Dihigo and Lázaro Sálazar; (opposite, bottom, left to right) infielders Anastacio Santiella, Horacio Martínez, Francisco Correa, Javier Pérez, Fermín Valdes, and Pedro Arango; and (below, left to right) pitchers Heliodoro Díaz, Cocaína García, Luís Tiant Sr., Rodolfo Fernández, John Stanley, Frank Blake, and John Taylor. These "Cubans" — like most of the Pompez-owned teams — had some of the "real items" in the lineup, headed by island immortals such as Oms, Dihigo, Sálazar, García, Fernández, and Tiant. Sálazar was a left-handed hitter and thrower who in his prime was a lesser model of Dihigo, doing yeoman duty both on the mound and in the outfield. Fernández was a hard-throwing righty who earned special notoriety for his Havana exhibition triumphs in 1937 over the touring New York Giants, Brooklyn Dodgers, and Cincinnati Reds. Tiant "the Elder" (father of big leaguer Luís Tiant, Jr.) was one of the craftiest among Cuban mound aces who tested the blackball circuit and was legendary for his magical pickoff move alone. Tiant's best season came in the New York Cubans' top campaign of 1935, a year in which he appeared in the East-West All-Star Game and also started (and lost) a hotly contested NNL final playoff contest (8-7 score) against Josh Gibson's Pittsburgh Crawfords.

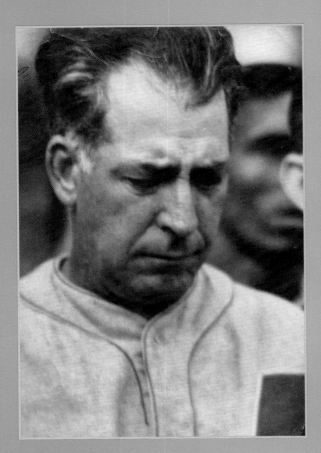

SOUVENIR

GRAN STADIUM CERVEZA TROPICAL

TEMPORADA AMERICANA 1937

MARIANAO - CUBA

¡welcome!

"New York Giants"
National League Champions 1936
and
"St. Louis Cardenals"

WILLIAM TERRY
MANAGER DE LOS "GIGANTES"

Official Souvenir Program

Featuring hall-of-fame hurler Carl "King" Hubbell (below center) and Cooperstown-bound slugger and manager Bill Terry (on scorecard), the popular New York Giants made another of their many visits to Havana in the winter of 1936-37, receiving a handful of drubbings from the local stars before splitting a pair of exhibitions in Tropical Stadium with Frankie Frisch and the also-touring St. Louis Cardinals.

One attraction of the visiting Giants was the presence on their roster of native Cuban moundsmen Dolf Luque (opposite, upper left) and Tomás de la Cruz. The pair were bested in the opener by unheralded Cuban southpaw Juan Eckelson, then embarrassed again 9-1 at the hands of Club Havana and its ace Basilo "Brujo" Rosell. After losing to yet another local mound legend, Ramón Bragaña, and yet another Cuban League outfit (Almendares), the big leaguers finally rebounded to gain a first victory over Fortuna, Cuban amateur champions that season. The local pitcher who finally tasted defeat was future Caribbean Series hero Agapito Mayor, still but a raw novice at the time. Hubbell later posted the Giants' only victory of the tour over a legitimate Cuban League club (Havana), but the New Yorkers' 2-4 overall mark was yet another embarrassment for barnstorming teams from the segregated big leagues up north.

¡ORO!

Cuba first rocketed into North American consciousness with winter-season island tours by big-league teams. While the first grand ballplaying tours encountered embarrassments (for the big leaguers, that is!) at the hands of local Cuban pitching phenoms named José Méndez and Eustaquio Pedroso during the winter seasons of 1908 and 1909, other such tours would nonetheless follow, and each would create substantial legends of its own. Somewhat unfortunately for the vacationing big leaguers, however, those legends almost always involved the surprisingly stellar performances by dark-skinned local ballplaying heroes.

It did not take turn-of-the-century big leaguers long to discover the pleasures of working winter vacations in the sunny "Gem of the Caribbean." After each new island visit an eloquent John McGraw or Frankie Frisch or some other big-league manager would return home with boundless praise for talented black Cuban baseballers, talented arms and powerful bats which the bug-eyed big league skipper lusted after for his own roster but yet could not hope to sign in a league still cursed by an odious "gentlemen's agreement" to shun blacks.

The bombarding of all-white major-league teams on off-season tours was not an event restricted to Cuban shores. Blackball historians have reconstructed enough boxscores from the black press of the '20s and '30s to estimate with confidence that the highly motivated Negro league clubs and touring black all-star teams may well have won nearly 60% of upwards of 400 such contests held around North America and throughout the Caribbean. But it was in Cuba that the winter league treatment often seemed roughest for the major leaguers. And it was in Cuba that some of the best forbidden ballplaying gems seemed to be hidden away from the eyes of big-league fans. When young Frankie Frisch of the Giants saw the Cuban Strongboy Cristóbal Torriente for the first time in 1920, he could only wish for a bucket of permanent whitewash to make the muscular slugger available for his own New York clubhouse. And when Babe Herman of the Dodgers witnessed a washed-up Méndez playing all nine positions with the Kansas City Monarchs in the '20s, he was equally stunned by the spectacle.

Four decades after the triumphs of Méndez and Pedroso, Cuba would again receive headline-grabbing attention as spring training base for the 1947 Brooklyn Dodgers featuring Jackie Robinson. While swarthy Cuban stars perhaps suffered more than any other group under the exclusionary "gentlemen's agreement" of the century's first half (for no place were there more blacks and near-blacks clearly capable of immediate stardom on the big-league circuit), it would ironically be Cuban soil that would now provide the perfect stage for prologue and opening act in Branch Rickey's and Jackie Robinson's bold big-league integration drama. Havana was the ideal launching pad for baseball's final steps toward racial harmony. After all, Cuba had long been a winter diamond paradise for showcasing black and white ballplayers upon the same level playing field.

In the decade following the Second World War (1946-56), North American baseball would become a semi-regular visitor to Fulgencio Batista's Cuba, and the bill of fare suddenly offered far more than mere spring training tuneups or occasional barnstorming tours by big-league outfits. Island visits by segregated barnstormers on the eve of a First World War or by the newly integrated Brooklyn Dodgers in the shadows of a Second World War had been mere prologues for a true Golden Era of Cuban baseball which now spanned the century's midpoint. Famed local teams representing Almendares, Marianao, Cienfuegos, and Club Havana staged a full decade of classic wintertime pennant races filled with homegrown island stars alongside an impressive smattering of North American big leaguers. For a brief span there were even competing leagues playing in the city's two sparkling showcase stadiums — El Cerro and La Tropical. And it was also the epoch when organized baseball arrived on the island for summertime play, with the International League Havana Sugar Kings. In sum, it was a glory-tinged era laced with names like Pedro Formental, Claro Duany, Orestes Miñoso, Conrado Marrero, Cisco Campos, Carlos Paula, Witto Aloma, Raul Sánchez, Pedro Ramos, Camilo Pascual, Rafael Noble, and Silvio García — plus stateside imports Rocky Nelson, Tommy Fine, Luke Easter, Tom Lasorda, Monte Irvin, and Dick Sisler — and it served as both apogee and swan song for Cuba's 20th-century professional baseball saga.

During its final glorious decade in the 1950s Cuba's Professional Baseball League was a true showcase for some of the best local diamond talent ever produced, much of it headed straight for the major leagues. Pictured here, the mid-'50s league all-star team posing in El Cerro Stadium included such island notables as Sandalio "Sandy" Consuegra (top, second from left), Sandy Amoros (top, fifth from left), Pedro Ramos (top middle, in jacket), Silvio García (top, fourth from right), Héctor Rodríquez (top, second from right), Ray Noble (bottom, far left), Minnie Miñoso (bottom, second from left), Ultus Alvarez (bottom, fifth from left), Mike Fornieles (bottom, second from right), Humberto "Chico" Fernández (far right), and Camilo Pascual (bottom, third from right). This was unarguably the proudest set of Cuban-born major leaguers to date.

Of the group mentioned here, only García and Alvarez failed to wear big league uniforms, yet the former — a versatile infielder-pitcher — was rumored in the mid-forties to be a top candidate for Branch Rickey's big-league integration scheme, and the latter a decade later was a renowned slugger who once led the Cuban circuit in longballs (with 10 round-trippers in 1956). Pascual, Ramos, and Miñoso were the most luminous of the lot as major leaguers. But Amoros also earned an irrepressible piece of World Series fame, Fornieles authored a remarkable 1952 pitching debut — a one-hitter in his first outing for the Washington Senators — and was also 1960's top relief ace (with the Boston Red Sox), and durable Consuegra was the American League pacesetter in winning percentage (16-3, .842) for the 1954 edition of the Chicago White Sox.

Miguel "Mike" González may well have been one of those old-time ballplayers whose career was far more notable for its longevity than for its impact on the record books. In 17 big-league seasons he served with senior circuit clubs in Boston, Cincinnati, St. Louis (twice), New York, and Chicago, gaining distinction only as the league's top defensive backstop three different years with the latter franchise. Over twenty seasons in the National League the rugged catcher managed to appear in better than one thousand games, yet for all those opportunities he stroked only 13 homers, batted in barely 250 runs, and hit the ball at a rather anemic .253 pace. These were hardly offensive numbers to brag of, even for a receiver more noted for his defensive role than for his offensive production.

Back home in Havana during winter seasons González was a much more imposing figure than he ever was on the big-league diamond. There he played for more than a quarter of a century (1910-36), all of it but three seasons with the Havana ballclub. He wielded a heftier bat (as a lifetime .290 hitter) and even managed a .432 average and batting title in 1933. And it was on native soil that he earned the highest accolades of his career as a long-time manager. Fourteen times (all with Club Havana) he won Cuban League pennants as a skipper, more than any other individual in league history. He was also one of six different Cuban managers (along with Nap Reyes, Fermín Guerra, Oscar Rodríguez, Clemente Carreras, and Tony Castaños) to direct his country's

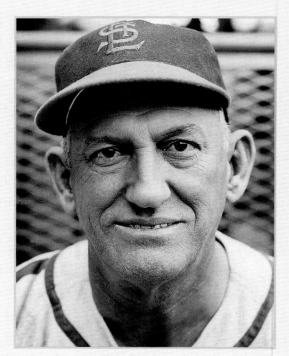

entry to victory in the first dozen-year phase of the winter league championship Caribbean Series. Managing alone assured his 1956 spot in the Cuban hall of fame.

But it was in another arena that Miguel González would earn his true niche. No one has ever had a better knack at being in the right place at the right time. That is to say, no ballplayer ever got quite so much mileage out of his often accidental roles as a pioneer and a relentless opportunist. When it came to making the big leagues González was beaten there by only two of his countrymen — Rafael Almeida and Armando Marsans. (Some leave 19th-century pioneer Steve Bellán aside, due to questions about the major-league status of the 1870s National Association.) González's 1912 debut with the Boston Braves put him one season ahead of José Acosta and Jack Calvo in Washington and two ahead of Luque (Braves) and Angel Aragón (Yankees). González pioneered once more when tabbed by fate and the St. Louis Cardinals as an interim manager in 1938 (8-8 record) and 1940 (1-5). But his most lasting page in the history books was reserved for his other roles with the Cardinals as both bench coach and scout. While functioning as the former it was third base coach González who franticly waved home a scampering Enos Slaughter with the winning run of the 1946 World Series, one of the most memorable plays in Fall Classic history. And it was again the flamboyant Cuban who (due largely to his limited English) coined the immortal phrase "good field, no hit" when filing a telegraphed 1924 scouting report on unknown catching prospect Moe Berg. It was, of course, a phrase which many times in the future would ironically be applied by fellow scouts to González's own Caribbean Basin countrymen.

MIGUEL A. GONZALEZ
MANAGER DEL "HABANA"

M. A. GONZALEZ

"REFRIGERACIÓN KELVINATOR
CASA CALUFF
J. A. Saco 356
SANTIAGO DE CUBA.

(34) MIGUEL L. GONZALES

"MIKE" GONZALES

This collage of Mike González images spans the immortal Cuban's colorful four-decade big-league and winter-league sojourn. Opposite bottom: Colorful artwork from *Bohemia* magazine, Cuba 1950. Opposite top: in uniform as coach with the world champion St. Louis Cardinals, 1946. Clockwise from top left: Promotional card distributed by Havana appliance dealer, 1940s; collectible Yuenglings Ice Cream postal card, USA 1928; Play Ball collectors card, USA 1940; pos-ing with shortstop Mosquito Ordeñana (left) and big league outfielder Dick Sisler (right) while managing the runnerup Havana ballclub, 1946. This was the year Sisler truly terrorized Havana winter league pitching, slugging a league-leading nine roundtrippers, including three circuit blasts in a single game off fellow big leaguer Sal "the Barber" Maglie.

NAPOLEON REYES

"REFRIGERACIÓN. KELVINATOR"
CASA CALUFF
J.A.Saco 356
SANTIAGO·DE·CUBA.

As a big leaguer Nap Reyes manned first, third, and the outfield with the New York Giants for only 279 games across four seasons (1943-45, 1950). As a winter-league regular in his native Cuba he also failed to reach true star status during seven seasons, batting .265 for his career and shining more on the defensive side than in the batters' box. In Mexico — where he fled from the big leagues in 1946 to join Jorge Pasquel's rebel circuit — he proved a far more potent batsman, hitting .332 in 1948 while doing double duty as a playing-manager for Puebla. When he took up managing fulltime, however, Reyes finally established his greatest legacy on the baseball diamond. In his homeland he directed two championship ballclubs under the banner of Marianao (1957, 1958), also leading that same club to consecutive triumphs in the prestigious Caribbean Series during those same seasons. To date Reyes remains the only manager ever to enjoy such back-to-back successes in the showcase winter league playoffs. When the proud Sugar Kings were forced to abandon their homeland for Jersey City in mid-year of 1960 it was again Reyes who managed the ballclub for their sad final half-season of gypsy existence. Add it all up and you have one of the most lofty careers in the annals of 20th-century Cuban baseball.

CIENFUEGOS

75.—Napoleón Reyes. Manager

This collage of '50s-era Cuban League stars includes Adrián Zabala (two photos below), Conrado Marrero (top right and opposite, top left), Sandalio Consuegra (opposite, top right and middle), Silvio García (two photos, opposite bottom), and Panchón Herrera (middle and bottom left). Zabala and Herrera are today the lesser-known of the quintet, although the former was a mid-'40s mound star with Almendares and a cup-of-coffee big leaguer with the New York Giants (4-7, 5.02 ERA), while the latter won an International League triple crown for Buffalo in 1959 (.329, 37 HRs, 129 RBIs) on his way to an able big-league career in Philadelphia. The colorful Herrera also sported a memorable moniker back home in Cuba, where his given first name (Panchón) was conveniently converted by fans to "Ponchón" to signify his propensity for striking out (strikeouts are "ponchados" in Spanish).

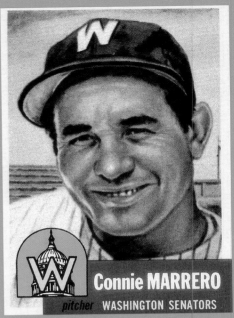

Connie MARRERO
pitcher WASHINGTON SENATORS

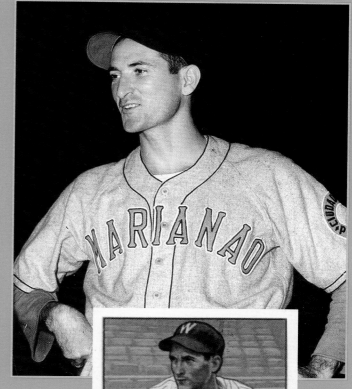

SANDALIO CONSUEGRA

5.—Silvio García. Coach.

RAY NOBLE

Cuban hall of famer Rafael "Ray" Noble enjoyed a brief three-season major-league sojourn with the New York Giants (1951-53) which contained few boasting points. He appeared in only 107 games and batted a mere .218 while serving as occasional replacement for durable Wes Westrum. There was, nonetheless, a token appearance as pinch hitter in two 1951 World Series games. Back in Havana it was a far different story for the popular slugger who over the seasons between his 1943 debut and late-'50s retirement accumulated the largest total of career roundtrippers (71) in Cuban League annals. Noble (pronounced NO-blay) suffered a fate familiar to numerous Latin ballplayers — that of being known by a name not his own. He was usually called "Sam" during his U.S. big-league years, a distortion of his Jamaican-born father's frequent references to him as simply "my son" (misheard by non-Spanish speakers as "Sam").

35.—Rafael Sam Noble

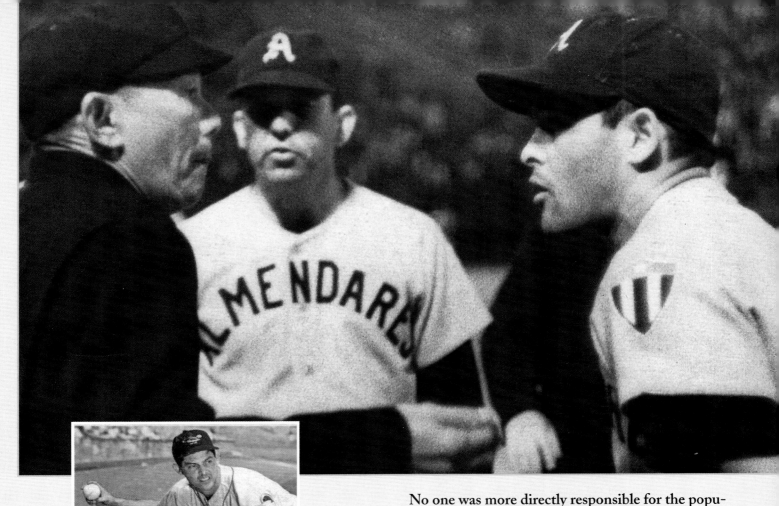

Ray Noble's U.S. (1952 Bowman on left) and Cuban (1957 Chicle Peloteros) bubblegum cards are displayed here (opposite, top), along with an action-filled shot in which the all-star Cienfuegos backstop cuts down a sliding Marianao runner at the plate in Havana's El Cerro Stadium. Willie Miranda's colorful 1957 Topps bubblegum card (above) overlays a Cuban League scene in which the talented Almendares infielder (right) joins his manager Bobby Bragan (center) in a heated discussion with hall-of-fame umpire Raul Atán.

No one was more directly responsible for the popular stereotypical 1950s image of "good field, no hit" Latin American infielders than was flashy Cuban gloveman Guillermo "Willie" Miranda. In nine American League seasons with Washington, Chicago, St. Louis, New York, and Baltimore, Miranda did preciously little damage with his Louisville slugger (be batted .221 overall) but a ton of damage to opponents with his vacuum-like glove (where only his deep range and efforts at making dangerous plays kept him from leading the league's shortstops in fielding percentage). Miranda's Baltimore manager Paul Richards was only one of many experts to rank this daring Cuban as tops among the league's shortstops. In Richards' view Phil Rizzuto and Luís Aparicio may have been more versatile, but neither matched Willie for truly spectacular glovework. Richards also noted that in both Baltimore (where Miranda started for four seasons) and New York (where he backed up Rizzuto) numerous fans came to the park just to witness Willie's magical infield displays. Willie also played twelve seasons in Cuba with Almendares, and again he demonstrated that his value to a ballclub was in the field (where his defense earned him honor as Almendares team captain), not standing in the batters' box (where his lifetime average was but .237).

ALMENDARES

COCAINA
GARCIA

"REFRIGERACIÓN KELVINATOR"
CASA CALUFF
J. A. Saco 356
SANTIAGO DE CUBA.

Héctor Rodríguez (two photos, opposite top, and at left) was widely considered by island baseball experts of the '40s and '50s to be perhaps the greatest defensive infielder in Cuban League history, and that reputation was enough to earn a brief shot with the Chicago White Sox in 1952. It was not enough, however, to guarantee much success in the big time for a light-hitting if flashy third baseman who did not reach the big time until he was past 32 years of age. Big-league third sackers are expected to provide offensive lumber as well as defensive leather, and it was Héctor's anemic bat against American League hurlers (.265 BA, 40 RBIs and but one homer in 140 games) that sealed his doom during his only major-league season. Herberto Blanco (bottom right) might have had a similar shot at the big leagues had he come along only a few seasons later, in time to benefit, like Rodríguez, from Jackie Robinson's pioneering trip across the color barrier. Instead the sharp-fielding and clutch-hitting infielder was destined to star only in the Cuban League (first with Santa Clara in 1941 and then with Havana for the bulk of his career), in Mexico (where he spread a .288 batting average over 11 seasons), and in the North American Negro leagues (1941-42).

There was more than one sterling pitcher named Gárcia on the Cuban circuit of the mid-1940s. While the more celebrated Silvio García was supplementing his impressive mound duties with stellar infield play for both Marianao and Cienfuegos and also catching Branch Rickey's eagle eye as a potential candidate for big-league integration, Manuel "Cocaína" García (two photos, opposite bottom) was spinning memorable mound performances of his own during the World War II era. The squat and swarthy southpaw paced the Cuban winter circuit in winning percentage twice (1943 and 1947), as well as in total victories in consecutive years (1943-44), and in complete games on yet another occasion (1945). The numbers alone suggest that between 1943 and 1947 there was no better hurler on the entire island than the stocky Club Havana righthander with the eye-catching nickname. The case for Manuel García was further advanced when he earned instant immortality by tossing the fifth-ever no-hit, no-run effort in Cuban League history, a December 1943 5-0 whitewashing of Club Marianao.

The seaport city often dubbed "the Athens of Cuba" holds its indelible place in the history of Cuban baseball. It was in Matanzas, after all, that lore and legend firmly places the game's initial introduction on the island. Visiting sailors reputedly demonstrated bats and balls and their functions for dock workers in the port city and had soon struck up informal games with the locals. These accounts of U.S. Marines teaching the national game to Cuban dock workers in 1866 may not be quite historically accurate. But there is far less controversy about the city's role in hosting the first reported organized game on the island. This took place on December 27, 1874, when ballclubs representing Havana and Matanzas met on the local clearing known as Palmar de Junco ("Junco's Palm Grove") for a one-sided match that counted among its famous participants the ex-big-leaguer Esteban Bellán and the ballplaying patriot Emilio Sabourín.

Matanzas is also birthplace to some of the island's most memorable, colorful, and accomplished professional "peloteros" (ballplayers). Armando Marsans called Matanzas home, as later did island big leaguers Minnie Miñoso, Bert Campaneris, José Cardenal, Leo Cárdenas, and José Valdivielso. One of the most impressive modern era ballparks today sits in Matanzas, and it is also one which boasts one of the country's proudest modern-era patriotic names (Victory at Girón Stadium, commemorating the failed Bay of Bigs invasion). Matanzas also once boasted a short-lived entry in the earliest years of professional Cuban League play, capturing a single championship during the 1893 season.

But it is on the amateur ballfields that the city of Matanzas has built its loftiest reputation. When amateur national tournaments were first launched on the island in 1914 it did not take long for a team from Matanzas (Bellamar de Matanzas in 1918) to capture a coveted championship banner. During the 1940s some of the best amateur league teams played there, including the Cuban champions of 1943 and 1945 carrying the banner of Deportivo Matanzas. Action (apparently a classic rhubarb at home plate) seen here is from a mid-1940s amateur championship contest staged at the famed Palmar de Junco ballpark site. In most recent decades Matanzas has also been back in the limelight with a highly competitive year-in and year-out entry in the modern-era Cuban League. Although Matanzas forces have yet to capture a Castro-era league championship, they have nonetheless recently boasted the league's batting champion (1997) in star outfielder José Estrada.

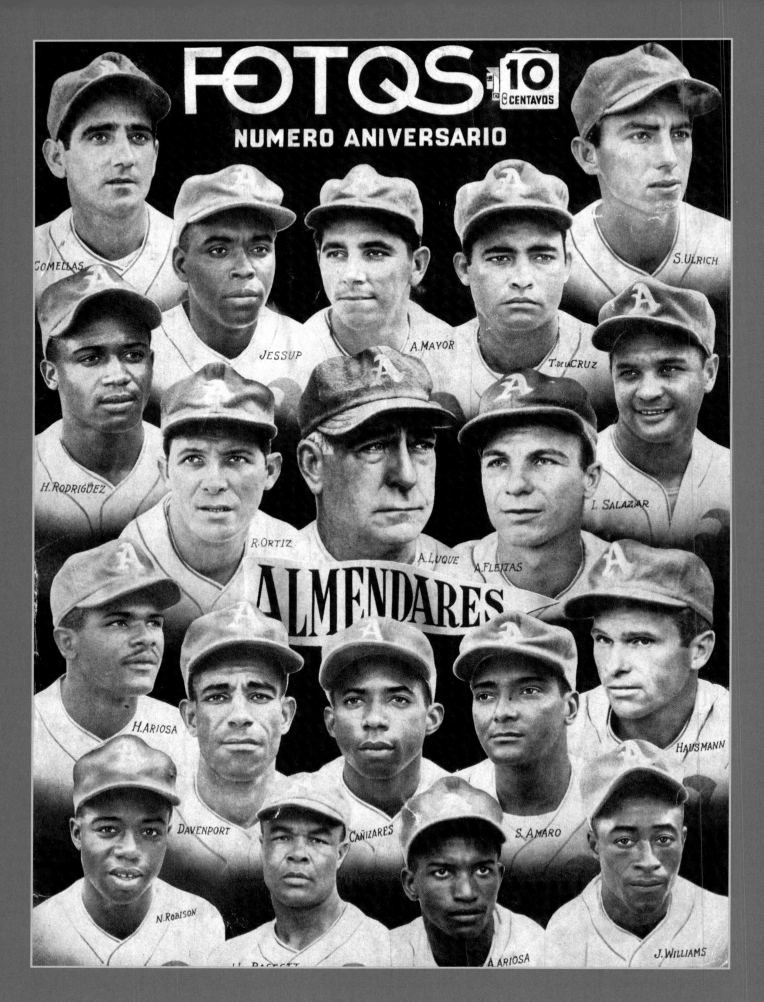

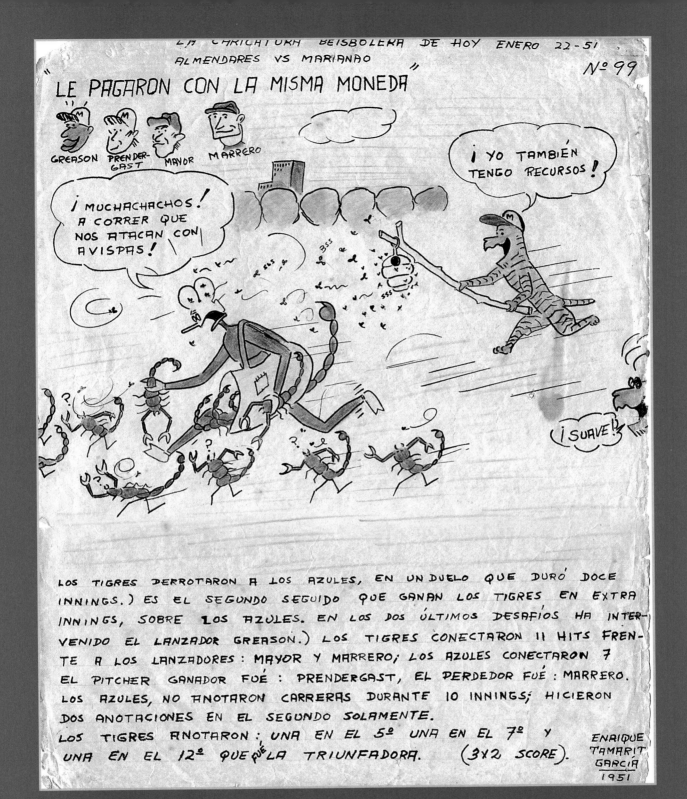

Almendares was a popular ballclub with legions of rooters from its inception before the turn of the century, even if over the years Havana would maintain a slight edge in overall championships. Sports cartoonist Enrique Tamarit García here humorously represents the "Alacran Grande" (the large scorpion, symbol of "Los Azules" of Almendares) helping his charges flee the feared Marianao Tiger in a league game played on January 21, 1951. A popular *Fotos* magazine cover (opposite) features members of the 1947-48 Scorpions ballclub, managed by veteran Dolf Luque (center), a talent-laden team whose heartbreakingly narrow championship loss (by a single game) to Club Havana would interrupt a string of Almendares titles in the late 1940s.

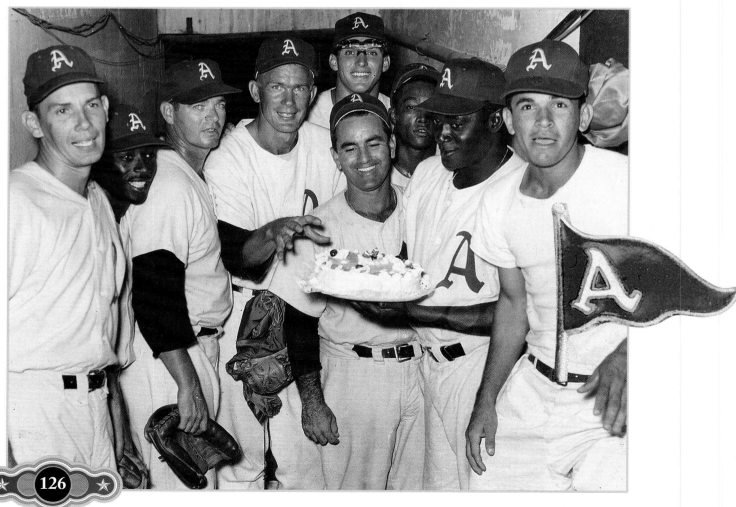

# EL QUE LE GANE AL ALMENDARES SE MUERE

## "HE WHO DEFEATS ALMENDARES DIES TRYING"

"Los Alacranes" (Scorpions) of Almendares boasted a proud tradition stretching back to the initial national championship season of 1878 and to their own first championship year of 1894. Over the 71 seasons of team history the blue-clad warriors of Almendares trailed rival Club Havana only by the slimmest of margins in both championships captured (30-25) and total games won (1,553-1,522). The narrow edge in victories enjoyed by Havana was to be credited in the end only to the three seasons (1882, 1888, 1889) in which the Alacranes failed to field a team, and Almendares thus in the end could boast the better winning percentage (.539-.537) and also the final three championships (1954, 1955, 1959) garnered by the two century-long rivals. Bright moments from a final decade of Almendares history shown here include future big leaguer Mike de la Hoz (opposite, top, center) caught in an informal moment with teammates, a mid-'50s birthday celebration (opposite, bottom) for coach Clemente "Sungo" Carreras, and the 1954 pennant winners (below) who cruised to a championship under manager Bobby Bragan.

Club Almendares - Campeón 1953-1954

1ª. FILA DE IZQUIERDA A DERECHA: GUILLERMO MIRANDA, ANGEL SCULL, SERGIO VARONA JR. (COACH), CLEMENTE CARRERA (COACH), BOBBY BRAGAN (MANAGER), AGAPITO MAYOR (COACH), REINALDO CORDEIRO (COACH), OSCAR SARDIÑAS, CONRADO MARRERO. 2ª. FILA DE IZQUIERDA A DERECHA: MANUEL FERNANDEZ (MASAJISTA), RAYMOND ORTEIG, GONZALO NARANJO, ASDRUBAL BARO, JIM WALSH, PATRICIO QUINTANA, HECTOR RODRIGUEZ, FORREST JACOBS, GUILLERMO JORGE (JEFE CUARTO), DR. JULIO DE ARCOS (ADMINISTRADOR GENERAL). 3ª. FILA DE IZQUIERDA A DERECHA: EARL RAPP, JOE HATTEN, SAM CHAPMAN, BOB MUNCRIEF, VIRGILIO R. CONTRERAS, OCTAVIO RUBERT, FERNANDO DIAZ, EMILIO CABRERA, CLIFF FANNIN, GLENN NELSON. SENTADO DELANTE: LUIS CIFRAN, (BAT BOY.)

CAMPEONES **Almendares B.B.C.** 1946-1947

DE LA CRUZ    JESSUP    C. MARRERO    J. COMELLAS    M. LANIER    A. MAYOR    ARIOSA    C. LEAL    L. SALAZAR

A. CAÑIZARES    DAVEMPORT    R. ORTIZ    H. RODRIGUEZ    A. LUQUE    FLEITAS    S. AMARO    HAUSMANN

RAMOS    GAINES    WILLAMS    GONZALEZ    MARTINEZ    O'NEILL    OXAMENDI    J. LEON    M. FERNANDEZ

PRESENTADOS POR    FOTOS    LA MEJOR REVISTA

**Base Ball Profesional**
1952 CAMPEONATO · 1953

"El que le gane al Almendares
se muere"

**Almendares**

In a pair of typical posed scenes from the early 1950s, long-time Alacranes outfielder Avelino Cañizares (left) snags a fly ball, while outfielder Francisco Campos (left) and catcher Chino Valdivia enjoy a moment (opposite top) of post-game clubhouse relaxation. Cañizares wore the smart blue and white flannels of Almendares for 11 seasons (1943-53), Campos shagged outfield flies in the early fifties at the same time he was seeing summertime spot duty with the Washington Senators, and Valdivia was one of the team's numerous unheralded role players.

Fermin Guerra (above and above right) stood in the spotlight of '40s-era Cuban baseball, not only for his durable service as catcher and manager with Club Almendares, but also because of his big-league tenure which included nine seasons and three American League teams. Guerra first broke into the big time as the twentieth Cuban major leaguer when he debuted with a single 1937 game in Washington.

Fermin "Mike" Guerra's ultimate hour of glory came when he directed two editions of the blue-clad Scorpions (Alacranes) to Cuban League championships (in 1949 and 1950) and also managed the first Caribbean Series championship outfit in 1949, when his Almendares ballclub swept Venezuelan, Panamanean, and Puerto Rican all-star squads in the friendly confines of El Cerro. Across its final two decades the always-popular Almendares team featured dozens of other memorable ballplayers, among them such stellar North American big-league imports as Willie Mays, Art Fowler, Bob Skinner, Bob Allison, Dee Fondy, Wally Post, Steve Souchock, Sam Jethroe, Ken Aspromonte, Tommy Lasorda, and Joe Coleman. Front-line Cuban "peloteros" who filled Almendares rosters between 1945 and 1960 included Roberto Ortiz, Octavio Rubert, Andres Fleitas, Héctor Rodríguez, Agapito Mayor, Willie Miranda, Connie Marrero, Santos Amaro, Santiago Ullrich, Orlando Peña, Angel Scull, and Tommy de la Cruz.

The true highlight season for Almendares came in 1947 during the first year of play at the new showcase Gran Stadium del Cerro and the most dramatic Cuban League pennant chase ever. A strong stretch run (12 victories in the final 13 games) built on stellar moundwork by import Max Lanier and natives Agapito Mayor and Tomás de la Cruz sealed a dramatic championship over runnerup Club Havana. Clutch victories over "Los Rojos" (2-1 and 9-2 behind southpaws Mayor and Lanier) during the season's final week ultimately settled the issue. Mid-'50s Almendares teams under Bobby Bragan were nearly as potent with their consecutive championships of 1954 and 1955 and their lineups fleshed out with U.S. imports such as Willie Mays (bottom right), Russ Nixon (below, right) and Lou Skinner (below, center). Santos "El Cangaru" Amaro (below, left) manned an outfield post for the 1947 league champions. Manager Dolf Luque and his victorious 1947 ballclub (opposite top) prepare to hoist their 1947 pennant. Luque was still around as a team official posing for a 1954 Almendares publicity poster (opposite bottom) which mockingly mourned a dead and defeated Club Havana Lion.

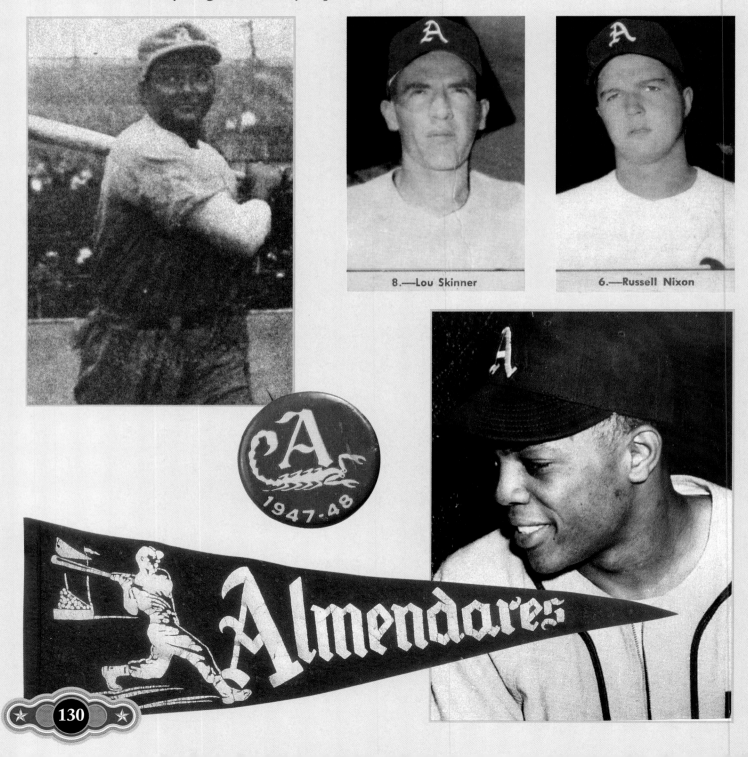

8.—Lou Skinner

6.—Russell Nixon

Two exciting and parallel action sequences highlight the fierce rivalry between Havana and Almendares, played out over many seasons of nip-and-tuck championship tussles and culminating with the memorable teams and individual stars fielded by both clubs in La Tropical Park and El Gran Stadium del Cerro in the 1940s and 1950s. In these game-turning moments Carlos Blanco of the Lions evades the tag of Fermin Guerra, Alacranes catcher (opposite), while Almendares runner Roberto Ortiz evades Havana backstop Sal Hernández (above).

To live in Havana during the first half of the 20th century was to commit one's emotional fortunes to "Los Azules" of Almendares, or to live and die instead with "Los Rojos" of Club Havana. The two baseball clubs were at the very heart of the city's sporting and social life and passions ran equally as deep among their rabid followers as they ever did between devotees of Brooklyn and New York big-league clubs during the same epoch. Like in so many other baseball hotbeds, this was a rivalry which split families, ruined friendships, and above all filled the coffers of the thriving Cuban Professional Baseball League.

# LA LEÑA ROJA TARDA PERO LLEGA

## "THE RED BEATING IS SLOW BUT INEVITABLE"

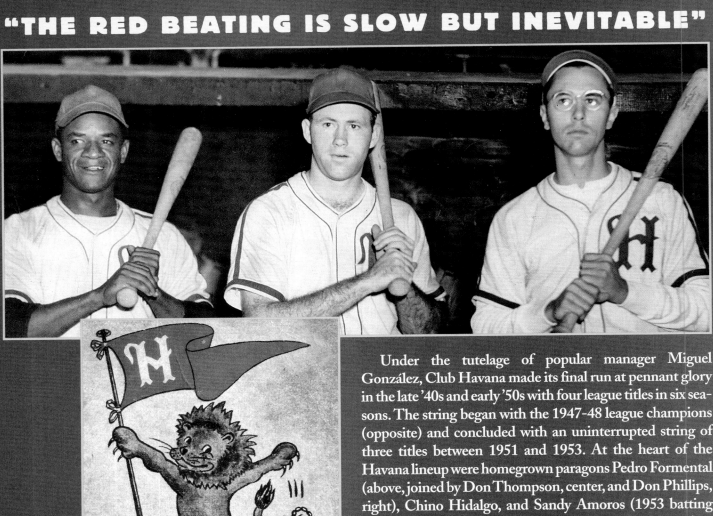

Under the tutelage of popular manager Miguel González, Club Havana made its final run at pennant glory in the late '40s and early '50s with four league titles in six seasons. The string began with the 1947-48 league champions (opposite) and concluded with an uninterrupted string of three titles between 1951 and 1953. At the heart of the Havana lineup were homegrown paragons Pedro Formental (above, joined by Don Thompson, center, and Don Phillips, right), Chino Hidalgo, and Sandy Amoros (1953 batting champion), but potent bats were also supplied by Negro leaguer Henry Kimbro (1948 batting champion) and major-league imports Hank Thompson, Lou Klein, Johnny "Spider" Jorgensen, and Steve Bilko. The pitching of this era was again split between island natives (Adrián Zabala, Carlos "Patato" Pascual, Limonar Martínez, Julio Moreno) and big-league mercenaries such as Hoyt Wilhelm, Bill Ayers, and Mario Picone. During this final '50s-era string of successes the proud Lions ballclub under skipper González would also boast a Caribbean World Series title (Cuba's second) captured during 1952 round-robin play in Panama.

Felicidades

TE DESEAN LOS Habanistas

**FOTOS**

10 CENTAVOS

SALVADOR HERNANDEZ MANAGER

MAC DUFFIE    CONSUEGRA    ULRICH    MARTIN    MEDIN

H. BLANCO    ESTALELLA    OLMO    KLEIN    C. BLANC

SAGUITA    MONTEAGUDO    P. GARCIA    MARTINEZ    IBANEZ

I. TORRES    NAVARRO    COCOLISO    NATILLA    ROJ

**CAMPEONES** DE **1947-1948**    **HABANA**   B B C   DE **LA LIGA NACIONAL**

Take away the 14 completed 19th-century championship seasons (there were several seasons that were either never started or never finished) and Almendares, not Havana, had the upper hand when it came to overall won-lost record and overall first-place banners collected. And all three other long-time league rivals claimed at least one championship after Havana hoisted its own final banner in 1953. But long-term bragging rights nonetheless belong to the forces of "Los Rojos" whose 1,553 victories and 30 first-place finishes best any and all rivals.

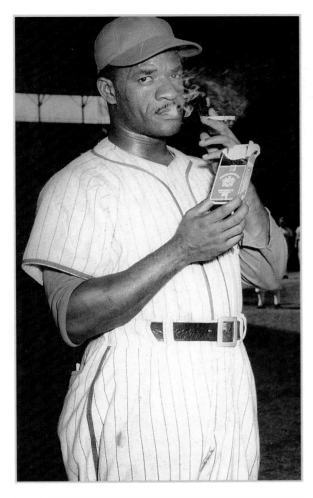

No local hero loomed any larger on the Havana baseball scene of the fifties than did talented outfielder Pedro "Perucho" Formental. Perico (for short) carried the bad rap of being a shameless braggart ("they call me Perico 300" — a reference to his facility at hitting for top averages) but usually backed up such boasts, copping one batting title in 1950 and hitting at or near the magical .300 mark on several other occasions. The strong lefty thrower and swinger spent the bulk of his Cuban League career drilling base hits and chasing outfield flies with the Havana Lions, though he broke in with Cienfuegos and wrapped up his dozen-year career with Marianao. Along the way he also played for the Triple-A Havana Sugar Kings, the Negro American League Memphis Red Sox (where he enjoyed his top averages of .341 in 1949 and .363 in 1950), three Mexican League ballclubs (Tampico, Veracruz, San Luís de Potosi) in the mid-'40s, and a collection of additional winter-league ballclubs in Venezuela and the Dominican Republic. Formental's lasting reputation nonetheless was built squarely on his abilities as a run producer in his own homeland. Perucho closed out his Cuban League career tied with Cienfuegos immortal Alejandro Crespo as the all-time RBI leader at 362 (Ray Noble would soon surpass them both with 372) and also once held the single-season RBI standard (57 in 1953, later tied by Rocky Nelson).

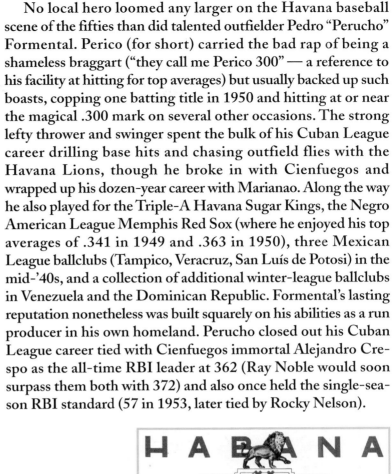

56.—Robert Bob Bluaylock

55.—Bill Muffet

Forrest "Spook" Jacobs (above left) had remarkably little to recommended him during his brief big-league visit. His tall cup of coffee consisted of but three seasons (1954-56) and only one of those (the first) could boast more than 30 games played. He was wraith-like in stature and also swung a limp bat which produced an anemic .247 cumulative batting average, only 199 total bases, and not even a single homer in 665 at-bats. Only his glove was adequate enough to make him a Philadelphia A's regular second baseman as a rookie. Even his nickname was more curious than truly memorable (it probably derived from his frail, ghostly appearance but could also have appropriately referred to his invisible statistics). But for all this impotence in Philly, Kansas City, and Pittsburgh, no visiting North American big leaguer or minor leaguer ever took better advantage of a brief visit to the sunny winterball climes of Havana than did the diminutive shortstop with the eerie nickname. On Cuban soil Jacobs magically transformed from Mario Mendoza into Richie Asburn, winning the 1956 batting title with Havana and also smacking the ball at better than a .300 clip in two previous seasons with Almendares.

Other North American imports also performed well for Club Havana, often far better than they did in big-league venues back home. Bob Blaylock (opposite top card) was one of a number of visiting major-league hurlers (St. Louis Cardinals) to don "Los Rojos" colors in the late '50s. Another was Billy Muffet (opposite bottom card) who was a solid starter with Havana in 1957-58, though he did pace the league in both losses and walks yielded that winter. When it comes to home-grown heroes, Lázaro Sálazar (opposite bottom) stands among true Cuban baseball giants, right up there with Havana teammate Pedro Formental and also with a list of legendary player-managers that includes Miguel González, Fermin Guerra, Martín Dihigo, Pelayo Chacón, and Adolfo Luque. Though his best seasons came between the mid-'30s and mid-'40s with Almendares (he won batting titles in 1935 and 1941, and was also the league's best hurler while hitting over .400 during the earlier season), the Cuban and Mexican league hall-of-famer was still taking cuts for Havana as late as the early '50s. Lesser local Havana stars also played memorable roles, among them Gilberto Torres (bottom left card) and Raul Sánchez (bottom right card). The former was an infielder and pitcher who sipped coffee in the big leagues with Washington, while the latter was a mound mainstay with Almendares, Cienfuegos and Havana and also hurled sporadically in the big leagues (Washington, Cincinnati) and with the Triple-A Sugar Kings.

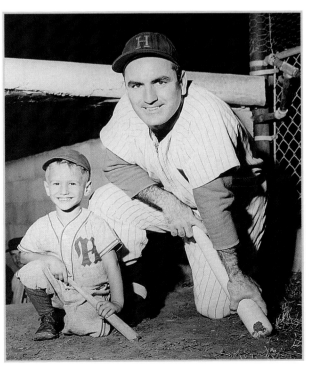

50.—Gilberto Torres

59.—Raúl Sánchez

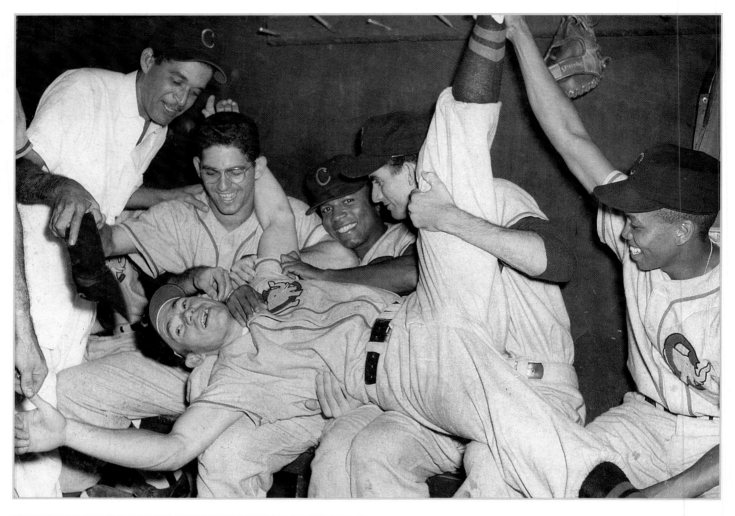

Is this a riotous victory celebration for the usually also-ran Cienfuegos Elephants ballclub, or simply a rare moment of tension-breaking frivolity? Whatever the occasion, that is 1955-56 league home run champion Ultus Alvarez (above) receiving some mock roughhouse treatment from his teammates.

At left, Cienfuegos backstop Ray Noble (left) and Havana hurler Mario Picone compare 1953 pre-game notes in a scene of fraternization that was just as rare for that era in Havana as it most certainly would have been in any big-league ballpark.

At right, a trio of on-field rivals, Havana hurler Cocaína García (left), Cienfuegos infielder Don Zimmer (center), and Zimmer's teammate Pedro Ballester engage in a pre-game batting-cage discussion. And the scene above suggests that the forces of Havana were just as capable of clubhouse revelry as were those of Cienfuegos. Since each club won three pennants during the league's final decade, such occasions for merriment had plenty of rationale in both camps.

# EL PASO DEL ELEFANTE ES LENTO PERO APLASTANTE

## "THE TREAD OF THE ELEPHANT IS SLOW BUT CRUSHING"

The youngest of the four Havana rivals was the green-clad Cienfuegos outfit, whose inaugural season had come in 1926-27 (a last-place finish) and whose first banner was earned under manager Pelayo Chacón in 1930. The final ledger for "the Elephants" was five first-place finishes, six seconds, seven thirds, and eight fourths, and a .480 winning percentage (732-793) which was the worst of the "big four" ballclubs. Nonetheless Cienfuegos owns the distinction of gaining the final two championships (1960, 1961) of Cuban League history. Pictured below are 1940s hitting star Alejandro Crespo (left and right) and U.S. pitching sensational Tommy Fine (center), author of the only no-hitter in Caribbean Series history.

Nap Reyes (above right) led Marianao to consecutive Cuban League titles in the late '50s and a pair of Caribbean Series championships those same two years, but a handful of seasons earlier he was playing for rival Cienfuegos. The 1945-46 Cienfuegos ballclub (below) captured the second-ever championship banner for "Los Elefantes" and featured Dolf Luque (middle row, center) as manager, Martín Dihigo (top row, center) as a pitcher in his second-to-last active season, and the pesky Nap Reyes (top row, sixth from right), who was traded that season from Almendares to Cienfuegos.

CLUB "CIENFUEGOS", Campeones Base Ball Profesional 1945-1946, luciendo los magníficos y vistosos trajes confeccionados por la famosa "CASA VASSALLO", la casa que viste campeones.
Sentados, de izquierda a derecha: Pagés, Colás, "Pollo" Rodríguez, Rodríguez Galí, Adolfo Luque (Manager), Florentino Pardo (Propietario), "Cheo" Ramos (Coach), Crespo, Gallart. De pie: Xiqués, Roque, Zabala, Berres, Farzoni, Gladu, Silvio, Dihigo, Maglie, Napoleón, Conrado, Tiant, Chile Gómez, Roger y Casanova (Masajista).

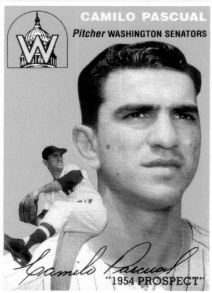

CAMILO PASCUAL
Pitcher WASHINGTON SENATORS

*Camilo Pascual*
"1954 PROSPECT"

Much of Cienfuegos' success of 1960 and 1961 was built on the arms of its two major-league star hurlers, Camilo Pascual (15-5 in 1960) and Pedro Ramos (16-7 in 1961). Pascual is pictured above with teammate Latigo Gutierrez, a promising pitcher who reached the Triple-A level with the St. Paul Saints of the American Association. The Topps reprint bubblegum card at left represents Pascual's 1954 rookie season in Washington.

Each ten-year span of the past half-century has featured a single dominant Latin American hurler — and each of these imported pitchers has in turn reflected the special ambiance of his own particular decade. The 1950s showcased the yeoman-like efforts of Camilo Pascual (opposite, top right), who labored nobly while compiling a confidence-shattering .297 winning percentage (28-66) with a hapless Senators team (1954-58) that could neither knock out base hits from the batter's box nor effectively knock them down in the field.

Had Pascual labored in Yankee Stadium rather than Griffith Stadium during the epoch of Yogi Berra, Whitey Ford, and Mickey Mantle, his name and not Juan Marichal's might well have been toasted regularly in hot stove discussions of Latin America's original pitching hero — to say nothing of likely enshrinement in the hallowed halls of Cooperstown. Ill-starred teammate Pedro Ramos (opposite, bottom, center) presented a similar saga. While Pascual's major-league career coalesced with the arrival of a more talented supporting cast behind him in Minnesota (where he became a 20-game winner), Ramos drew new blood from a late-career transition to the bullpen with the New York Yankees.

Camilo Pascual's older brother Carlos (below) went by the nickname "Patato" and earned a 1950 one-season cup of coffee with the Senators. Pete Ramos poses below with 1961 Cienfuegos hitting stars George Altman (U.S., left) and Borego Alvarez (Cuba).

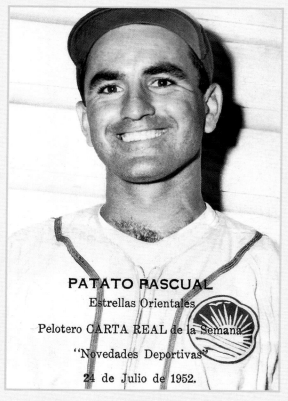

PATATO PASCUAL
Estrellas Orientales
Pelotero CARTA REAL de la Semana
"Novedades Deportivas"
24 de Julio de 1952.

Big-league veteran hurlers Max Surkont (below left; Boston Braves and Pittsburgh Pirates) and Luís Aloma (below right; Chicago White Sox) provided part of the American-Cuban flavor of early-'50s ros-ters for Cienfuegos. Above, future big-league journey-man catcher José "Joe" Azcue is greeted by Cienfuegos teammates after a late-'50s circuit blast.

If Cienfuegos and Marianao were the newest and least-celebrated of the four grand Cuban League tenants in the '40s and '50s, they nonetheless accounted between them for five of the final six league championships leading up to Cuban professional baseball's demise in 1961. A collage of Marianao personalities on this page includes (clockwise from top left) Rollie Hemsley (ex big-leaguer and coach), Zoilo Versalles (the first big-league MVP from Latin America), Silvio García (here demonstrating his daring baserunning), and Claro Duany (a .300 hitter in both 1948 and 1951).

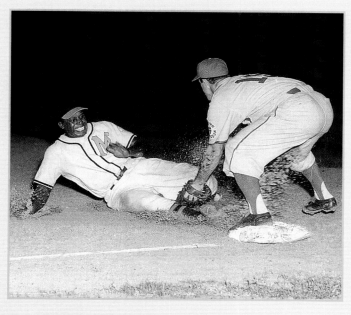

# MARIANAO CIUDAD QUE PROGRESA

## "MARIANAO—CITY OF PROGRESS"

Of the four annual rivals for island diamond glories the Tigers of Marianao boasted perhaps the least-celebrated tradition and the smallest contingent of partisans among Havana's throngs of baseball *fanaticos*. But even Marianao loyalists had numerous heroes and even occaional championships to celebrate. The club (known as "the Grey Monks" around 1949) entered the Cuban League with a considerable bang, winning the championship banner in its maiden outing (1923) with a team that featured such notables as player-manager Merito Acosta, Manuel Cueto, Pelayo Chacón, Emilio Palmero, and that year's best pitcher, Lucas Boada. Over their 27 seasons in the circuit the orange-and-brown-clad Tigers claimed four championships, finishing second six times, third on seven occasions, and dead last in 10 seasons. The overall ledger for the club was 729-861, an impotent winning percentage of .458. Early 1950s stars Chiquitín Cabrera (right) and Quincy Trouppe pose together below, while the full 1946-47 team, featuring Miñoso, Estellela, and Conseguera, appears on the facing page.

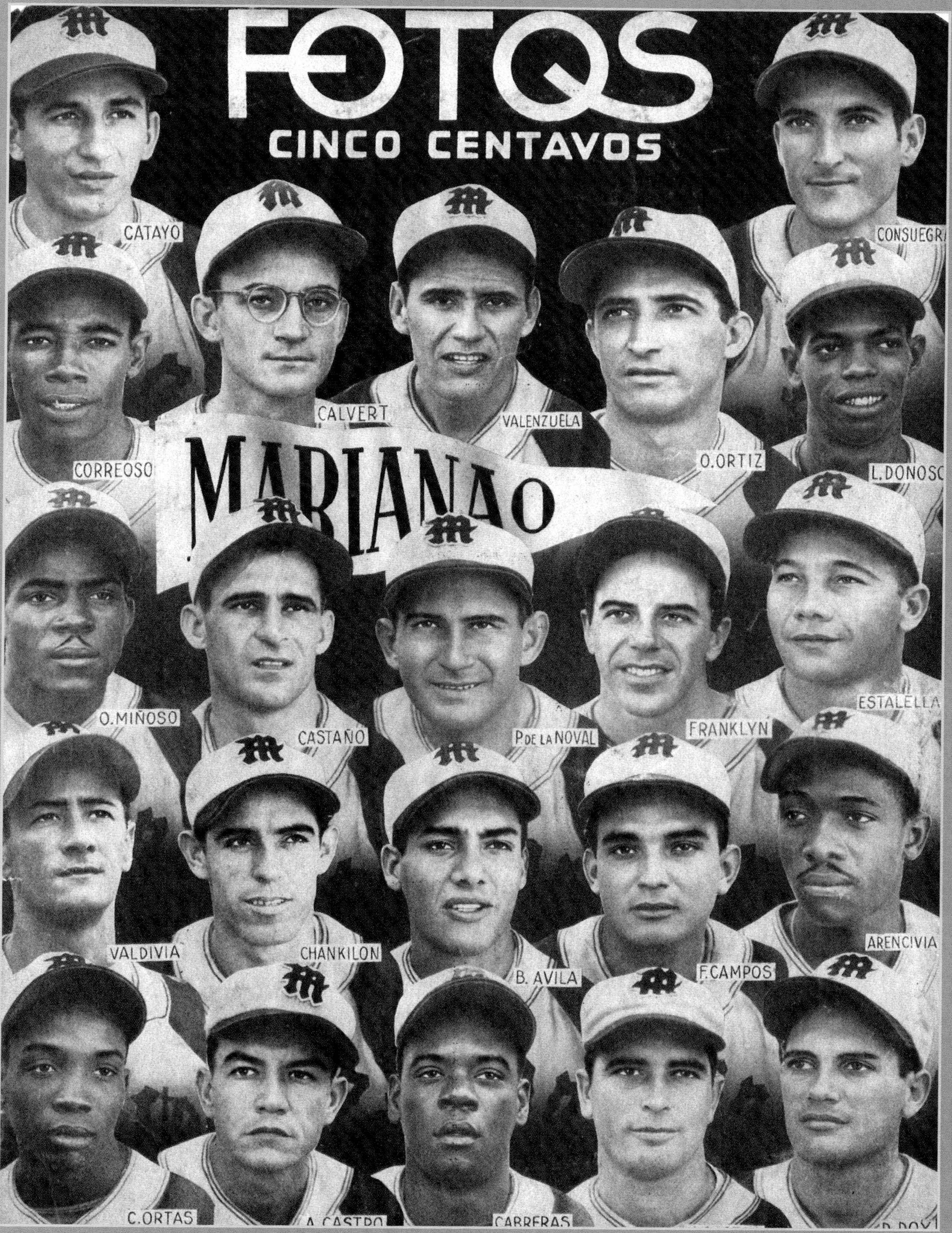

FOTOS
CINCO CENTAVOS

MARIANAO

CATAYO
CONSUEGRA
CALVERT
VALENZUELA
O.ORTIZ
CORREOSO
L.DONOSO
O.MIÑOSO
CASTAÑO
P.DE LA NOVAL
FRANKLYN
ESTALELLA
VALDIVIA
CHANKILON
B.AVILA
F.CAMPOS
ARENCIVIA
C.ORTAS
A.CASTRO
CARRERAS

At left, Francisco Salvent (left) and Juan Delis enjoy a light moment during the championship 1956-57 winter season, as do (below) Lorenzo "Chiquitín" Cabrera (left) and Carlos Blano during the same pennant-winning campaign. Cabrera enjoyed his finest hour with a record .619 BA in the 1951 Caribbean World Series.

Club Marianao's most successful epoch came during the Cuban League's swan song seasons of the late fifties, when the suddenly revived Tigers captured consecutive titles in 1957 and 1958 under skipper Nap Reyes. The first of these two pennant winners celebrates here (opposite, bottom) after their title-clinching victory ended a 20-year drought. The biggest sluggers for the Marianao team during its peak late-'50s seasons were big leaguers Miñoso (1957 batting leader), Milt Smith (1958 hitting champ), and Solly Drake, but another up-and-coming star was first baseman Julio Becquer (opposite, top, center and left).

79.—René Friol

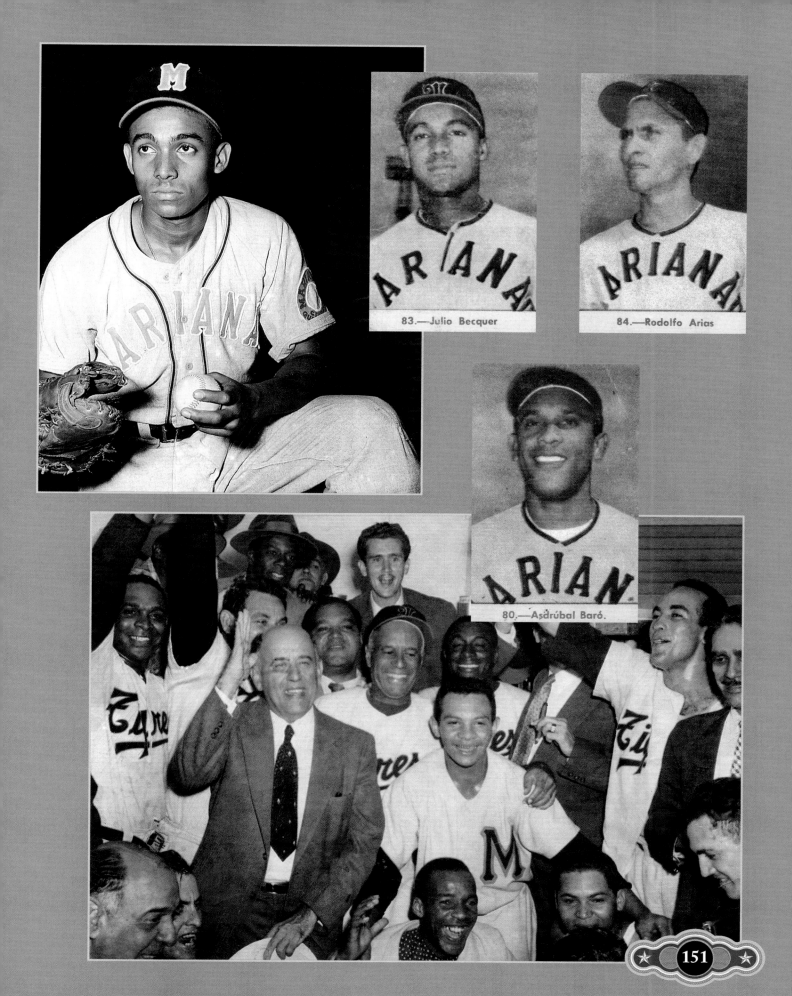

83.—Julio Becquer

84.—Rodolfo Arias

80.—Asdrúbal Baró.

# PAPA JOE'S CUBAÑOLAS

Washington baseball historian Morris Bealle once observed that Joe Cambria hadn't done so badly as Clark Griffith's "one-man scout force" and that he would soon do even better if he could somehow get over his apparent predilection for "Cubanolas" among the numerous recruits he signed.

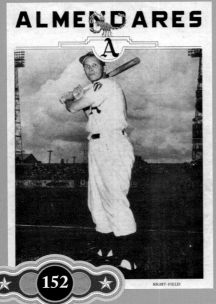

Roberto Ortíz (left), Roberto Estalella (right)

Maverick scout Joe Cambria (named "official scout" for Cuba and Puerto Rico in 1949, and then for the West Indies and South America in 1954) combed Latin American soil for potential big leaguers to serve his Washington Senators employers. The result was a seemingly endless stream of Havana imports that turned Clark Griffith's teams into a Cuban invasion force in the nation's capital. "Papa Joe" (as he was known by the Havana locals, who even named a popular cigar brand after him) is even widely (if falsely) reported to have scouted and nearly signed a promising young pitching prospect of the early 1940s named Fidel Castro.

Cambria created the "Cuban Connection" for Clark Griffith's lowly Senators (alias Nationals) in the imme- diate postwar period. His first signee, Bobby "Tarzan" Estalella (opposite, bottom right) — a legendary long- ball slugger back on own his native soil — was a fan- favored yet lead-fingered third sacker who managed but 44 round trippers (alongside 41 errors) and a respectable .282 batting average over parts of nine big-league cam- paigns (half of those with Connie Mack's Athletics dur- ing the talent-thin WWII years). But Washington fans of the late 1930s had so much fun watching the gritty Estalella knock down enemy grounders with every part of his anatomy except his glove hand that they often phoned the ballpark in advance to find out if the "Hand- some Cuban" was in the lineup before making the trek out to the Griffith Stadium grandstands.

32.—Julio (Jiquí) Moreno

LUIS ALOMA

JULIO BECQUER
FIRST BASEMAN—WASHINGTON SENATORS

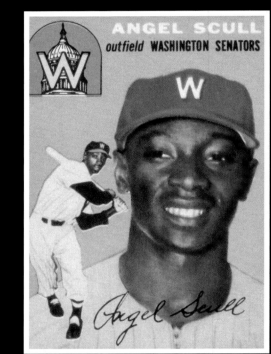

ANGEL SCULL
outfield WASHINGTON SENATORS

Angel Scull

MIKE GUERRA

CONRADO MARRERO

MIKE Fornieles
BALTIMORE ORIOLES PITCHER

Sanchez
CINCINNATI REDLEGS PITCHER

82.—Juan Delis

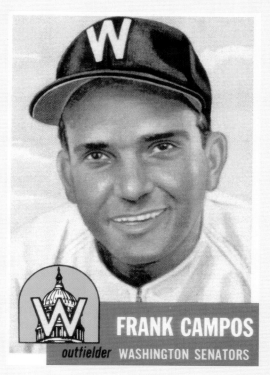

**FRANK CAMPOS**
*outfielder* WASHINGTON SENATORS

The considerable honor roll of Latin American ballplayers residing in Washington in the 1950s begins, of course, with the solid pitching of Pedro "Pete" Ramos (67-92 for the Senators between 1955 and 1960) and Camilo Pascual (53-77 over the same period). Other strong-armed Cuban pitchers rounded out the bulk of the Senators' always-under-manned staff throughout the decade: Sandy Consuegra was 20-16 over three seasons before being dealt to Chicago in 1953; Conrado Marrero compiled a 39-40 career mark in the first five seasons of the '50s; Mike Fornieles registered an impressive rookie 1.37 ERA in brief action before departing for service with the Chicago White Sox (in a fortuitous exchange for eventual Washington ace lefthander Chuck Stobbs). Luís "Witto" Aloma, another Cuban hurler who debuted in 1950, never made it to Washington, which might explain how he achieved the best mound record (18-3, 3.44 ERA) of any of his countrymen.

And then there were endless utility players such as José Valdivielso, Carlos Paula, Francisco Campos, Juan Delis, Mike Guerra, Angel Scull, and Julio Becquer. In all, almost two dozen Latin-born ballplayers (mostly Cubans) appeared in major-league action for the Clark Griffith Senators during the cellar-dwelling ballclub's final topsy-turvy decade in the nation's capital.

He may have had the best curveball in the majors during the "Fabulous Fifties" of big-league slugging, but Cuban ace Camilo Pascual (left) won less than a third of his decisions for the talent-thin Senators during his first half-dozen big-league seasons. Despite his fabulously futile record, Pascual was still respected by fans and peers alike as one of the most fearsome righthanders in the circuit. And once the lowly Senators donned a new disguise as the much-improved Minnesota Twins, Pascual also performed a chameleon act largely unmatched in baseball history. Ensconced in the Twin Cities and revived by a contender, the once hapless Pascual turned in sterling 20-11 (1962) and 21-9 (1963) campaigns, also leading the league in strikeouts for three straight seasons (1961-63).

If "Pistol Pete" Ramos (below) was not as effective over his total career as his sidekick Pascual, winning nearly 60 fewer games and never approaching a 20-victory season, he was every bit as unforgettable. What was most memorable about Ramos — off-field antics aside — was his personal contribution to baseball's long-ball slugging of the '50s. No one in all baseball history has given up home runs in more charitable fashion. Pistol Pete allowed the highest number of homers per innings pitched (one homer in every 7.48 frames) in big-league history, outdistancing Denny McLain (one per 7.79), Mudcat Grant (one per 8.36), and Don Newcombe (one per 8.55) for this dubious honor.

30.—Pedro Ramos

Cuba was a black baseball paradise, from the earliest North American Negro leagues inroads of Torriente and Méndez in the teens and twenties to the mid-century island performances of dozens of dark-skinned major-league rejects immediately before and after Rickey and Robinson's bold experiment in Brooklyn. Among the final waves of star Negro leaguers in Cuba were such shadowball legends as Max Manning (right), Cleveland "Chiflan" Clark (above right), Henry Kimbro (above center), and the recently resurrected Buck O'Neil (above left, in Almendares uniform). O'Neil (today a celebrity after his narrator's role for the popular Ken Burns PBS-TV documentary on baseball history) was only a brief visitor to Cuba, where he batted but .216 during the 1946-47 season. Kimbro, by contrast, spend a decade's worth of winters in Havana, slugging his way to one island batting crown in the late '40s and providing most of the heavy hitting for a 1948 Havana championship ballclub. At the beginning of the same decade, nine seasons earlier, the muscular Kimbro was also a Cuban basestealing champion while playing for Almendares. Manning pitched the last four seasons of the 1940s with Havana and logged 27 complete games and a 27-33 overall ledger, while Clark debuted in the U.S. with the New York Cubans in 1945, fresh off a spectacular winter season in which he hit .361 for champion Almendares. The hotshot center fielder was also a Cuban League all-star during the 1946 winter campaign.

HABANA

A tradition of itinerate Cuban ballplayers traveling the summer blackball circuits which began full-force in the teens and twenties was yet alive and well — even if perhaps breathing its last gasps — during the wartime years of the early and mid-forties. Those baseball-thin World War II seasons also saw little if any drop in blackball talent streaming to Cuban shores during the winter months. In the Negro National League the New York Cubans (also then called Cuban Stars) were still a big New York box office attraction, playing home games in the storied Polo Grounds and featuring headline ballplayers like those featured on the 1944 poster below (hall-of-famer Ray Dandridge, top left; Dave Barnhill, bottom left; Terry McDuffie, top right; and Dominican Juan "Tetelo" Vargas, bottom right). The 1945 New York Cubans (opposite top) boasted such full-blooded Cuban stars as Martín Dihigo (top, fourth from left), Orestes (not yet "Minnie") Miñoso, Ray Noble, and Luís "the Elder" Tiant (middle, third from left). Back on Cuban shores the winter season featured blackball standouts such as Terry McDuffie (opposite, center left), Jess Jes-

sup (opposite, mid-center), and Lenny Hooker (opposite, center right). A veritable Negro league all-star team also could be found performing in Cuba each winter, such as the one collected on the bottom of the opposite page and including: Terry McDuffie (far left, Almendares), Quincy Trouppe (third from left, Marianao), Lennie Pearson (fourth from left, Almendares), Willie Mays (third from right), Joe Black (second from right, Cienfuegos), and Ray Dandridge (far right, Marianao). Mays signed with Almendares for the 1950-51 season but never took the field for a league game due to an injured foot. Black, who debuted spectacularly in the majors at age 28 in 1952 with rookie of the year honors, foreshadowed his heady Brooklyn debut by pacing the Cuban League in victories (15-6) earlier that same winter. McDuffie played the outfield but excelled as a pitcher and was a fan favorite in Cuba during his eight winters in Havana. The stocky righthander would pitch 135 games on the island, winning 37 (second only to Ray "Jabao" Brown among Negro leaguers) but also dropping 43 for a lifetime below-water mark.

Perhaps the top blackball performer of the '40s-'50s to grace the Cuban winter league during its final decades was Cooperstown hall of famer Ray "Talua" Dandridge (opposite, two bottom photos) who played 11 seasons in Havana — beginning with Cienfuegos in 1939 and ending with Marianao in the early fifties — and banged out a lifetime .282 average on the island. Talua also sparkled at third base, as he did for years with the Newark Eagles, with various Venezuelan and Mexican winter ballclubs, and during five Triple A seasons in the American Association and Pacific Coast League. Other Cuba-tested blackballers from the north included Lennie Pearson (left two photos) who won three RBI titles with Havana, and Marvin Williams (bottom right), a slugging Mexican League star. Raul López (below, left) was a native Cuban southpaw who broke in with the New York Cubans one season before the demise of the Negro National League.

Negro leaguer Connie Johnson (below) posted a 12-11 record with Marianao in 1954-55, between big-league stops in Chicago and Baltimore. Much-traveled Quincy Trouppe (top right) was a catcher with the same Cuban club four winters earlier.

Cuba's near-complete domination of world championship tournaments sponsored by the International Baseball Association (IBA) began long before Fidel Castro's revolution of the late 1950s had brought a sudden end to professional leagues on the island. Cuba had already been a major player in all but a handful of the first 14 IBA tournaments conducted between 1938 and 1953, hosting six "mundiales" (1939-43, 1952), winning seven of the events (1939-40, 1942-43, 1950, 1952-53), and taking runner-up medals (second in 1941 and third in 1951) on two other occasions. Across the '40s and early '50s Cuba managed to register a medal-winning performance (finishing in the top three) in all but one (fourth place in Venezuela in 1944) of the competitions it entered. The world championship amateur tournaments were suspended for eight years after the 1953 gathering in Caracas, and when play resumed in Costa Rica in 1961 (with Cuba again claiming a gold medal) the Castro-era of total amateur emphasis had by then replaced the pre-revolution epoch in which amateurism was only the underpinning and not the true showcase of the Cuban baseball scene.

There were many stellar individual performances in the IBA world tournaments of the 1940s, a large portion of them by celebrated Cubans. Julio "Jiqui" Moreno was the champion tournament pitcher on two occasions, and catcher Andrés Fleitas twice won individual batting honors. Ramón "Dumbo" Fernández of Venezuela would register eight consecutive base hits in the 1944 round robin, Cuba's Limonar Martínez blanked Mexico on only 63 pitches in 1943, and Panama's Cecilio Miller stole 14 bases in the 1950 tournament. But no star shown any brighter than that of Cuba's own Conrado Marrero. Marrero's personal career apex arguably arrived with the IBA world championships of the early 1940s. First there was the tense championship matchup with Team Venezuela in La Tropical Stadium on October 22, 1941. The diminutive Cuban righthander squared off against Daniel "Chino" Canónico in a classic duel which fell ultimately to the visitors 3-1 on three first-inning tallies. Marrero would gain his sweet revenge and his country's grateful adulation a year later (October 4, 1942) when he returned to the hill to face a Venezuelan lineup sporting Luís Aparicio at second base and the same Canónico on the hill. This time Marrero spun a memorable 3-hitter of his own in the 8-0 victory.

Of the many Cuban ballplayers to earn their earliest attention on the fields of IBA tournament play none did so with a grander splash than Conrado Marrero. Despite limited big-league successes in the early '50s, Marrero remains one of Cuba's largest baseball icons. And the reputation he built mainly on the home front in the '40s was largely earned with stellar performances within the Cuban and international amateur ranks. The stocky 5'7" future big leaguer (Washington Senators, 1950-54) and Cuban League champion pitcher (Almendares, 1948) first carved out his niche in 1938 in the Cuban UAA league, twirling for Club Cienfuegos and tossing no-hitters in both 1938 and 1942. Eventually he won still greater plaudits around the island with a pair of masterful IBA tournament performances on the hill for his native Cuba, starring in the gold medal showdown games in La Tropical Stadium in both October 1941 and October 1942.

Opposite: Cuban manager Renaldo Cordeiro (left) examines the lineup card for his 1943 entry in the VI Campeonato Mundial de Béisbol Aficionado (VI IBA World Championships) held in Havana. Below left: Conrado Marrero wearing his Almendares uniform in the late 1940s. Below right: Nap Reyes as a member of the Cuban National team for III Campeonato Mundial (1940) in Havana. Reyes played third base and batted .297 for a Cuban team that captured the country's second straight IBA gold medal.

On the eve of a 1947 big-league campaign when "all hell broke loose in baseball" (to use Red Barber's famed book title phrase to describe that season), Branch Rickey and his Dodgers prepared for their testing of the integration waters with a 47-day sojourn in cosmopolitan Havana that was to serve as the team's spring training camp and simultaneous shelter from the prying New York press hot on the heels of the breaking Jackie Robinson story. The Dodgers were no strangers to Havana during the spring season — they had also held their spring training rituals there in March 1942, that time in La Tropical Stadium (a festive visit commemorated on these pages by artist-journalist John Groth with his panoramic painting from the pages of *Collier's* magazine). But it was the 1947 visit that would provide perhaps the most celebrated island stopoff by visiting big leaguers since the one-time visit of Babe Ruth in 1920 and those of Ty Cobb (1910) and Christy Mathewson (1911) back in the heart of the dead-ball era.

For all the commotion that Robinson would bring to organized baseball only a month later with his historic debut on the National League scene, this Havana visit also coincided with a period of turmoil for Cuban baseball itself. The Cuban League, which had flourished with only occasional war-induced interruptions since the previous century, was now about to come apart at the seams just after reaching its own most glamorous epoch. The threat to organized baseball represented by Jorge Pasquel's rebel Mexican League had resulted in the banning from organized baseball of those players who had jumped to Mexico, among them a considerable number of Cubans. One immediate result would be two separate Cuban seasons during 1947-48, one in La Tropical ballpark featuring "ineligibles" and another (more official and successful) title chase at the new El Cerro Stadium featuring remaining "eligibles" among the visiting and native professionals. But in the late winter of 1947 — despite these gathering storm clouds of labor dispute and this fanfare surrounding Robinson and the Dodgers — most Cubans were only interested in one unfolding baseball story of much narrower local import. The same final week of February which witnessed the arrival of the Brooklyn ballclub also celebrated the windup of perhaps the most dramatic pennant chase in Cuban annals: a tense series of deciding games between Almendares and Club Havana which culminated a dramatic charge to the finish by a victorious Almendares ballclub managed by Dolf Luque.

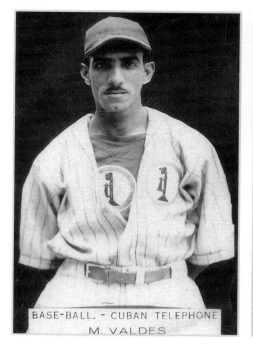

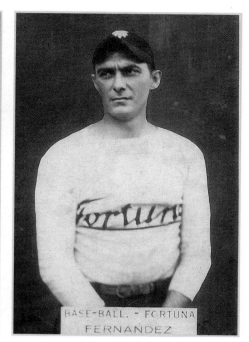

BASE-BALL. - CUBAN TELEPHONE
M. VALDES

BASE-BALL. - FORTUNA
GARROS

BASE-BALL. - FORTUNA
FERNANDEZ

# HISTORY AND TRADITION OF CUBAN AMATEUR BASEBALL

Amateur Cuban championships were launched in 1914 (the same year Dolf Luque debuted in the majors) and continued across the decades until 1960 (the very year that Fidel Castro debuted as leader of a new revolutionary Cuba, one in which amateur baseball would overnight replace professional baseball as the new Cuban national pastime). The very first National Amateur League title was captured by the Vedado Tennis Club ("Los Azules") which bested Havana Institute, Marianao Society, and Cuba Athletic Club over the 16-game schedule. Across the years strong teams representing the Vedado Tennis Club (seven titles), Fortuna Sport Club (four titles), Universidad (five championships), Teléfonos (four victories), and Hershey (seven championships) were the most frequent island champions. But perhaps it was Club Teléfonos (Cuban Telephone Company) that in the end boasted the most storied history from pre-Castro Cuban amateur baseball. This celebrated team debuted in 1925 in the Intersocial League (which played in the ancient Víbora Park in Havana) and later moved to both the Amateur Athletic Union circuit and the National Amateur League, where it won titles in 1931, 1950, 1951, and the final season of 1960. In the decade of the '30s this team would boast Narciso Picazo, who ranks alongside Agapito Mayor as the best southpaw found anywhere in the annals of Cuban amateur baseball. Ten years later it would feature another mound legend, Juanito Decall, who once defeated the visiting big-league Boston Red Sox in what remains perhaps the supreme moment for Cuban amateur baseball.

Although many a living veteran Cuban baseball historian might find room for argument here, it is frequently concluded that Cuba's most memorable amateur season came with the nip-and-tuck campaign of 1943 (opposite page), one in which Deportivo Matanzas, coached by Pipo de la Noval, edged out the defending champion Military and Navy team (Circulo Militar y Naval) of manager Evelio Miranda on the season's final day to capture the bitterly contested tournament title. Among that season's outstanding pitchers were future big leaguers Sandalio Consuegra (9-1, with a 0.97 ERA), Conrado Marrero (7-1), Limonar Martínez (11-3), and Julio Moreno (20-6), but less-notable lefty Daniel Parra (18-6) and untouchable Pedrito Díaz del Yara (6-0) also flashed brilliance. Top offensive stars during that 1943 season were Hiram González (.424 BA), Armenio Torres (28 RBIs) and Daniel Day (28 runs scored). The memorable summer of amateur play was capped with a memorable fall performance by the national team selected from UAA tournament ranks. The Cuban squad coached by Reinaldo Cordeiro breezed to victory in the world amateur championships staged in La Tropical Stadium with a 9-3 overall record. Team pitching stars included Redro "Natilla" Jiménez, Isidoro León, Sandalio Consuegra, Julio "Jiqui" Moreno, and Rogelio "Limonar" Martínez. Other members of the gold medal squad (Cuba's fourth, and second consecutive) included infielders Virgilio Arteaga, Angel Fleitas, Luís Suárez, and Quilla Valdés, outfielders Francisco Quicutis, Bautista Aristondo, Ernesto Estévez, and Alberto Morera, and catchers Rogelio Valdés and Rouget Avalos.

Amateur competitions fired Cuban rooting passions throughout the decades between and including the two World Wars. During this four-decade epoch Cuba boasted a rich proliferation of amateur and semipro circuits and tournaments that were also incubators for the talent which would eventually rise to fill the professional ranks. In additional to the Amateur Athletic Union (UAA) league (which produced national teams for IBA world championships) and National Amateur League (which crowned an annual national champion), there was also a juvenile amateur league, Pedro Betancourt winter league, intermunicipal league, sugarworkers league, industrial laborers league, several interprovincial leagues, and a large handful more. Many climbed the ranks to national-level stardom,

and from the National Amateur League over the course of the years came such future notables as Andrés Fleitas, Roberto Ortiz, Vicente López, Evelio Hernández (holder of an amateur record of 22 strikeouts in a single game), Conrado Marrero, Agapito Mayor, Adrián Zabala, Octavio Rubert, Willie Miranda, Napoleón Reyes, Roberto Estelalla, Limonar Martínez, Wito Alomá, and Pedro Pagés — Cuban League and big-league luminaries each and every one. One of the proudest moments for the Cuban amateur ranks came in the spring of 1941 when an all-star squad from the NAL rudely defeated the visiting Boston Red Sox (including Dom DiMaggio, Jimmie Foxx, Joe Cronin, and Bobby Doerr) 2-1 behind the superb pitching of unheralded amateur leaguer Juan Decall.

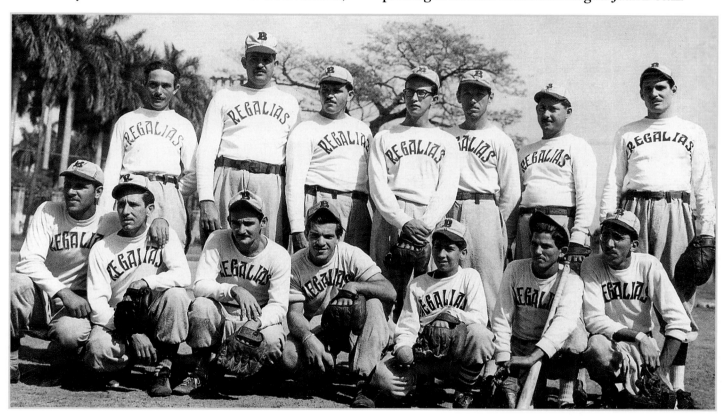

Each decade provided thrilling annual competitions for the National Amateur League (NAL) championship banner. One represetive team from the 1920s pictured here is the Lilobama Sports Club (opposite, top), proudly displaying their team banner. NAL winners of the 1920s were Cienfuegos (1920), Fortuna (1921, 1922), Universidad (1923, 1929), Policía (1924), and the Vedado Tennis Club (1925, 1926, 1927, 1928). The competitive tradition continued in the '30s, a decade represented visually here by the 1933 NAL champion Regla ballclub (above). Thirties-era amateur championship teams included Universidad (1930), Teléfonos (1931), Hershey (1932, 1934, 1935, 1938, 1939), Fortuna (1936, 1937), and Regla (1933). The most intense and competitive NAL tourna-

ments were perhaps those contested during the wartime decade of the 1940s. A well-equipped and snappily attired '40s-era amateur ballclub pictured here is the Lucky Seven Sports Club outfit (opposite, bottom). NAL championships in the forties were won by Hershey (1940, 1948), Cienfuegos (1941), Círculo Militar (1942), Deportivo Matanzas (1943, 1945), Círculo de Artesanos (1944), Universidad (1946, 1949), and Deportivo Rosario (1947). These seven different national championship ballclubs of the 1940s would represent the largest number from any single decade in the near half-century of pre-Castro-era Cuban amateur tournaments.

The victory in XI Campeonato Mundial, which was handed to Cuba belatedly by Mexico City officials in October 1951, was quickly muted when the defending champions themselves arrived on Mexican soil for World Championships XII one month later. The favored Cubans swept nine of 10 opening-round games (losing only to Puerto Rico), then surprisingly fell in two of three final-round matches (losses to champion Puerto Rico and runnerup Venezuela and a single victory over the Dominican Republic). A tense moment from the 1951 world championships in Mexico City (left) features an unidentified Cuban runner evading the catcher's tag in some classical bang-bang home plate action.

After a three-year absence from IBA world championship play (1945, 1947, 1948) the Cubans returned with a vengeance in 1950, sweeping to victory in the early-December tournament (Campeonato Mundial de Béisbol Aficionado XI) staged in Nicaragua that year. The 1950 IBA tourney actually ended with something of a raging controversy when Puerto Rico was disqualified for using professional ballplayers. Results from the final round were thus nullified and Cuba was belatedly declared the series winner. IBA resolution of the matter did not take place until a special FIBA meeting in Mexico City eleven months after the close of tournament play. During preliminary-round action the Cubans (paced by pitching ace Juan Izaguirre) had tied the Dominicans and Venezuelans with identical 9-2 round-robin records, but had also beaten their two closest competitors head-to-head.

Members of the 1951 bronze medal Cuban team (left), which stumbled briefly in Mexico City, included (left to right) shortstop Olivares, first baseman Cárdenas, third baseman García, outfielder Figarola, shortstop Seijo, outfielder Cordova, and second baseman Suárez. IBA world championship action would return to Havana in 1952 (XIII Campeonato Mundial) and the host Cubans would be ready to bounce back and reclaim the title they had squandered in Mexico City a year earlier. Of the 1951 players pictured at left, three (Suárez, Olivares, and García) would return for the gold medal victory party. An Ambrosia photo album (opposite) from 1943 contains players from that year's victorious Cuban entry in the IBA world championships, including future professional pitching stars Sandalio "Sandy" Consuegra (top row, second from right) and Julio "Jiqui" Moreno (second row down, second from left).

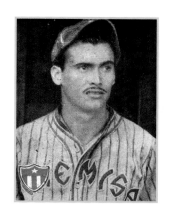   

  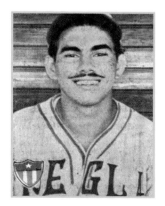 

Avelino Cañizares (top right and center, in black cap) was a Cuban-born glue-fingered shortstop who plied his trade on his native island with both Cienfuegos and Almendares, and in the U.S. Negro leagues with Quincy Trouppe's Cleveland Buckeyes, but who flashed perhaps his truest brilliance in Mexican League play throughout the '40s with teams like Tampico, Torreón, and Veracruz. Another stellar Cuban infielder to find a comfortable home on Mexican summer diamonds was Havana and Cienfuegos veteran Pablo García (top left). García suffered a tragic moment in Mexico during the summer of 1952 as one of a dozen Cuban ballplayers seriously injured when a Monterrey Sultans team bus crashed head-on with a truck carrying seven tons of unprocessed corn. While individual Cuban leaguers found pro successes in the land of mariachi during the late '40s and early '50s, island amateur "peloteros" tasted a rare and painful defeat there (opposite) with their third-place finish in the 1951 IBA world championship tournament.

# THE CUBAN COMET

On May Day of 1951 a 29-year-old jet-skinned rookie outfielder from Cuba was destined to become the first black ballplayer to don a Chicago White Sox uniform for official American League play. He was hardly a normal rookie, of course, given his advanced age and his two earlier trials at the big-league level in Cleveland (he played 17 games in 1949 and during the previous month of April 1951). To the unrestrained joy of long-suffering Chisox supporters crammed into the bleachers, as well as those glued to their radios throughout the Windy City, this pioneering "rookie" was also destined to debut with a bang and a flash rarely seen during three dark decades of South Side baseball that had followed the curse of the 1919 Black Sox World Series scandal. And the castoff rookie did not disappoint. In his first at-bat for his new Chicago team, Saturnino Orestes Armas Arrieta Miñoso ("Minnie" for short) pounded out a home run off Yankee ace Vic Raschi.

Miñoso's full career (one that stretched nearly thirty seasons in the majors, Cuba, and Mexico) would from beginning to end be marked by tantalizing near-miss brushes with the highest levels of diamond fame — painfully close encounters with achievement and celebrity far greater than what actually materialized. Here was the most colorful dark-skinned Cuban ballplayer of the post-Robinson integration years. Yet Miñoso's flashy style and dramatic flair translated most often into huge efforts at doing precisely what was needed to win ballgames for his team. He played with a reckless abandon aimed always at achieving nothing short of victory; his was a flair with a clear work ethic. He stole bases with a game on the line, harassed pitchers with daring base-running ploys, took extra bases, and made impossible wall-crashing catches. For this he was always appreciated by fans and teammates, yet never quite so celebrated around the league as was his equally flashy rival, Vic Power from Puerto Rico. Even in the local popularity polls he could never quite rival teammate Nellie Fox, always a favored son in the eyes of Chicago's ballpark diehards.

Whatever they called him, American League fans were soon in love with Saturnino Orestes Armas Arrieta "Minnie" Miñoso. Larry Doby, the American League's first black pioneer, possessed a stable temperament that made him far more like Jackie Robinson's teammate Roy Campanella — a quiet revolutionary determined to lead by strong, silent slugging and soft-spoken clubhouse diplomacy. Miñoso — Doby's teammate for a brief spell in 1949 before being traded to the White Sox two seasons later — burned instead with Robinson's dignified fire. The "Cuban Comet" also burned up the American League basebaths with three consecutive stolen base titles (1951-53) earned in an age when base speed was of little premium and rarely employed as an offensive strategy of preference. The flashy style he brought to the game was guaranteed to cement Miñoso's reputation with fair-minded fans, just as it would further fan the flames of hatred among those spectators and opponents who could not stand to see such a flashy black man upstaging everyone else on the field of play.

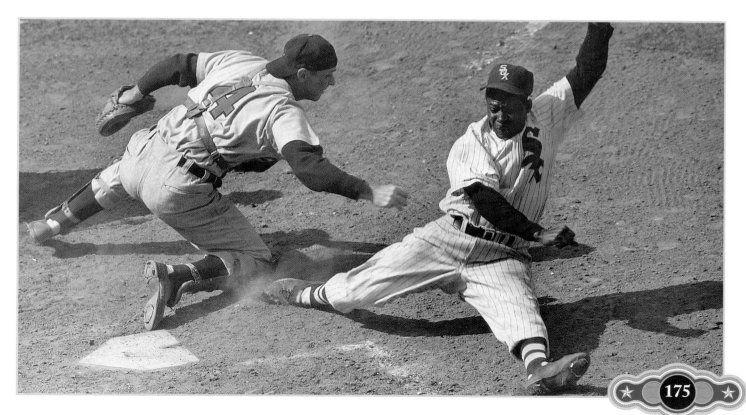

O. MIÑOSO

"REFRIGERAIÓN KELVINATOR"
CASA CALUFF
J. A. Saco 356
SANTIAGO DE CUBA.

If Miñoso was often overlooked, overshadowed, and just plain underappreciated throughout his lengthy baseball sojourn, he certainly left a mark both at home and abroad that was difficult to deny for very long. In a career that seemed to stretch on and on without pause on both sides of the Caribbean, Miñoso finally overwhelmed his critics and naysayers with mere longevity and the weight of amassed ballplaying numbers. Combine his big-league years with those in Cuba (as a star for the Marianao Tigers from 1946 to 1961) and Mexico (from the mid-'60s to mid-'70s), and few ever played so well for so long.

Diminished by the color barrier, which robbed him of perhaps five productive early-career seasons, Miñoso's 17-year big-league numbers today fall slightly short of Cooperstown standards in most eyes. He won stolen base titles but never copped a hitting crown; he fell short of 2,000 base hits (though only by a handful); his career batting average in the end was also a hair's breadth under the magic .300 level.

Minnie Miñoso might well stand as one of the greatest stars of all-time if his total stats in organized baseball were summed into a single listing. That is in part because Miñoso's seemingly endless career continued on in the Mexican League for nearly ten more summers (well beyond the age of 50) after his regular big-league tenure had ended in 1964. The records earned in Mexico and on the winter circuit are rarely seen by today's students of big-league history but are enough nonetheless to nail down a certain measure of immortality.

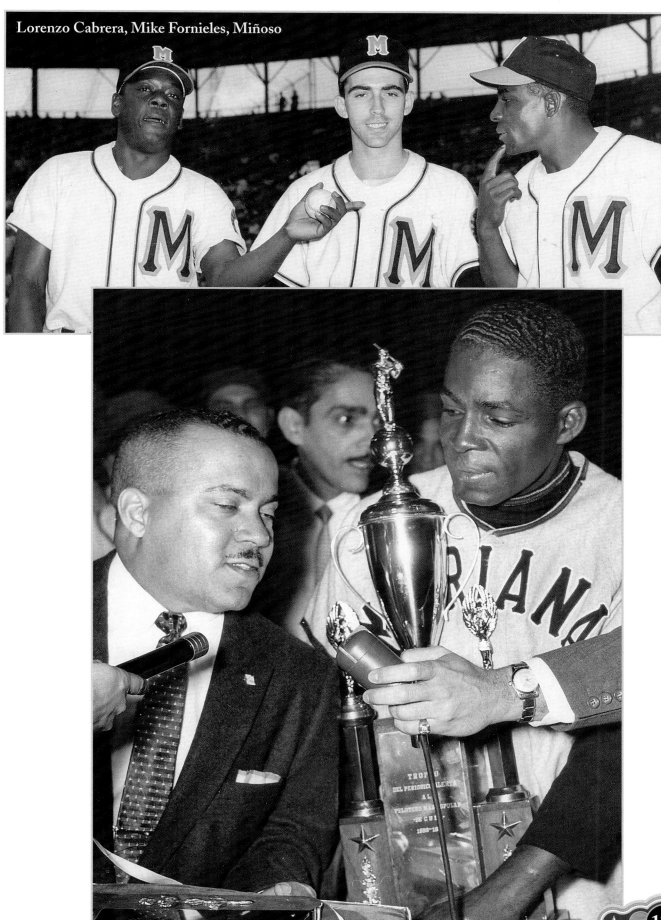

Lorenzo Cabrera, Mike Fornieles, Miñoso

What about the strange moniker of "Minnie"? Here the surviving story seems to be altogether muddled. Even Miñoso cannot give an adequate accounting. First there is the story attributing the nickname to Joe Gordon, the veteran Indians second sacker who reputedly hung the designation on his rookie teammate in the 1949 Cleveland spring training camp. Others (though not Boudreau himself) contend that Lou Boudreau, Cleveland manager, first used the alliterative nickname with his young Cuban third baseman. Some have suggested that it was used in the Cleveland camp as a shorter and easier form of Miñoso; others that it referred to a smallish ballplayer who was under six feet in height. Then there is Miñoso's shadowy story of a visit to a Chicago dentist's office. Miñoso suggests (in his biography *Extra Innings*) that he heard his dentist calling to someone named Minnie and thought he himself was being addressed, when it was the doctor's receptionist who was being hailed. This would in no way account for how the colorful name quickly spread among Chicago fans and Miñoso watchers everywhere around the league. As with the best of baseball legends, all parties seemed early on to have adopted a tacit conspiracy of silence on the matter. Whatever the truth, the fictions and fantasies always seemed better still.

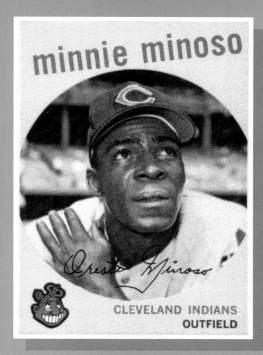

minnie minoso

CLEVELAND INDIANS
OUTFIELD

MINNIE MINOSO

It is for his headlining debut season of 1951 that Miñoso is perhaps best remembered. Throughout a sensational first full-time summer, the nearly middle-aged rookie tore up the American League, inspired a climb in the standings for the longtime doormat White Sox, and singlehandedly put Cuban baseball on the big-league map. By season's end, he had defined a new age of hit-and-run daredevil baseball in the Windy City and revived a long-slumbering baseball franchise in the process. The pre-Miñoso Chicago White Sox had been a sixth-place ballclub in 1950, as they had been in 1949 and 1947 (they finished dead last in 1948).

After Miñoso came on the scene with his rookie explosion of 1951, the same Chicago club climbed to fourth (their first time in the first division in more than a decade), then nestled into a comfortable position as pennant contender with five straight third-place finishes. Although Minnie Miñoso was not there to finish the pennant drive of 1959 — he had been traded back to Cleveland for hall of famer Early Wynn — he was clearly the inspired team leader who had launched the once-hapless Chicago outfit to full recovery after four decades of debilitating Black Sox swoon.

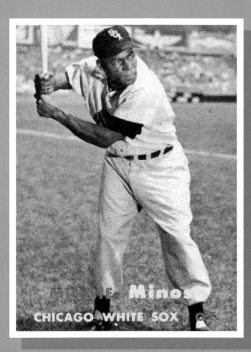

CHICAGO WHITE SOX

It was somewhat of an ironic misfortune that the Cuban Comet's original big-league debut in 1949 should have been with Bill Veeck's racially mixed Cleveland Indians, a team already featuring two headline-hogging blacks named Larry Doby and Satchel Paige. Doby earned a lion's share of notoriety as the first American Leaguer to represent his race; and the venerable Paige was already a full-blown Negro leagues legend who, while far past his pitching prime, was nonetheless as much a celebrity in Cleveland as he had long been everywhere else. Had Miñoso's debut been staged with any other junior-circuit ballclub, it might thus have stirred far greater media and fan attention than it ever could have with Bill Veeck's already-integrated Cleveland Indians.

Chico Carrasquel, Miñoso, Bobby Avila

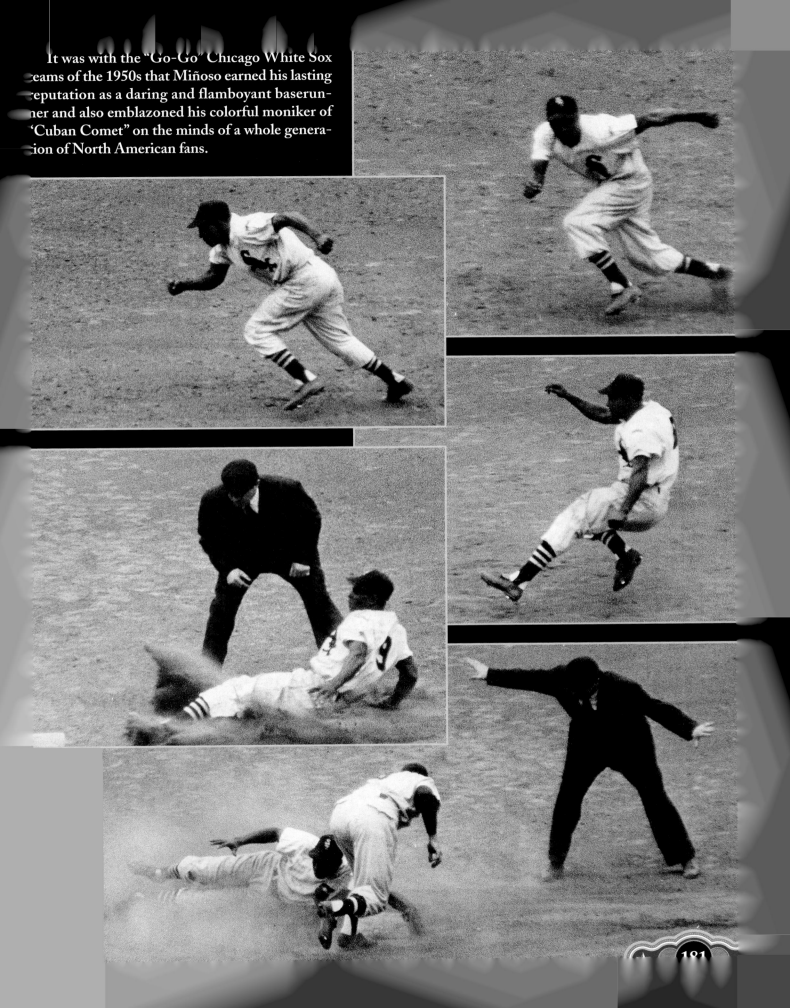

It was with the "Go-Go" Chicago White Sox teams of the 1950s that Miñoso earned his lasting reputation as a daring and flamboyant baserunner and also emblazoned his colorful moniker of "Cuban Comet" on the minds of a whole generation of North American fans.

181

¡REBELDE!

# FIDEL'S REVOLUTIONARY BASEBALL

July 24, 1959, was a landmark date in Cuban baseball history. On tap that night was of one of the most memorable exhibitions of amateur ballplaying ever witnessed in Havana's El Cerro Stadium. It was also destined to be a night that would signal a crucial crossroads for Cuba's baseball future. Fidel Castro himself took the mound that evening to pitch a brief two-inning exhibition with his hastily assembled army "Barbudos" team. The opposition was provided by a military police squad and the occasion was pre-game entertainment for a Sugar Kings-Rochester Red Wings International League contest. A single night later another extra-curricular event would be staged as supplement to a second Sugar Kings-Red Wings matchup — the first grand celebration of "July 26th" (a newly sanctioned patriotic holiday in honor of the 1953 Moncada affair) since Castro and his revolutionary movement had seized power from deposed President Fulgencio Batista. Fidel hurled valiantly in the July 24th exhibition, pitching two full innings and even batting once. That would be the sum total of the future president's limelight pitching career. But it would be enough to launch events that would soon change the face of baseball on the island forever.

As relationships between Castro and Washington, D.C., deteriorated in late 1959 and early 1960, the Havana International League ballclub soon found itself on shaky ground. Reported gunfire at the July 26th ballpark festivities — one night after Castro's celebrated mound appearance — caused suspension of a league game and sounded alarms throughout organized baseball that Havana might no longer be a hospitable home for professional competitions. The league championships (with Richmond) and Junior World Series against the American Association champions from Minneapolis were successfully staged on the island at the end of the 1959 summer season. But by mid-year of 1960 the Sugar Kings had been arbitrarily pulled from Havana by league moguls and relocated overnight (July 13, 1960) in Jersey City, New Jersey. The Cuban winter league also played its last round of games in the first weeks of 1961.

Baseball did not — as some thought it might — cease as a national sport in Cuba under Fidel's revolutionary regime. Instead it found new and vibrant life, with fresh young players, bold new administrative leadership, and a revitalized revolutionary mission. A drastically revamped Cuban League of full amateur status was in place for the 1962 season. The games now looked a bit different, but Havana's showcase El Cerro Stadium (soon expanded in size and renamed Estadio Latinoamericano) was still the main venue. Comfortable new concrete stadiums were also built in Matanzas, Pinar del Río, Santa Clara, Camaguey, Santiago, and elsewhere around the island. Aluminum bats and designated hitters came into the league by 1976. There were numerous and sometimes confusing changes in the lineup of teams and in the organization of championship seasons over the next quarter-century and more. But baseball on the island continued to thrive in full isolation from professional circuits in neighboring countries. Impressive talent was developed and engaging stars — only seen outside their homeland during occasional appearances with the Cuban national team — emerged and flourished. There were names like Wilfredo Sánchez, Lino Betancourt, Felipe Sarduy, and Agustín Marquetti to liven the 1960s. The 1970s and 1980s produced legendary pitchers (Braudilio Vinent) and sluggers (Lázaro Junco) who were the equal of many a big-league phenom. And the game still thrives in the mid-nineties, despite a few recent setbacks related after one fashion or another to the country's deteriorating economy in the face of an unpopular (and some say immoral) United States trade and travel embargo. With the emergence of superstars such as Omar Linares, Orestes Kindelán, Victor Mesa, Germán Mesa, and Pedro Luís Lazo — as well as a small handful of young refugee talent that has fled northward to the big leagues — Cuban baseball still easily outdistances that of any other Caribbean nation as an island talent font.

| HAVANA-CUBAN'S (104) | HAVANA-CUBAN'S (118) | HAVANA-CUBAN'S (117) |
|---|---|---|

**ANTONIO LORENZO**
Pitcher

**MANUEL (CHINO) HIDALGO**
Short stop

**ORLANDO (TANGO) SUAREZ**
Catcher

| HAVANA-CUBAN'S (102) | HAVANA-CUBAN'S (103) | HAVANA-CUBAN'S (113) |
|---|---|---|

**OSCAR RODRIGUEZ**
Manager

**OCTAVIO RUBERT**
Pitcher

**MARIO DIAZ**
Catcher

| HAVANA-CUBAN'S (123) | HAVANA-CUBAN'S (107) | HAVANA-CUBAN'S (121) |
|---|---|---|

**JULIO (Jiquí) MORENO**
Pitcher

**AGUSTIN DELAVILLE**
Outfielder

**FRANCISCO GALLARDO**
Infielder (2ª Base)

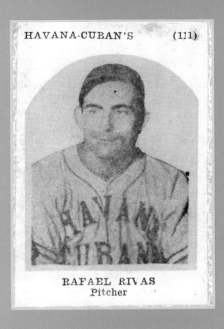

HAVANA-CUBAN'S (111)

RAFAEL RIVAS
Pitcher

HAVANA-CUBAN'S (106)

HECTOR ARAGO
Tercera Base

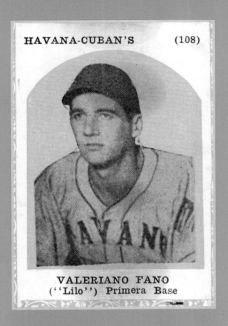

HAVANA-CUBAN'S (108)

VALERIANO FANO
(''Lilo'') Primera Base

Fidel's remarkable revolution of 1959 dramatically changed the face of Cuba for decades to come — on the nation's ballfields as will as in every public and private corner of national life. An inevitable if tragic break in formal diplomatic relations between Castro's government and the United States would mean a quick end to professional baseball in Cuba by the second season of the sixties. First the International League pulled the plug on its Havana franchise, seemingly at the very moment when the ever-popular Sugar Kings were finally peaking as a true league power. Cuba's winter-league circuit, with its loose connections to major league baseball, was a second victim, forced out of business at the end of the 1960-61 season. Castro's revolutionary path toward first socialism and later communism as a governing ideology would nonetheless still leave important space for baseball on the Cuban national agenda. Yet the new Cuban baseball scene would henceforth be a radically different one.

The decade-and-a-half that preceded revolutionary change in Cuba had witnessed the professional winter league in Havana enjoying perhaps its finest hour. Cienfuegos, under manager Tony Castaño, walked off with the final two championships, winning a record 48 games in 1960. Longball slugging was the order of the day and Borrego Alvarez (Cienfuegos) and Panchón Herrera (Havana) wielded the heaviest lumber. Havana's International League Sugar Kings (1954-60) also simultaneously piqued Cuban baseball pride and thus drew heavy fan turnouts at El Cerro Stadium during the summer months. Bobby Maduro's Sugar Kings would by the late '50s assure that summertime minor-league baseball in Havana had equal billing with wintertime Cuban League play.

But the Sugar Kings were not by any means Cuba's first venture into organized baseball, nor owner Maduro's either. Entry had come a decade earlier with the Havana Cubans franchise of the Florida International League, a circuit which also included teams in such Florida locations as Tampa, Miami, Miami Beach, West Palm Beach, and Key West. Maduro was again the ballclub owner and native Cubans again filled most of the roster spots. The team was strong enough to garner four consecutive FIL titles in a thriving nine-team circuit that was Class C level from 1946 to 1948 and Class B from 1949 on. The Washington Senators counted the Havana Cubans among their affiliations during the early '50s and future big leaguers Juan Delis (.299 BA) and Julio Becquer (.294 BA) swung heavy bats during the club's final 1953 season. But the strong suit for the Havana Cubans was always pitching, much of it also destined for the big-league club in Washington. Conrado Marrero posted spectacular seasons between 1947 and 1949, winning 70 games in those three years and posting ERAs of most stingy proportions (1.66, 1.67, 1.53). Marrero also hurled a spectacular no-hitter against Tampa in 1949, while Julio Moreno (19-4 in 1947) and Sandy Consuegra (8-2 in 1950) also used the Cubans ballclub as their big-league stepping stone. Collectors cards displayed here are from the Montiel "Los Reyes del Deporte" ("Kings of Sports") promotional album and feature Havana Cubans players of the inaugural 1946 season.

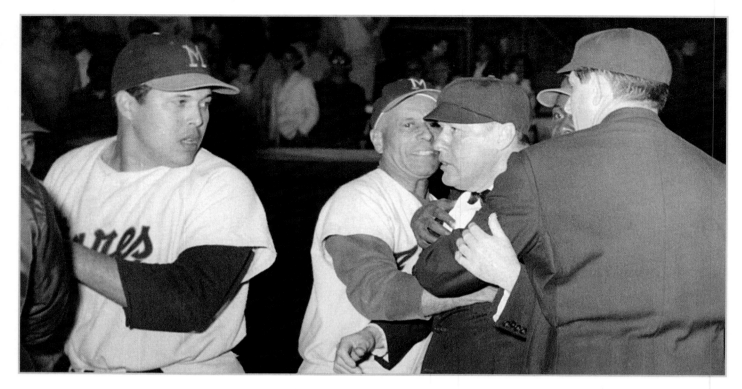

In English-language diamond lingo it is known as a "donnybrook" pure and simple, while in Cuba it is normally called a "pelea" — the Spanish noun for fistacuffs. Or perhaps even more colorfully a "cámara húngaro" (literally "Hungarian room"). Whatever you call it, it is a scene perhaps more fitting for blood sports like football in the United States or hockey in Canada. Above, legendary umpire Amado Maestri (who once ejected league mogul Jorge Pasquel from the ballyard in Mexico City) must be restrained from settling the score with Marianao's Juan Groguirre, who has apparently already peppered the man in blue with some choice verbal taunts. Below, Marianao skipper Nap Reyes receives an assist from a willing official in corraling his own enraged player Adolfo Arias. Both scenes are from Havana action in the late '50s.

In the hot Cuban climate tempers will flare at the mere drop of an insult or perhaps in the instant of an arbiter's questionable call. In the scenes below, Oscar Rodríguez goes nuts over an unacceptable umpire's call in the 1956 winter campaign. The action on this page is a traditional "before and after" sequence which has the enraged Cienfuegos coach heatedly gesturing his side of the story (top) and then losing control altogether as he is barely restrained by a contingent of teammates which includes star southpaw hurler and cup-of-coffee big leaguer Adrián Zabala at the far right.

This scene of dramatic disagreement on the diamond in Habana's El Cerro Stadium during the 1952-53 Cuban winter season is perhaps more notable for the personalities involved than it is for the heatedness of the angry exchange. Squaring off verbally at the left are Almendares manager and pitching legend Conrado Marrero and U.S. umpire Ed Runge, himself a major-league regular. Visible above Marrero's left shoulder is shortstop Willie Miranda, who remains on the fringes of the disagreement. Also prepared to back up their skipper at the right are coach Clemente Carrera (restrained by umpire Amado Maestri), Ultus Alvarez, Asdrúbal Baró, and Hector Rodríguez. Marrero's playing days were almost all behind him at the time of this unsavory diamond scene. Carrera and Baró would enjoy less-than-distinguished professional careers, though the latter would reach the Triple-A level twice with Omaha and the Sugar Kings. But Rodríguez and Miranda were, of course, more luminous figures. The former was one of the best-ever defensive infielders on Cuban soil, though he would fail to impress in his single big-league season (1952) as a light-hitting third baseman with the Chicago White Sox. The latter spent the entire decade of the '50s with a collection of American League teams (Washington, Chicago, St. Louis, New York, Baltimore) and has been acclaimed by many as the flashiest defensive shortstop ever, short of 1980s National League all-star Ozzie Smith.

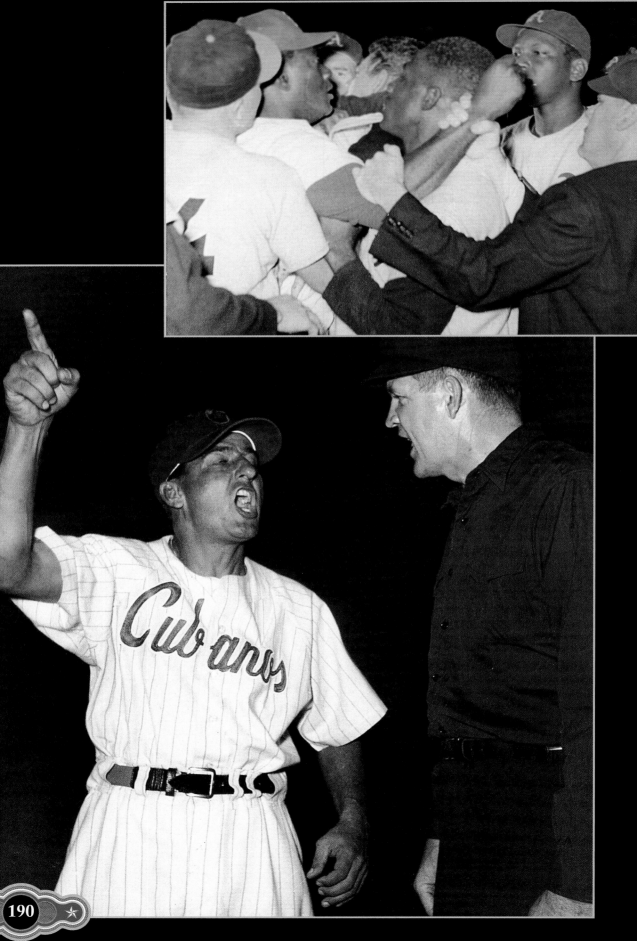

"Peleas," or donnybrooks, are common to baseball on all levels, and on these pages we witness such disruptions of diamond play at three levels of competition — professional winter-league play, international amateur tournament competition, and the once-popular pre-revolution Cuban amateur circuit. A staredown between Connie Marrero and Ed Runge has escalated into full-scale warfare (opposite, top) as Marianao's Minnie Miñoso is forced to restrain Almendares coach Clemente Carrera and umpire Amado Maestri rushes in from the right to restore order and separate the combatants. The action is more verbal (opposite, bottom) in a scene from International League action, where Sugar Kings manager Regino Otero hotly contests a point with a clearly unsympathetic official. Otero not only managed the Triple-A Sugar Kings to their first postseason appearance in 1955 but also further distinguished himself as a skipper in the Cuban League, Mexican League, and Venezuelan League, winning a record seven championships in the latter circuit. His brief major-league appearance consisted of 14 games with the 1945 NL champion Chicago Cubs. As the action captured here suggests, Otero was one fiery Cuban skipper who always made certain that umpires appreciated his particular point of view.

Sometimes the men in blue are not themselves a sufficient force to quell such misguided enthusiasm from players and managers, as clearly is the case below, where police have entered the field to aid in restoring order during an interrupted Cuban amateur-league (Liga Nacional de Amateurs) contest between Marianao and Matanzas. This disorderly scene took place during the 1946-47 season on the hallowed grounds of Estadio Palmar del Junco in Matanzas (historic site of the first recorded game in Cuba back in 1874).

Big-time organized baseball arrived in Havana in 1954 when Bobby Maduro's Class B Havana Cubans were transferred up the organizational ladder into the thriving Triple-A International League, joining cities such as Toronto, Montreal, Buffalo, Rochester, and Richmond in pro baseball's top minor-league circuit. Maduro had been a driving force behind securing minor-league baseball on the island back in 1946 and had been largely responsible as well for the building that same year of La Gran Estadio del Cerro, Havana's showcase downtown ballpark. Now he was again in the driver's seat when Cuba's political and baseball capital took a major step toward the long-held dream of true major-league status. Among the several field managers to direct Sugar Kings fortunes were former big leaguers Regino Otero (1954-1956) and Pedro "Preston" Gómez (1959), along with Tony Pacheco (1958) and Tony Castaños (1960). In early seasons the team was an inevitable also-ran, though it did feature a handful of players who were previously or eventually significant big-league names (especially Raul Sánchez, Conrado Marrero and Saul Rogovin). By the end of the decade, however, the SKs peaked (with Mike Cuéllar, Tony González, Elio Chacón, and Leo Cárdenas in the lineup) during a run to 1959 postseason glories. Fan support was high — with more than 300,000 fanaticos cramming El Cerro Stadium in 1955 — and always enthusiastic. Even Fidel, once in power, saw the team as an import symbol of Cuban national pride and also of Cuban national achievement.

Napoleon Reyes (left, middle, and right) earned his fame on Cuban diamonds as a heavy-hitting second baseman long before the arrival of the Triple-A Sugar Kings. But with the International League team there would be yet a new role for the popular Reyes. He had become a regal manager by the early 1950s, earning distinction in that capacity in the wintertime Cuban League, with Marianao, as well as in the Caribbean Series (directing Marianao to back-to-back victories in 1957 and '58) and the Venezuelan League. With the Sugar Kings he served as coach during the final partial season in Havana. And when the plug was pulled on the franchise by International League honchos during the middle of the 1960 season, it was Reyes who was asked to take managerial control of the relocated club during the second-half of the campaign in Jersey City.

This collage of scenes provides a broad panorama of Sugar Kings history. Raul Sánchez (opposite, top) was a mainstay hurler during the team's first three seasons, posting a 22-22 overall mark but twice winning in double-figures before moving on to the parent Cincinnati Reds. The Sugar Kings were known throughout the decade for strong pitching always neutralized by light hitting. Sánchez, Emilio Cueche, and later Mike Cuéllar were among the best Havana moundsmen. And even veteran Connie Marrero took a fling on the hill as a fill-in starter with credible 7-3 (1955) and 3-1 (1956) ledgers. President Fulgenio Bastita (opposite, bottom, second from left) was a frequent spectator in the grand-stands in the years before the outbreak of Castro's rebellion in 1956. Manager Regino Otero (below) animatedly argues a point during colorful diamond rhubarb action. Otero was at the helm when the team debuted and remained through the first three seasons, directing the club to a pair of surprising successes (78-77 in fifth and 87-66 in third) over its first two campaigns.

Havana's Sugar Kings would provide a new home for a number of old Havana baseball standbys. One was Pedro Formental, long a celebrity on the Cuban winter baseball landscape. The popular portside-hitting and throwing outfielder had captured a Cuban League batting title with Havana in 1950 and also starred over the years with Cienfuegos (1943-46) and Marianao (1954). His total of 56 career homers remains the record for Cuban League batters swinging from the left side of the plate. The league standard for righties was owned by backstop and brief major leaguer Ray Noble, another Cuban veteran who would also grace the Sugar Kings roster. In the scene on the facing page Formental rounds third after a timely home run in El Cerro Stadium during the 1955 campaign, his second and last with the Triple-A ballclub. Other familiar faces in the Sugar Kings lineup were Vicente López, Vicente Amor, Conrado Marrero, Julio Moreno, Juan Delis, Ray Noble, Fermín Guerra, Roberto Ortíz, Angel Scull, and Andres Fleitas, among others. Amor, Formental, Marrero, Moreno, Noble, and Scull — along with imports Pompeyo Davalillo, Clint Hartung, Johnny Lipon, and Ken Raffenberger — played on the 1955 edition of the team, which is pictured below. It was this 1955 squad, the middle of three teams managed by Otero, which surprised the entire league up north and even the fans back home with a winning season's record (87-66, third place) and brief playoff appearance, from which it was quickly ousted in five games by the powerhouse Toronto Maple Leafs.

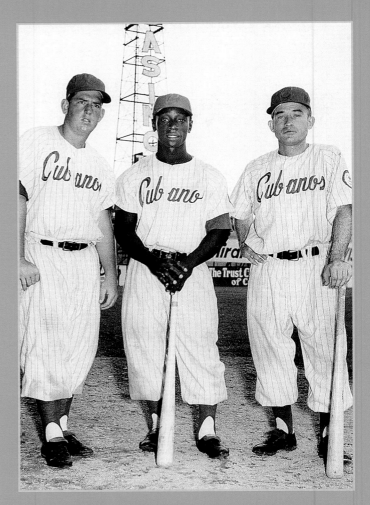

The parade of Sugar Kings stars continued in the mid and late '50s. Conrado Marrero (opposite, bottom, in dugout with trainer Natilla Jiménez) was the most popular figure, alongside Pedro Formental and Ray Noble from the ranks of the oldtimers. Marrero was enjoying the final hour of a career in which he had starred in local and international amateur play between 1938 and 1945 with teams from Cienfuegos, anchored the staff of the Class B Havana Cubans of the Florida International League for three seasons (1947-49, with two campaigns of 25 wins), visited the big leagues with the Washington Senators in the early '50s (39-40 over five summers), and hurled and even managed in the Cuban winter league with Almendares through the mid-'50s. Tony González and Angel Scull were a pair of up-and-coming prospects, and one would make it fairly big in the major leagues while the other would ultimately fail to make the grade. González (opposite, top left, left, with Luís Zayas, right) would one day post impressive big-league numbers which included 1,485 hits and a .286 batting average for 12 seasons. With the Phillies he was a league leader in outfield fielding percentage in 1962, 1964 and 1967. González was also a mainstay with the SKs when he manned center field and contributed 20 homers, 86 RBIs, and a .300 batting average during the 1959 season.

Fleet outfielder Scull (opposite, top right, between Forrest Smith, left, and Don Nichols) had his major-league dreams cut short by severe injury while a crack Washington prospect. He had been pencilled into the Senators starting outfield during 1954 spring training before a broken leg shut down any potential big-league action. Scull rebounded for a successful minor-league run with Triple-A Atlanta and the Mexican League, also copping a Cuban winter league batting title (1955) with an impressive .370 average. Juan Delis (below) was also one of the grandest among Sugar Kings heroes. The fleet-footed Delis shared first base with Julio Becquer during the SKs' maiden season, then returned from a 1955 cup of coffee with the Senators to play an infield and outfield utility role. But the highlights would come with the 1959 season, ironically played out in the midst of revolutionary chaos and also under the pressures of imminent International League rejection. During that final full summer new stars had come onto the scene with slugging first baseman Borrego Alvarez, flyschasers Dan Morejón and Carlos Paula, backstop Jesse Gonder, and infielders Cookie Rojas and Leo Cárdenas. The team jelled despite an ugly incident on July 25th, when an overzealous revolutionary celebration drove players scurrying from the field during an important mid-year weekend series with the archrival Rochester Red Wings.

Beisbolito
Revista Programa de la Liga Internacional

SUGAR AAA KINGS

FOREST SMITH

1ª Edición  10¢
DEL 18 DE ABRIL AL 1º DE MAYO DE 1956

No minor-league team at any level or in any locale ever experienced a wilder or wackier season than did the Sugar Kings during a memorable 1959 campaign played against the backdrop of revolutionary fervor in Cuba. Revolution and its aftermath had gripped the entire country in the months immediately before baseball play opened in late April. Throughout the summer Castro and his revolutionary leaders were familiar faces in El Cerro Stadium, just as they were everyplace else around the Cuban countryside. The team barely survived not only a tough pennant race (winding up nine games behind frontrunner Buffalo and three below runnerup Columbus) but also a memorable political incident that had transpired in late July. Chaos finally and unfortunately broke out smack in the midst of pennant fever on a late-July evening, just one night after Fidel's ballyhooed ballpark pitching exhibition with his "Los Barbudos" army team.

El Cerro Stadium was jammed with *guajiros* (Cuban peasants from around the countryside) and *barbudos* (Castro's soldiers) who had gathered for a special night of revolutionary celebrations marking a first post-revolution commemoration of the 1953 Moncada garrison attack at Santiago. Diamond action had been stopped on the stroke of midnight — with the game still knotted in the 11th frame — for purposes of raising banners and singing the national anthem. Sudden and sporadic gunfire from enthusiastic revelers next broke out everywhere in and around the ballpark, and it continued unabated even after ballplaying was resumed. When a stray bullet fired skyward grazed the batting helmet of Rochester third base coach Frank Verdi and another singed the shoulder of SKs' shortstop Leo Cárdenas, both ballclubs hastily sought shelter. The incident nearly put an immediate end to pro baseball in Cuba when the traumatized Rochester team left the country in panic, refusing to play the next day's scheduled match. The season continued nonetheless, and the Sugar Kings soon rebounded on the field to surprise everyone, including themselves, during the league's Shaughnessy Cup playoffs, first sweeping Columbus in four straight and then besting Richmond for the league title. Havana was miraculously able to boast a championship team for the first and, sadly, the only time.

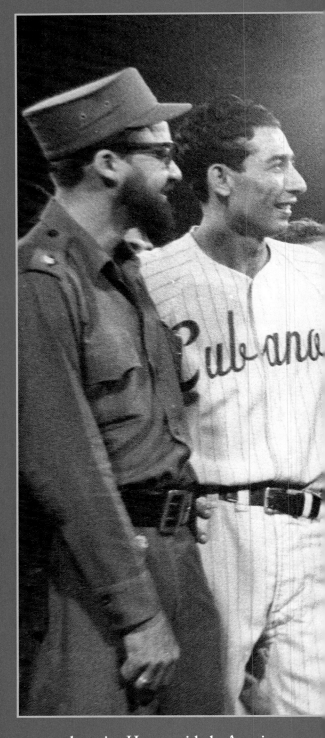

Fidel (center) visits the Sugar Kings late in the 1959 championship season, posing here with Rochester manager Clyde King (far right) and national sports chief Guerra Matos (far left). It was the postseason of that very year, however, which witnessed the greatest hours of the Sugar Kings saga. Those triumphs came with the excitement of Junior World Series play, a tradition dating back before World War I and this time matching International League postseason champion Havana with the American Association kingpin Minneapolis Millers. Minneapolis was led by playing manager Gene Mauch and featured rookie sensation Carl Yastrzemski at second base. The Millers and SKs split a pair of snow-plagued games in Minnesota before weather conditions convinced officials to revamp the remaining schedule. The series was finished up in Havana, where the home club took a 3-1 series lead before dropping two and setting up a dramatic Game 7 showdown. If the weather was plenty hot down in Cuba, the diamond action thus proved even hotter.

There were later some much exaggerated reports about the role of Fidel's revolutionary army in the outcome of the championship games. Stories circulated that armed Castro loyalists occupied the dugouts and box seats and thus intimidated Minneapolis ballplayers. But such accounts seem to have little basis in fact — especially the one that contended that Castro himself passed the Millers' bullpen on the way to his seat before the final game, patted the revolver on his hip, and announced confidently that "Tonight, we win!" The Sugar Kings simply made the big hits and thus won all the big games with late-inning rallies. Dan Morejon drove home the winning run in the bottom of the eleventh in one pivotal contest (Game 4), then delivered the major blow, a Game 7 series-clinching single in the bottom of the ninth, sending veteran pitcher Raul Sánchez scurrying home with the deciding tally, barely ahead of Tom Umphlett's desperate heave from center. It was perhaps Havana's finest baseball hour, though tragic circumstances lay just around the corner.

CUBANS AAA SUGAR KINGS

BEISBOLITO

CAMPEONES
1959
LIGAS MENORES

At left, Sugar Kings manager Pedro "Preston" Gómez receives an award in El Cerro Stadium from Fidel's official representative, Guerra Matos, right, after Havana's exciting Little World Series triumph over the American Association champion Minneapolis Millers. Matos served as first national sports director for Castro's revolutionary government, which had come to power earlier that same year. Looking on in the background are Havana players Enrique Izquierdo (left), Leo Cárdenas (second from left) and Tony González (center).

Government sports director Matos appears in one baseball setting (right), mugging for the camera with a famed revolutionary comrade named Cienfuegos (Comandante Camilo Cienfuegos, center), and in another (below) performing official duties alongside members of the team bearing that same name. In the latter scene Castro's number-one sports official presents a check from the revolutionary government to members of Cuba's professional ballplayers association, represented by popular Marianao outfielder Minnie Miñoso (far right). The Cienfuegos players in this scene — admiring a 1959 league championship banner — are Cienfuegos catcher Ray Noble (left) and pitcher Camilo Pascual.

The most popular myth surrounding Cuban baseball is undoubtedly that involving Fidel as a legitimate big-league pitching prospect. Most fans have run across the Castro baseball legend in one or another of its many familiar forms. The story usually paints Castro as a promising talent who was scouted in the late '40s or early '50s and nearly signed by a number of big-league clubs. One widely circulated version is the one that involves famed Clark Griffith "bird-dog" Joe Cambria and the Washington Senators, but the New York Giants and New York Yankees are just as often mentioned as the teams which missed out on turning Castro into Camilo Pascual. It is a grand story and has been swallowed hook, line, and fastball by many. If only scouts had been more persistent — or if only Fidel's fastball had a wee more pop — the history of the Western Hemisphere over the past half-century would likely have been reshaped. Or so goes the wellworn propaganda. One author, David Truby writing in *Harper's* magazine, even provides a handful of fictionalized scouting reports from the likes of talent hawks Howie Haak and Alex Pompez. The barren truth is that Fidel was indeed a crack high school athlete, one who excelled more at basketball than pitching, but who did show up at two of Cambria's open Havana tryout sessions in 1945 in order to impress his classmates. Cambria was never equally impressed, however, and no pro contract was ever offered to the future revolutionary leader.

The impetus for stories of Castro as serious big-league prospect seem to flow as much from his later fascination with the game as they do from phony stories about a hot schoolboy prospect. There are the records of numerous exhibition appearances at stadiums in Havana and elsewhere across Cuba during the first decade following takeover by the revolutionary forces. The most renowned event was Fidel's single appearance on the mound in El Cerro Stadium wearing the uniform of his own army pickup team, aptly named "Los Barbudos" ("the Bearded Ones"). Rarely, however, have the North American press or stateside baseball historians ever gotten the story quite straight.

The famed Barbudos game took place in Havana on July 24, 1959, before a crowd of 25,000 "fanaticos" and as a two-inning preliminary to an International League contest between the Rochester Red Wings and the local Sugar Kings. A contemporary newspaper account in the Rochester *Democrat and Chronicle* is the best source for details of the evening's colorful events, and also for the most familiar Castro pitching photo republished on numerous occasions. Castro hurled both innings and was captured on the mound (above) in several photos which would later become the only widely seen images of Cuba's Maximum Leader turned into a baseball pitcher. Almost the entire public impression of Fidel as moundsman is built upon these photographic images. Fidel struck out two batters, one with the aid of the umpire on a generous call which had "El Jefe" dashing to the batter's box to shake hands with the cooperative arbiter. Castro is reported to have "needlessly but admirably" covered first base on an infield grounder (the mark of some true latent mound skills), to have bounced to short in his only turn at bat, and to have demonstrated surprisingly good mound style — "wild but fast, and with good motions."

Another legendary link between Castro and pitching prowess is the often anthologized story told to *Sport* magazine writer Myron Cope in 1964 by ex-big-leaguer Don Hoak, a clearly apocryphal tale in which Hoak reputedly enjoyed an unofficial at-bat against Castro, the Havana University law student and budding revolutionary leader. As Hoak recounts the story, his unlikely and unscheduled at-bat against young Fidel came during his own single season in the Cuban League, which the ballplayer conveniently misremembers as being the winter season of 1950-51. Hoak's account involves a game between his own Cienfuegos club and the Marianao team starring outfield legend Pedro Formental. During the fifth inning and with Hoak occupying the batter's box, a spontaneous anti-Batista student demonstration suddenly broke out, with horns blaring, firecrackers exploding, and pro-revolution forces streaming directly onto the field of play.

Hoak's account continues with the student leader, Castro, marching onto the mound, seizing the ball from an unresisting Marianao pitcher, and tossing several warm-up heaves to catcher Mike Guerra. Fidel then barks orders for Hoak to assume his batting stance, famed Cuban umpire Amado Maestri shrugs agreement, the American fouls off several wild but hard fastballs, batter and umpire suddenly tire of this charade, and a bold Maestri finally orders military police ("who were lazily enjoying the fun from the grandstand") to brandish their riot clubs and drive the student rabble from the field. Castro left the scene in Cope's words "like an impudent boy who has been cuffed by the teacher and sent to stand in the corner." It was all a politically correct enough and most entertaining tale, but yet one with no basis whatsoever in hard fact. Loopholes is the Hoak account are so numerous and extreme — Maestri was not an umpire to ever permit such high jinks, Batista was not even in office in 1951, and Fidel was still in prison on the Isle of Pines during Hoak's actual Cuban season, which was 1954 — as to suggest that ballplayer Hoak and author Cope could only have concocted the whole saga with tongues firmly planted in cheeks.

Fidel and baseball have remained intimately linked for the forty years of Castro's reign in Revolutionary Cuba. But it was only as "El Presidente" and Maximum Leader — not as legitimate ballplayer — that Fidel Castro emerged as one of the most remarkable figures of all Cuban baseball history. It was Fidel who was the guiding spirit and formal architect behind the reconstruction of the country's national pastime in the radically altered form of a thriving amateur league known as "the National Series," which debuted in 1962. Fidel's vision of baseball and all other sport as a showcase for revolutionary training and national pride lies behind the juggernaut Cuban national teams which have dominated several decades of international play. Fidel was never Cuba's Walter Johnson or even its latter-day Dolf Luque; he was instead something closer to a cross between the mythic founder Abner Doubleday and the marketing genius A.G. Spalding. Without ever launching a serious fastball (opposite) or swinging a potent bat (right), Castro — like Judge Kenesaw Mountain Landis north of the border a generation earlier — had far greater impact on his nation's pastime than a whole generation of leather-pounding, lumber-toting ballplayers.

Above, Fidel (left) and his one-time catcher, Commandant Camilo Cienfuegos, are captured by the camera moments after the famous "Los Barbudos" exhibition in El Cerro Stadium on July 24, 1959. There was clearly never any doubt about who called the pitches that night, but Cienfuegos truly stole the moment with his memorable line concerning ballplaying with his revered commander and Cuba's Maximum Leader. "I never oppose Fidel in anything, including baseball," quipped the astute revolutionary general when asked by reporters why he had turned down the assignment of pitching for the opposing military police team during the two-inning exhibition.

Fidel's bearded and fatigues-clad revolutionary leaders were ubiquitous ballpark fixtures during early-1960s baseball seasons, especially at amateur Cuban League games staged in Havana and other league cities. Che Guevara (opposite, bottom) and Raul Castro (below) were both anxious to take their cuts in public, with the better batting form not surprisingly displayed by Fidel's own brother. An Argentinean by birthright, Che hardly cut a noble baseball figure, yet he nonetheless showed his own fascinations for the national game of his adopted homeland.

At right is an historic program for the July 1959 game in El Cerro Stadium when Fidel pitched for "Los Barbudos" and Camilo Cienfuegos donned catching gear for two innings to receive the Maximum Leader's lively fastballs. Castro was reported by a baseball writer with the Rochester (NY) *Democrat and Chronicle* — on hand for the main attraction Red Wings versus Sugar Kings contest — to have practiced all day in his hotel room for his brief stint against a squad of local military police.

While Clemente, Cepeda, Marichal, and Camilo Pascual stood head and shoulders above dozens of utility-role Latin big leaguers throughout the '60s, the field was more crowded with Spanish-speaking "franchise players" by the mid-1970s. At the forefront of this new invasion was a trio of Cuban imports featuring two of the sport's most fearsome sluggers and one of its most flamboyant and effective hurlers. Pedro "Tony" Oliva (below) was the last "impact" player to flee Cuba on the heels of the Castro revolution and also the last big-name recruit for popular Washington Senators bird dog Joe Cambria. Oliva's career began with a true star-burst in Minnesota as the only big leaguer ever to win batting titles in his first two seasons, and also with an American League rookie record 217 hits. By the early 1970s Oliva was a well-established star, having earned a third batting title in 1971 and knocking out a league-best 204 safeties to launch the new decade a season earlier. Unfortunately, Oliva was often unfairly overlooked by U.S. fans — like Clemente and Cepeda before him — and his later career-slowing injuries — like Clemente's — were often dismissed as goldbricking.

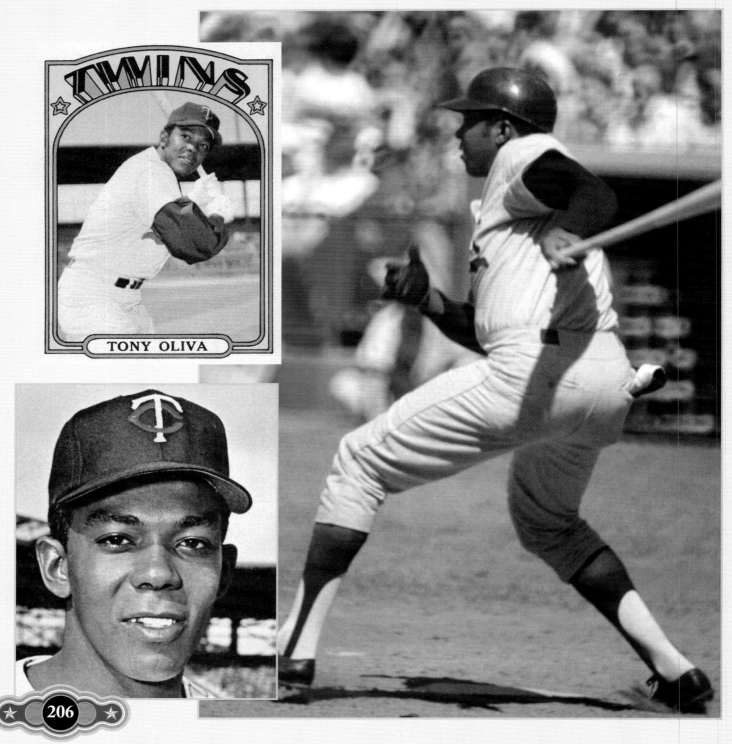

TONY OLIVA

TONY PEREZ

It is only part and parcel of the hidden tragedy of modern Latin ballplayers that so much controversy has swirled around Cooperstown candidates such as Orlando Cepeda and "Tany" (Antanasio) Pérez. While the San Francisco slugger was finally inducted in 1999, the backbone of Cincinnati's big red machine of the mid-'70s has simply fallen victim to cruel happenstance. It was the fate of Pérez to play on a team where he was but one among a half-dozen candidates for canonization (including the flashier stars named Pete Rose, Joe Morgan, and Johnny Bench). But it will always remain difficult for Cooperstown voters to ignore the record of a slugger who retired as the 14th-best RBI man in major-league history, owned nearly 3,000 base hits and nearly 400 homers, and reigned with rival Cepeda as the all-time Latin American major-league home run king. For a full decade (1967-76) he anchored a big red machine batting order almost without parallel, six times topping 100 RBIs. Throughout his decade in Cincinnati's infield Pérez and the Reds managed four pennants, and his greatest single season (1970) precisely coincided with and matched Bench's, thus providing the champion Redlegs with one of the greatest single-season slugging tandems ever suited up in the same lineup.

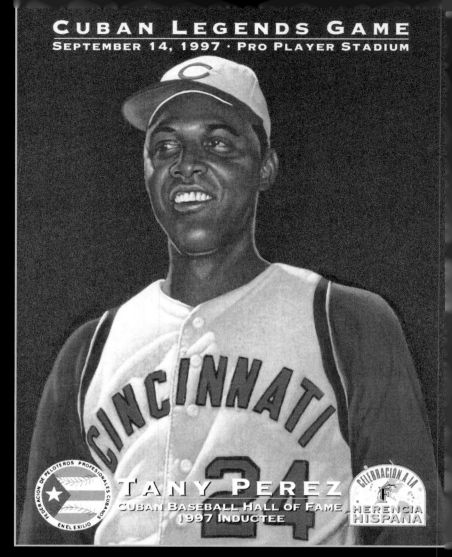

TANY PEREZ
CUBAN BASEBALL HALL OF FAME
1997 INDUCTEE

"Looie" Tiant Jr.'s baseball career was sealed by birthright and family heritage, yet also marked by an agonizingly slow start and dogged after retirement by an unfortunate set of persistent ironies. The younger Tiant (left, with the Red Sox and near right with the Twins) flashed early brilliance just as his famous father had three decades before. Signed to a professional contract in the Mexican League by former Cleveland Indians batting champion Bobby Avila, Tiant quickly established a Pacific Coast League record for winning percentage (15-1, .938) before joining the big-league club midway through the 1964 season. His debuts in Cleveland and Minnesota were a sad tale of unfulfilled potential, however. Tiant won 20 only once for the Indians (in 1968, when he posted a brilliant 1.60 ERA) but then lost 20 in 1969 and was peddled promptly to the Twins. Tiant's earliest claim to fame was thus a dubious distinction of having duplicated an unwanted feat of acclaimed countryman Dolf Luque. Like Luque his early hallmark was that he had dovetailed seasons when he first won and then lost 20 games.

Tiant would achieve true stardom only with a fateful stop in Boston (1971-78) and a niche as one of that history-rich franchise's most popular players ever. The rolly polly righty with the twisting mound delivery was assured a prominent place in diamond history by his memorable 1972 and 1975 seasons alone. In the former campaign Tiant again reigned as ERA champ (1.91). During the latter he paced the pennant-winning Bosox with 18 victories, then earned a crucial series-tying complete-game win in Game 4 of the fall classic. Tony Pérez would belt three homers for victorious Cincinnati in that same World Series, Mike Cuellar in Baltimore a half-dozen seasons earlier was first among Latin pitchers to capture a Cy Young Award, and Tony Taylor would amass more than 2,000 hits (mostly in Philadelphia) across a durable two-decade career that peaked in the late '60s and early '70s. Yet no other Cuban would quite dominate the 1970s like the colorful, cigar-chomping flamethrower named Luís Tiant.

MIKE CUELLAR

210

Today's showcase Cuban League arose from the ashes of professional baseball, which had suffered a sudden and inglorious death on the island in the summer months of 1960. But Cuban diamonds did not lie dormant for long. Under the guiding influence of Castro himself a brand-new Cuban baseball establishment was molded in the first few seasons of the sixties. And it was a baseball world with a considerable number of remarkable differences. Professionalism was banned, ballpark admission was now free to the public, wooden Louisville Sluggers were eventually traded (by 1976) for Japanese-made aluminum models, modest state-of-the-art stadiums were built with volunteer revolutionary labor, and home-sewn Batos-brand baseballs were the new tools of Cuban batters and hurlers. These Cuban batsmen and moundsmen were still a potent collection of talented stars, even if the focus was now on the pride of national competion (at home in the Cuban League and abroad on the national team in world amateur tournaments) rather than on earning professional contracts. Among the grandest of these new Cuban stars were Agustín Marquetti (opposite and left), a southpaw-swinging Havana first sacker who banged out prodigious roundtrippers in the early '70s, and Braudilio Vinent (below), a 221-game winner in the 1970s and '80s who remains Cuba's career pacesetter in complete games, shutouts, and innings pitched.

From its outset in 1962 the new Cuban League has boasted its unique features. One is the strict regional structure of its province-based circuit and national championship series. Teams are geographically fixed with players drawn only from each team's immediate locale. Players are not switched willy-nilly from roster to roster as in the North American professional leagues. There are no trades in the Cuban League, a practice consistent with the country's socialist notion that ballplayers are not mere chattel, or so much ballclub property, to be bought or sold at a club owner's whim. Fan loyalties run deep due to this regional organization, as do the heated intersectional rivalries.

The current Cuban League setup includes four divisions of four teams each, further divided into western and eastern zones (comparable to U.S. American and

National leagues). A postseason playoff tournament involving four divisional winners and four runners-up is similar to the U.S. League Championship Series format, and the championship round which concludes each National Series is (like the majors) a best-of-seven affair. League structure has altered somewhat over the years (Cuba itself was resegmented into 14 provinces in May 1975) and so has the seasonal organization. But the basic scheme has remained largely intact since 1962.

Cuban League seasons are the means for selection of national teams for international competitions at the world senior level (such as Pan American Games, IBA World Championships, Intercontinental Cup, and Olympic tournaments). Traditionally there have been two seasons in Cuba — a provincial round (usually 39 games for each of 14 teams) followed by a superprovincial round (54 games for a smaller group of combined all-star clubs). The first round, or National Series, (1998 was National Series XXXVII) was prelude to a Select Series competition for the coveted Revolutionary Cup, usually contested between four larger zones (Occidentales, Havana, Centrales, and Orientales). With the most recent 1998 schedule, however, the two-season format was scrapped and replaced with a longer, single 90-game schedule stretching from early November to late April.

The biggest Cuban stars of recent decades have been sluggers Antonio Muñoz (1967-90), Wilfredo "El Hombre Hit" Sánchez (1967-84), and Lázaro Junco (1978-95), along with flamethrowing hurlers Aquino Abreu (1962-70) and Braudilio Vinent (1969-88). Muñoz, a first baseman with Las Villas, still holds CL records for games played and runs scored, as well as doubles, total bases, and RBIs. *Sports Illustrated* writer Ron Fimrite, upon seeing Muñoz in 1977, dubbed him a lefthanded Tony Pérez. Sánchez was the first CL batsman to reach 2,000 hits, a feat that earned his colorful nickname. Junco long held the career homer mark with 405 roundtrippers. And Abreu was especially brilliant in January 1966 when he matched big leaguer Johnny Vander Meer's feat of back-to-back no-hitters, thus performing perhaps international baseball's most overlooked heroic pitching feat.

A collage of first-generation Cuban League stars pictured here includes a trio of CL and national team heroes. They are: outfielder Elpidio Mancebo, Mineros 1962-77 (above, left), infielder Walfrido Ruíz, Industriales 1965-78 (above, right), and pitcher Alfredo García, Henequeneros 1965-76 (right). García led the league in victories (12) in 1970, while Mancebo was twice (1968, 1970) a league pacesetter in bases on balls received and also once held a CL single-season record for doubles (26 in 1969). He received more free passes than any Cuban Leaguer of the sixties. Ruíz in 1968 established a single-game Cuban League record for sacrifice flies, stroking three in a contest against Henequeneros. Also pictured here are several Cuban-issue stamps of the 1980s and 1990s, which celebrate the country's proud, long-standing record in international baseball tournament competitions.

Cuban League stars pictured below, with their teams and years of league play, include: Antonio Jiménez, Industriales 1959-72 (top left), Agustín Arias, Orientales 1962-74 (top right), and Eulogio Osorio, Industriales and Havana 1961-77 (bottom right). All three would proudly represent their country in various international tournaments during the first post-revolution decade.

Arias was a slick-fielding shortstop on the 1970 Cuban national team, which captured a gold medal at the eleventh annual Central American and Caribbean Games. Jiménez several times during the 1960s paced the Cuban League in runs scored and in 1963 banged out the most triples, while Osorio was twice the league's leader in doubles.

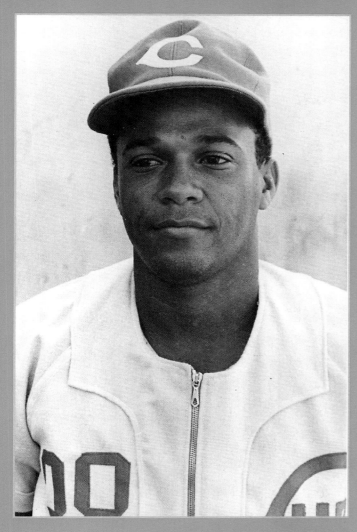

Cuban League stars pictured on this page are: Rigoberto Rosique, Henequeneros 1964-79 (top left), Rolando Macías, Azucareros 1963-79 (bottom left), and Roberto Valdés, Orientales 1963-78 (top right). Rosique was one of the most talented batsmen of the first decade of Cuban League play.

Among stars of the 1960s, Rosique owned the fourth-highest batting average (.288 in National Series play) and was also among the most skilled at drawing free passes (third in the league over the first nine seasons). For the same decade, Valdés posted the best ERA (1.39) while Macías was third in wins with 50.

JUEGOS OLIMPICOS BARCELONA '92

¡PATRIA!

# BASEBALL AND THE COLD WAR

Among great sports dynasties, any long-toothed fan is most likely to mention dominant professional teams such as baseball's New York Yankees, basketball's Boston Celtics, or hockey's Montreal Canadiens. In the amateur ranks, collegiate juggernauts come to mind such as the footballers of Notre Dame and the '70s-era basketballers of Coach John Wooden at UCLA. There was also the interminable reign of USA basketball in the Olympic Games before the disorienting shock of that still-controversial 1972 loss to an underdog Russian national team in Munich. Yet on the grand stage of worldwide competitions the most impressive dynasty of all has unquestionably been the one which the Cubans launched on the amateur baseball front in the early 1960s and which has rolled on largely unmolested and almost without serious interruption ever since.

Baseball teams — even the very best baseball teams — rarely win above 60% of the time. Cuban ballclubs competing on the international scene have, nonetheless, made a true mockery out of any such standards of normalcy. Since the early days of the Castro-led revolution Cuban amateur baseball has more than withstood the tests of time. New stars are rolled out almost annually with production-line efficiency: ace pitcher Braudilio Vinent and longball bashers Antonio Muñoz, Agustín Marquetti, and Armando Capiró in the '70s; sluggers Victor "El Loco" Mesa, Lázaro Junco and Luís Casanova and crafty hurler Omar Ajete in the '80s; and all-world third baseman Omar Linares in the '90s. The Cuban national team would capture an incredible 80 of 81 games played at the highest levels of international tournament competition between a surprise opening-round 1987 Pan American Games upset loss to the U.S. in Indianapolis (the Cubans later captured the gold medal in a rematch with the seemingly overconfident Americans) and their 1996 Olympic gold medal triumph in Atlanta. Including world junior-level games, Cuba's record over the same stretch was an unimaginable 144-1. Along the way Cuban teams have demonstrated their unchallenged superiority at every turn by winning eight of nine International Cups; six straight IBA world championships; four consecutive Central American and Caribbean Games tournaments; the 1987, 1991, and 1995 Pan American Games titles; and both the Barcelona and Atlanta Olympics. With such resounding victories the Cuban juggernaut has remained the envy of the entire amateur baseball world, if not also of the entire professional baseball world.

Cuba's amateur baseball triumphs are hardly a new occurrence and indeed stretch back to the very beginnings of world championship play in the 1930s and to the establishment of round-robin Caribbean Basin competitions a decade later. But under Fidel's revolutionary regime baseball became a proud instrument for demonstrating superiority of the island nation's state-sponsored sports programs. Any neutral observer soon had to admit the view expressed by exile Cuban historian Louis Pérez, that baseball — the quintessential North American game — has most effectively served Fidel Castro's Cuban Revolution — a quintessentially anti-American embodiment. Few North Americans, however, pay much attention to amateur baseball and fewer still follow international competitions. Despite their lopsided triumphs at Pan American venues and Olympic tournaments, the greatest among Castro-era Cuban ballplayers have remained completely unknown to North American fans while nonetheless enjoying the status of national heroes back home. Yet by the mid-nineties the scene was slowly changing. The slugging prowess of Omar Linares and Orestes Kindelán at the Atlanta Olympics inspired renewed North American interest in Cuban talent. The appearance of a new flock of refugee Cuban stars in the big leagues of late — especially flashy shortstop Rey Ordoñez (Mets) and half-brother pitching sensations Livan Hernández (Marlins) and Orlando "El Duque" Hernández (Yankees) — has also reawakened burgeoning international audiences for potent Cuban baseball skills. And during the past season a highly competitive and groundbreaking exhibition series against the big-league Baltimore Orioles has clinched the lofty status of Cuba's national pastime.

Cuban baseball since the revolution boasts a legacy of homegrown stars whose feats unfortunately remain only whispered rumors away from the island — most especially in big-league venues to the north. Augustín Marquetti, Antonio Muñoz, Lázaro Junco, Pedro Rodríguez Jova, and Wilfredo Sánchez ("El Hombre Hit") are a quintet of '60s and '70s-era sluggers whose reported on-field heroics and prowess with the lumber (albeit metallic "lumber") fire the imaginations of North American scouts and ballpark denizens who never saw them play even a single inning. But in recent decades one island star has surpassed them all and also has enjoyed a far more visible international stage for his rare diamond exploits. The Olympic baseball arena (officially launched in 1992 with the first gold medal competitions) has today entrenched Omar Linares as a recognizable figure outside of Cuba's narrow confines. Among the initiated few following the international baseball scene, some have even boldly touted this grandest Cuban star of the 1990s as "the greatest third baseman found anywhere on the planet."

American ballfans who made the effort to camp out in Atlanta's Fulton County Stadium for 1996 Olympic competitions came away undoubtedly carrying two lasting (and perhaps mildly surprising) impressions. Cuba's national team, which easily swept the tournament to collect their predicted gold medallions, was every bit as good as rumors in the sporting press had warned. And slugging third baseman Omar Linares — seemingly a cross between Brooks Robinson and a politically correct Albert Belle, as one U.S. writer cleverly phrased it — was also every bit as brilliant as his mountain of advanced press clippings. Linares put on an awesome individual show of longball slugging, first in the showdown game with Team USA when he cracked a mammoth opening-inning roundtripper, and again during the championship faceoff with Japan in which he socked three more dingers to clinch a championship victory. Here was not only a naturally gifted ballplayer with major-league skills, but also a gritty athlete who time and again rose to heroic feats in the sudden-death pressures of international tournament competitions. In two of the most important games ever played by the Cuban baseballers — as in so many similar moments in the past — it was Linares who brilliantly carried the Cuban team and the Cuban dreams of politically tinged victory squarely on his own broad shoulders.

The legacy of Omar Linares in the Cuban League is one of grandiose proportions. For 15 years the muscular third sacker has starred for the hometown Pinar del Río team and has repeatedly expressed his interest in playing nowhere but on the soil of his cherished homeland. Linares is through and through a devoted patriot as well as a diamond nonpareil. The island's combination of Mays, Mantle, and DiMaggio (with a large dose of Brooks Robinson and Mike Schmidt thrown in) has five times won batting titles with .400-plus averages (during 65- or 85-game seasons). His lifetime average has hovered above .375 and his rocket arm and infield range make him a complete ballplayer in the field (where he has played both third and short). Equally grand is his performance on the world stage for more than a dozen seasons. Linares batted better than .500 in his first world amateur championship action as a raw youngster of fourteen. A year later he was the youngest Cuban League starter in history. Olympic partisans are most familiar with the exploits of "El Niño" in Barcelona and Atlanta (where he slugged eight roundtrippers, including three in the gold medal finale). Between those gold medal curtain calls came numerous tournament MVP performances — most notably those in the 1993 IBA World All-Star Game at the Japan Tokyo Dome and the 1987 Intercontinental Cup tourney staged in Havana. Omar Linares has not only been Cuba's greatest diamond prize of the modern era, but also indisputably major-league baseball's greatest loss.

Linares (featured in a photo collage on these pages) provided late-inning slugging to key a 1996 gold medal victory in Atlanta versus Cuba's longtime rivals from Japan. The Cuba-Japan shootout would remind international observers of previous world championship battles between the two powers during the late '80s and early '90s. Linares was, as usual, the most luminous hero. As in their heralded matchup with the Americans a week earlier, the Cubans jumped to a commanding lead early, but the Japanese made a game of it with a fifth-inning grand slam which knotted the count. The tournament longball onslaught then continued full force in the sixth and seventh frames. In the end eight roundtrippers by the Cubans (of 11 total in the game) were sufficient to run the international victory string to 143 straight in world tournament competitions. For fans whose perspective reached beyond the U.S.-based majors, there was no longer any question about the greatest dynasty in baseball history — or maybe even sports history as a whole. As it had been for a century or more, Cuban baseball was once again an unmatched exemplar for the diamond sport. And Omar Linares was also again Cuba's most power-packed star.

CUBA 1994

Occidentales

TERCERA BASE/THIRD BASE
OMAR LINARES

Linares is a member of a talented baseball family, as well as a powerhouse Cuban League team of recent years. Brother Juan Carlos Linares (a lefty-hitting and throwing outfielder and .300-plus career hitter, posing with Omar, right, in the photo above) has also starred with Pinar del Río throughout the mid-'90s. The pair's father, Fidel Linares, was a Cuban League stalwart of an earlier generation who led the circuit in base hits in 1963. The two Linares brothers have kept Pinar del Río at the apex of the Cuban League scene for much of the current decade.

If Omar Linares has missed out on a professional big-league career, he has nonetheless enjoyed his moment to shine brightly against the "capitalist" professionals on their own stage. In the first game between Cuban leaguers and big leaguers in four decades, it was Linares who thrilled delirious Havana fans in Estadio Latinoamericano and momentarily sunk the Orioles' hopes by stroking the key eighth-inning hit to tie the historic game and send the affair (an eventual Baltimore victory) into extra frames.

While Linares — a native of Pinar del Río — is western Cuba's greatest baseball product during the Castro epoch, another prodigious slugger has in recent years emerged from the island's eastern sector. Santiago Province native Orestes Kindelán has climbed above the 400 plateau in career dingers (430 as of mid-1999) to overhaul Lázaro Junco as the island's all-time home run threat. The bull-like six-footer who swings from the right side has starred for more than a dozen campaigns with the Santiago de Cuba team of his native province and led that squad to recent consecutive postseason championship showdowns with two-time defending titlest Pinar del Río, and then finally to a 1999 league title. And the always laconic Kindelán (he lets his bat do his talking) has also pounded rival international pitching during most of Cuba's uninterrupted string of world championship, Intercontinental Cup, Pan American Games, and Olympic triumphs of the past decade.

Kindelán reached his apex as an international slugger with his amazing power surge at Fulton County Stadium during the 1996 Olympics. His nine mammoth homers outpaced more-celebrated teammate Linares, and Kindelán would likely have been Cuba's number-one Olympic hero in Atlanta had it not been for the three-homer game which Linares saved for the gold medal showdown with Japan. Kindelán himself also contributed a vital longball in the tournament finale. And two of his earlier blasts into the third deck of Fulton County Stadium were among the longest ever hit in the quarter-century-old major-league ballpark. Among Cuba's present baseball icons, only Linares and perhaps Santiago teammate Antonio Pacheco have been as valuable or as decorated on the international scene as has this muscular designated hitter who remains the pride of Santiago de Cuba.

In opposite-page action (top) Orestes Kindelán follows Omar Linares (10) across home plate after smacking one of his tournament-leading nine circuit blasts during 1996 Olympic competition. This clutch game-clinching blow came in semifinal action versus Nicaragua. Though employed almost exclusively as a power-swinging designated hitter (opposite, bottom) in recent seasons — both with Cuban national teams and with the Cuban League entry representing Santiago de Cuba — Kindelán has also performed as a dependable and sure-handed first baseman (above) and also as a fill-in catcher.

PRIMERA BASE/FIRST BASE
**ORESTES KINDELAN**

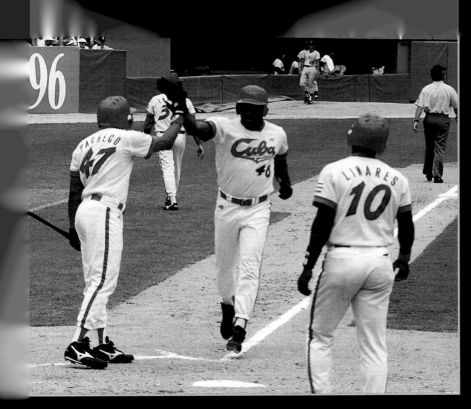

The career Cuban League home run ledger now stands as follows: Kindelán (430 in 17 seasons), Lázaro Junco (405 in 18 seasons), Omar Linares (377 in 16 seasons), Antonio Muñoz (370 in a record 24 seasons), Romelio Martínez (370 in 14 seasons) and Luís Casanova (312 in 17 seasons). Armando Capiró (1973) was first to smack 20-plus in a season, Junco still holds the record for years leading the league with seven, and Kindelán has been only twice the league pacesetter. Yet Orestes Kindelán is leaving earlier Cuban sluggers far in his wake when it comes to career productivity, and the big designated hitter from Santiago will likely have a few more seasons to pad his record numbers.

Orestes Kindelán (left, and sliding below) is now Cuba's all-time home run basher, having overhauled former record holder Lázaro Junco in 1997. Santiago's star attraction follows in a tradition earlier established by Augustín Marquetti (once the single-season record holder with 19 at the end of the league's first decade) and sustained in the '80's and early '90s by Matanzas-native Junco, owner of one of Cuban baseball's most deadly and compact swings. While Kindelán and Junco are of almost identical physical stature (six feet and a shade under 190 pounds), Kindelán is built more in the mold of a '50s-vintage big-league fence-basher, with bulging forearms and little foot speed. He boasts a body molded like Frank Thomas or Cecil Fielder, but his slugging approach has been always well-balanced like Thomas's and never one-dimensional like Fielder's. Kindelán is no wild hacker: while his strikeout totals (886) more than double his home run output, his selective swing has produced a career average well above .300.

Modern-day Cuban fans don't collect bubblegum trading cards of their diamond heroes. Such nostalgic trappings are absent in large part due to the economic crisis sweeping present-day Cuba. Collectable cards and photos from earlier baseball eras nonetheless remain popular items with tourists in Havana's numerous flee markets and book shops. And a 1994 limited-edition Cuban baseball card set — featuring Cuban League and national team standouts of the 1993-94 season — was produced for promotional purposes by a Canadian printer and made available to Cuban collectors by the public relations arm of INDER, the Cuban national sports authority. These cards (samples of which appear on this and other pages in this chapter) feature players in the uniforms of four all-star squads (Orientales, Habana, Centrales, and Occidentales) which competed for the coveted Revolutionary Cup during 1994's early-summer Select Series playoffs, following the regular wintertime National Series schedule.

CUBA 1994

Orientales

LANZADOR/PITCHER
**JORGE OCHOA**

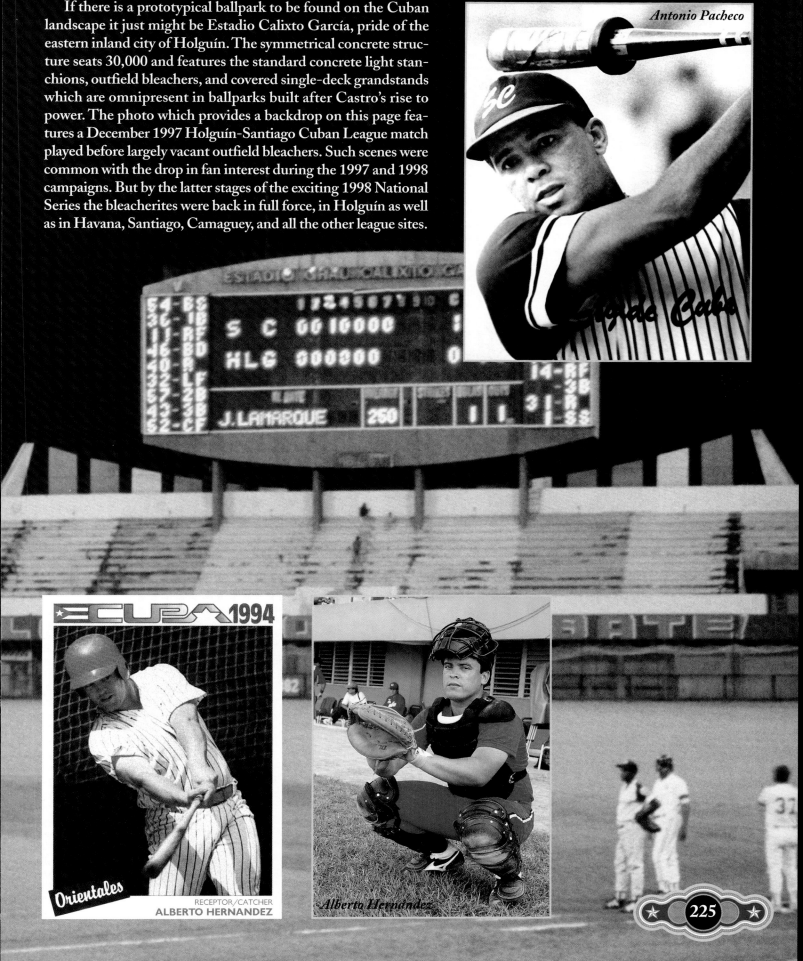

If there is a prototypical ballpark to be found on the Cuban landscape it just might be Estadio Calixto García, pride of the eastern inland city of Holguín. The symmetrical concrete structure seats 30,000 and features the standard concrete light stanchions, outfield bleachers, and covered single-deck grandstands which are omnipresent in ballparks built after Castro's rise to power. The photo which provides a backdrop on this page features a December 1997 Holguín-Santiago Cuban League match played before largely vacant outfield bleachers. Such scenes were common with the drop in fan interest during the 1997 and 1998 campaigns. But by the latter stages of the exciting 1998 National Series the bleacherites were back in full force, in Holguín as well as in Havana, Santiago, Camaguey, and all the other league sites.

*Antonio Pacheco*

RECEPTOR/CATCHER
**ALBERTO HERNANDEZ**

*Alberto Hernández*

Tense Cuban League game action (opposite, bottom) here takes place in Holguín's Estadio Calixto García between teams from Holguín and Santiago de Cuba. While most Cuban League ballparks offer little or nothing in the way of concession stands or roving grandstand vendors for the purchase of snacks or memorabilia, Holguín's stately ballpark does boast the rare distinction of beer vendors. Beer sales are hardly needed, however, to feed the wild enthusiasm and vocal spontaneity of Holguín fans, who remain among the most lively on the Cuban baseball scene. And if beer is an anomaly in the picturesque Holguín ballpark, the prominently displayed revolutionary slogan which adorns the third-base grandstand wall is not. Such slogans are also displayed (opposite, top) on the centerfield wall in Santiago, as they are in just about every Cuban park.

Cuban fans — like their counterparts throughout Mexico and the entire Caribbean — are a fun-loving throng who provide almost as much color and explosive action as the sporting spectacle which is unfolding before them. Musical instruments and noise makers of all types add to the grandstand din, which is an integral part of the Cuban ballpark scene. The exploits of top stars such as Victor Mesa (top) are greeted everywhere on the island with festive celebrations of unbridled enthusiasm. The celebration captured above is taking place among bleacher patrons in Santiago de Cuba and perhaps represents little more than some exciting home-team play, or maybe only the arrival in the batter's box of one of the local crowd's special favorites.

Eastern provinces boast some of Cuba's hottest baseball centers and thus not surprisingly some of the country's most classic and altogether characteristic ballparks. Stately Estadio Guillermón Moncada (above) located in picturesque Santiago de Cuba, at the island's far southeastern corner, features lush green-colored and cantilevered grandstands, stately inlaid dugouts and box seats along the foul lines, and towering electric light stanchions, all of which work in harmony to provide this particular stadium with a classic 1950s-era major-league or 1990s-era minor-league appearance.

With a well-earned reputation for running both his mouth and the basepaths with a reckless abandon, centerfielder Victor Mesa (below, right and opposite, bottom left) of the Villa Clara team has been dubbed affectionately "El Loco" by Cuban fans. A star on the 1992 Barcelona Olympic gold medal-winning squad, Mesa has approached the all-time Cuban base hit record (he fell just short of 2,000) and has overhauled the career base-stealing mark (550). A powerful righthanded swinger at 6'2", Mesa also owned more than 200 career homers and a lifetime batting average above .310 in National Series play. Luís Ulacia (below, left) paced the way with three hits during the historic March 1999 Havana encounter with the big-league Orioles. And those who saw Eduardo Paret (opposite, bottom right) in Atlanta realize that current New York Mets standout Rey Ordoñez would likely never have earned a regular spot on the Cuban national team even if he had not abandoned his native country for the big leagues.

CAMPO CORTO/SHORTSTOP
**LUIS ULACIA**

JARDINERO/OUTFIELDER
**VICTOR MESA**

Estadio Victoria de Girón (background) in the northern coastal city of Matanzas bears the name of one of revolutionary Cuba's proudest moments, the victory at Playa Girón during the abortive 1961 Bay of Pigs invasion by U.S.-sponsored anti-Cuban forces. This park was fittingly also a frequent stage for diamond heroics from several of Cuba's brightest national-team stars. The list must include Antonio Muñoz, Luís Ulacia, Victor Mesa, and Eduardo Paret. Muñoz (right and opposite top) is affectionately known as "El Guajiro" ("the peasant") and has in recent years served as a coach/trainer for Cienfuegos during National Series play. A slugging star in his own right throughout the '70s and '80s, he was also one of Cuba's most exemplary athletes of the revolutionary era. Muñoz remains a league career record holder in a half-dozen offensive categories: games, innings played, runs scored, doubles, total bases, and runs batted in. He also captured two league home run titles. But he is best remembered and revered for a dramatic ninth-inning circuit clout during the 1980 world championships gold medal game in Japan.

ENTRENADOR/TRAINER
**ANTONIO MUÑOZ**

LANZADOR/PITCHER
**ARIEL PRIETO**

*Habana*

CAMPO CORTO/SHORTSTOP
**GERMAN MESA**

*Habana*

CUBA 1994

*Habana*

LANZADOR/PITCHER
**VLADIMIR NUÑEZ**

Cuba's showcase ballpark today remains the venerable Estadio Latinoamericano located in the downtown El Cerro section of Havana. For today's visiting fan who is a refugee from the North American baseball scene this proud park provides a true nostalgic magnet, one featuring the lost flavor of baseball straight from the Golden Age '50s. There is total absence of ballpark commercialism, of course, and thus the emphasis at Estadio Latinoamericano is on diamond action pure and unadulterated. Neon foul polls which cast an eerie glow during nighttime games are the single visible modern touch. Huge throngs like the one attending this 1970s Cuban League game have been a staple of the proud ballpark's half-century history.

What is today known as Estadio Latinoamericano was once known as El Gran Estadio del Cerro (El Cerro is a hilly downtown section of Havana). The noble park was built in 1946 for $2 million, inaugurated on October 26 of the same year, and originally held 30,609 fanaticos. This venue was home to the Cuban winter league in its final decade of play, as well as to the International League Sugar Kings of the 1950s. Jackie Robinson and the Brooklyn Dodgers held spring training on this site in preparation for a groundbreaking 1947 National League campaign. After the 1959 revolution Havana's ballpark would be transformed into a showcase structure for the new amateur Cuban League and would in the process undergo several radical transformations. It was expanded in the early '70s to a 55,000-seating capacity with the addition of sprawling outfield grandstands. Fresh green paint and yellow revolutionary slogans on outfield fences also refurbished the overall physical appearance. During the '60s and '70s the park was also home to some rousing play in international amateur tournaments. And today it serves as home field for two teams — Industriales and Metropolitanos — competing each season as capital city entries in the Cuban League National Series. Among the numerous stars to call this ballpark home have been Pedro Cháves (opposite, bottom left), the first righthanded batter to twice capture league batting titles, Pedro José Rodríguez (opposite, center), first to capture three consecutive Cuban home run crowns, and current Industriales fan favorites Juan Padilla (opposite, bottom right), a valued utility man on several '90s-vintage Cuban national teams, and Germán Mesa (opposite, top right), a glue-glove shortstop so magical on defense that comparisons with Ozzie Smith are hardly a stretch.

CUBA 1994

*Occidentales*

JARDINERO/OUTFIELDER
**JUAN CARLOS LINARES**

CUBA 1994

*Occidentales*

LANZADOR/PITCHER
**EISLER LIVAN HERNANDEZ**

Cuban ballparks are a pure delight for the rare and fortunate visitor from North America. There is not a hint of the commercialism that has converted big-league and even minor-league parks into substitute shopping malls and entertainment complexes. There are no obtrusive billboards on outfield fences — though there are some outfield political slogans featuring revolutionary wisdom — and there are no ear-splitting electronic scoreboards filling the air with rock music and artificially orchestrated cheerleading. The focus remains on the ageless simplicities of a baseball game itself.

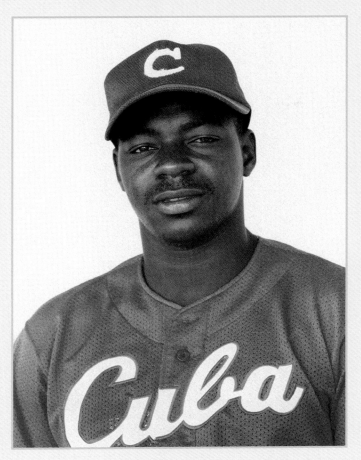

The crowd scene (opposite, bottom) captured here is from the always-raucous Pinar del Río ballpark, where knowledgeable boosters find nothing in the form of concession vendors or scoreboard promotions to distract them from the diamond action. Regional spirit is the byword in Cuban stadiums, since players represent the provinces of their birth or residence and are thus never traded from one franchise to another. Such highly charged rivalries as those between Industriales and Pinar del Río, Havana's Metros and Havana Province, Villa Clara and Camaguey, or Holguín and Santiago result in numerous game-ending onfield celebrations like the one seen below following a 1997 Pinar-Industriales postseason game.

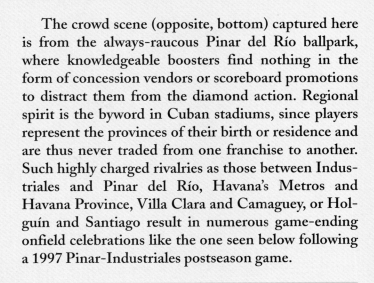

Pedro Luís Lazo (above) and Juan Manrique (right)

The dominating team of the past several seasons in Cuba has been the Pinar del Río ballclub, managed first by Jorge Fuentes and later by Alfonso Urquíola. Over the past two seasons Pinar has proven nearly invincible behind the savvy pitching of Pedro Lazo and the consistent hitting of Omar Linares, his brother Juan Carlos Linares, Daniel Lazo, Yobal Dueñas, and a contingent of additional hefty fencebusters. While Omar Linares has been Pinar's biggest cannon for more than a decade, there have been other stars as well for the green-clad team from Cuba's western-most city. Dueñas (opposite, top right) is one of the country's most promising up-and-coming second basemen and recently captured a league batting title. Catcher Juan Manrique, an Olympic starter in Atlanta, is considered to have the strongest arm among the island's backstops. But the showcase players have been Linares and Lazo, an intimidating 6'3" righthander who first flashed on the scene at age twenty-one in the 1994 National Series, posting a 10-3 record and 2.93 ERA. The Pinar team also boasts one of the most picturesque among Cuban stadiums — Estadio Capitán Sán Luís, named for a revolutionary hero of the province — plus some of the island's most rabid and vociferous fans. An evening at Capitán San Luís is almost guaranteed to provide not only swift baseball action but also a true fan fiesta of spirited rooting.

Pinar dominated 1997 Cuban League play in both the regular season National Series and also in postseason playoffs. The scene here takes place during the opening game of the 1997 National Series semifinals round, in which Pinar swept Havana's popular Industriales ballclub in four straight. The contest was a brilliant 2-1 pitching duel between Pedro Lazo and young Industriales ace José Contreras, one of the highlight games of the entire four-month season. A year later it would be a repeat of such league dominance by the Pinar team under its new manager Alfonso Urquíola. During the regular season of 1998 Club Habana (which represents Havana Province and not the capital city) seemed to pose a challenge, especially with the masterful pitching of 20-game winner José Ibar. In the capital city Industriales was also on the rebound, with the pitching of Contreras and a bevy of other young stars. And in the Oriente there were strong teams as usual in both Santiago, where Orestes Kindelán continues his slugging, and Camaguey. But when the postseason championships began it was Pinar that again rose to the top under their rookie manager and long roster of veteran stars.

The International Olympic Committee capped years of arduous planning by granting official status to baseball on October 13, 1986. The first official medal competitions were thus scheduled for Barcelona in summer 1992, and with the appearance of baseball on the Olympic scene the Cuban national team was now provided with its grandest stage yet for international triumphs. The juggernaut Cuban team, which had not lost a major international tournament since 1987, would be paced in Barcelona by slugging center fielder Victor Mesa and all-world third baseman Omar Linares, as well as such top pitchers as Omar Ajete, Giorge Diaz, Orlando "El Duque" Hernández, and Lázaro Valle. Before the opening pitch was thrown the team, managed by Jorge Fuentes, was an overwhelming favorite to extend Cuban baseball domination onto the prestigious stage of Olympic competition. A gold medal finale followed form and provided the expected one-sided route, with the Cubans prevailing 11-1 over Chinese Taipei, setting off anticipated flag-draped celebrations for a crack Cuban team.

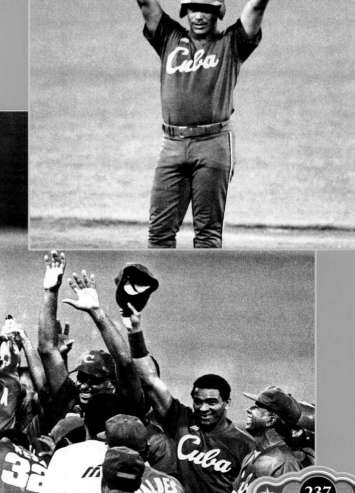

LANZADOR/PITCHER
**OMAR AJETE**

SEGUNDA BASE/SECOND BASE
**ANTONIO PACHECO**

RECEPTOR/CATCHER
**JUAN MANRIQUE**

DIRECTOR/MANAGER
**JORGE FUENTES**

The list of top Cuban stars on the international scene in the 1990s reaches far beyond the half-dozen names of Linares, Kindelán, Lazo, Valle, and Victor Mesa. Omar Ajete, for one, was a mound star in Barcelona and in the National Series before his left arm weakened due to repeated injury. Owner of a potent 90-92 mile-per-hour fastball, the formidable southpaw came within one pitch of a no-hit, no-run game during the 1987 Pan American Games. Versatile infielder Antonio Pacheco is an intelligent and complete player who was considered "unofficial" captain of both the Barcelona and Atlanta Olympic squads. Pacheco's career batting average in the National Series (the Cuban annual 50-plus-game season) hovered around .333 until injuries and age slowed him after the 1994 campaign. Germán Mesa was the starting shortstop of the Cuban national team between 1989 and 1995 and widely considered the best amateur shortstop in the world. A clever batter, Mesa was an even more outstanding fielder. When Mesa was dropped from the Cuban national team due to off-field problems in 1996 (suspicion of dealing with a major-league agent) he was replaced by flashy Eduardo Paret and the Cuban infield hardly missed a beat. Paret proved in Atlanta to be an even more spectacularly defensive wizard than Mesa or big-league defector Rey Ordoñez of the New York Mets. He also led the Cuban League in stolen bases in 1997 before his own brief suspension the following season. Outfielder Luís Ulacia and catcher Juan Manrique also displayed potential major-league skills with their showcase Olympic performances during the Atlanta Games.

The architect of Cuba's proudest international triumphs — 1992 and 1996 Olympic gold medal victories in Barcelona and Atlanta — was national team manager Jorge Fuentes. Fuentes has also been a major force in Cuban League play as manager of the Pinar del Río team, which stars Omar Linares and Pedro Luís Lazo. Fuentes is acknowledged in Cuba as a brilliant tactician who demands the respect of players and fans alike for his intelligent managing on the stages of both the National Series and world international competitions. The Pinar native has managed his region's team to Select Series championships in 1982, 1984, 1988, and 1991 and also to National Series titles in 1982, 1985, 1987, 1988, and 1997. His 15 years of managerial experience reached its apex, however, with the undefeated Olympic squads that he directed in Barcelona and Atlanta.

Let's talk baseball dynasties. We might start with Casey Stengel's Yankees, the "Boys of Summer" Brooklyn Dodgers, or the Bronx Bombers of the '20s behind Ruth and Gehrig, or perhaps a sometimes-overlooked Yankee edition of the late '30s with Gehrig and DiMaggio at the fore. Most of the baseball-playing world, however, reserves its reverence for the powerhouse Cuban national teams that have dominated the amateur version of the game for more than three decades, a good part of that time under the direction of recently deposed manager Jorge Fuentes.

Cuban baseball in the amateur ranks has long withstood the test of time. The stars are rolled out with production-line efficiency: pitcher Braudilio Vinent and

This collage of national team and Cuban League stars includes (clockwise from top left) 1997 batting champion José Estrada, skilled outfielder Daniel Lazo, 1995 home run king Miguel Cáldes, and current major-league refugee Rolando Arrojo.

fence-bashers Agustín Marquetti and Armando Capiró in the '70s, sluggers Victor "El Loco" Mesa and Luís Casanova alongside crafty southpaw hurler Omar Ajete in the '80s, and all-everything third baseman Omar Linares in the '90s, sustained by an ample roster of long-ball-blasters that has featured Orestes Kindelán, Antonio Pacheco, Luís Ulacia, and José Estrada at the top of the list. Cuba is 98-2 in major international tournament games since 1987. Their pair of official losses came at the hands of Team USA, during early-round action of the 1987 Pan American Games in Indianapolis, and Japan, in the finals of the 1997 Intercontinental Cup in Spain. The Cubans quickly rebounded from the first of these embarrassments to capture a tense rematch with the U.S. for the '87 Pan American gold medal. And they fought back from the second with an impressive nine-game unbeaten sweep during the recently completed IBA World Championships in Italy. By summertime 1998 the unmatchable record would now stand at an incredible 17 gold medals won during 18 senior world tournaments (Olympics, Pan Am Games, Intercontinental Cup, IBA World Championships) contested over the past 10 years.

International domination by the teams dispatched from Havana would reach its zenith in the decade of the 1990s, a period stretching from Olympic gold in Barcelona (1992) to IBA world championship gold in Italy (1998). Yet the Cuban baseball machine has nonetheless always been a dynasty in transition. Older stars such as Victor Mesa and Omar Ajete have been rapidly phased out and a host of new faces have arisen to replace them with clockwork efficiency. Foremost among the new arrivals of most prominence stands 1997 Cuban League batting champion José Estrada, who displayed clear signals of future brilliance in Atlanta. Another promising supernova is Miguel Cáldes, a fleet flychaser who had already displayed his power potential with a home run championship a season before manning the Olympic outfield in Atlanta with Estrada and veteran Luís Ulacia. On the pitching front, the arm injuries suffered by Barcelona stars Ajete and Giorge Diaz and the big-league defections of Rolando Arrojo, Osvaldo Fernández, and a pair of Hernández brothers have now opened the door for Pedro Luís Lazo (bottom left). Lazo blazed his fastball as both a starter and top reliever in both '96 Olympic and '98 IBA competitions.

The reigning question throughout international baseball circles in the 1980s and 1990s has been when (or if) the quarter-century of Cuban domination will ever begin to wither. The overthrow of baseball's international kings has been anything but easy or even possible. Cuba's national squad seems to be just like the Russian hockey teams of the '70s and '80s, both red-clad and relentless. Southpaw Omar Ajete owned a devastating heater clocked at 92 mph, and when this faded between Barcelona and Atlanta, then the wily and smoke-throwing Pedro Luís Lazo proved every bit as invincible. Second sacker Antonio Pacheco hits every bit as hard as Omar Linares, banging out a .400-plus average during eight summers of international play. The Cuban juggernaut may never have been more impressive than in Barcelona a half-dozen years ago. In nine games it outscored opponents 95-16, while hitting .404 with a .646 slugging percentage. The team ERA was an awe-inspiring 1.27. Cuba trailed once in the entire tournament, when Team USA surprised with five runs in the opening frame of a game in which the Cubans were ahead for good by the fourth. If tradition is any accurate predictor, Cuba may well be expected to remain all-powerful for the forseeable future. The introduction of professional players for the Sydney Olympics of 2000 may not even be enough to unseat the mighty Cubans on the field, though such a departure may well cause them to withdraw from any tournament tainted by professional athletes.

One of the keys to Cuban successes on the world baseball stage has been the depth of seemingly endless talent flowing directly from the Cuban League onto the annual editions of the Cuban national team. Behind the showcase names like Linares, Kindelán, Pacheco, and Lazo there are the less prominent names and faces of a fleet of stellar diamond performers who would be the envy of any other country's national squad. Even defections of up-and-coming stars seduced by the perhaps-unpure dollars of the North American professional circuit have hardly had a major impact. Retirements and forced suspension of other top Cuban Leaguers have seemed to do almost as little to weaken the Cuban national team roster. While one may shudder to think of a Cuban Olympic squad in 2000 featuring a pitching rotation of Livan and "El Duque" Hernández alongside Rolando Arrojo and Osvaldo Fernández (opposite, top left) — plus a middle infield anchored by Rey Ordoñez, Eduardo Paret, and Germán Mesa — those who have remained behind seem equally as potent. Lesser stars like the ones pictured on these pages have filled in admirably in Barcelona and Atlanta, as well as in recent Intercontinental Cup and IBA World Championship battles staged in Spain (1997) and Italy (1998). Hurlers Jorge Luís Valdés (below, left) and Giorge Diaz (below, right) are already hardened international moundsmen. Backstop José Raul Delgado (opposite, bottom left) is a solid defensive catcher who saw considerable action as a starting receiver in Barcelona. Gabriel Pierre (opposite, top right) is a near-.300-hitting third baseman who is one of the Cuban League's most solid performers in all aspects of the game. Ermidelio Urrutia (opposite, bottom right) has served numerous national teams over the past decade as a solid defensive outfielder and .315 lifetime hitter. Rugged first sacker Lourdes Gourriel (opposite, center) reached his career peak as MVP of 1989 Intercontinental Cup play when he posted a .435 BA while slugging at a .913 clip and homering and driving in four runs in the championship game.

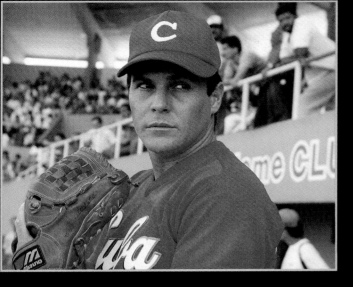

Current big leaguer Orlando "El Duque" Hernández (below) set a still-standing record for career winning percentage (126-47, .728) during his ten years in the Cuban League. Eduardo Paret (left) starred at the plate and at shortstop in Atlanta as a controversial replacement of all-time Cuban great Germán Mesa.

Cuba's vaunted national team arrived at the second Olympic games baseball competitions staged in Atlanta sporting an incomparable and almost mind-boggling record in world championship play. There was of course the laughably easy sweep of the first Olympic field in Barcelona four years earlier. There were the eight of nine world championships won since 1976, as well as every Pan American Games title contested since 1963. The Cubans also owned seven of eight Intercontinental Cup victories, as well as most of the world junior titles over the past half-century. And most impressive of all, perhaps, was the solid victory over a "dream team" of the world's best amateurs in the IBA World All-Star Game held in the Tokyo Dome on June 7, 1993. In that matchup — one pitting the Cuban gold medal squad versus an all-star group from other Barcelona competitors (including Japan, Korea, Taipei, and the USA) — Omar Linares once more flashed his awesome talent with a perfect day at the plate (homer, double, and sacrifice fly) and thus earned game MVP honors. Osvaldo Fernández (soon to defect to U.S. professional baseball), Omar Ajete, and Giorge Diaz stymied opposing hitters from all parts of the world. The Cuban team, backed by this kind of relentless powerhouse performance, once more had to be the overwhelming favorite when play opened in Atlanta.

The Cuban juggernaut hardly disappointed in Atlanta. Cuba ran through the field undefeated yet again, though there were close games with Japan (8-7), Nicaragua (8-7), and the USA (10-8) leading up to the final medal round. Linares and Kindelán, not surprisingly, led the offense with a home run barrage of titanic proportions. Aluminum bats in the hands of such vaunted sluggers led to a daily onslaught on the Fulton County Stadium upper deck. Kindelán launched one ball where none had been hit since 1971 in big-league play. The tournament highlight would come during an opening-week Sunday afternoon matchup with the underachieving group of American collegians comprising Team USA. The Americans had expected to fare much better than their out-of-the-money showing in Barcelona and were bent on restoring a tarnished reputation. A crowd of 45,000 expected an aluminum-inspired slugfest and that was exactly what they got. Cuba jumped to a 10-2 lead in the fifth, with Linares and Ulacia cracking back-to-back homers in the first. Omar Luís started for the Cubans and was effective if not brilliant until he tired in the middle frames. Team USA eventually rallied, but Pedro Lazo would effectively close the door in the ninth. For fans prone to nostalgia, the game had a distinct aura of the fifties about it, with no electronic scoreboard entertainment or blaring rock music to blur the exciting diamond play. The difference was that this was something major-league action could never provide — a true "world series" matchup between the world's two foremost baseball-loving nations.

# ¡NUMEROS!

# PRE-CASTRO (PROFESSIONAL) CUBAN LEAGUE STATISTICS

## CUBAN PROFESSIONAL LEAGUE RECORDS (1878-1961)

### YEAR-BY-YEAR CHAMPIONSHIP RESULTS

Managers in boldface were also U.S. major-league players (Key: # = non-Cuban manager)

| Year | Championship Team | Manager/Director | Record (W-L-T) | Pct. |
|------|-------------------|------------------|----------------|------|
| 1878-79 | Havana | **Esteban Bellán** | 4-0-1 | 1.000 |
| 1879-80 | Havana | **Esteban Bellán** | 5-2-0 | .714 |
| 1880-81 | NO OFFICIAL SEASON | | | |
| 1881-82 | SEASON NOT COMPLETED (DISPUTE BETWEEN HAVANA AND CLUB FÉ) | | | |
| 1882-83 | Havana | **Esteban Bellán** | 5-1-0 | .833 |
| 1883-84 | NO OFFICIAL SEASON | | | |
| 1884-85 | Havana | Ricardo Mora | 4-3 | .571 |
| 1885-86 | Havana | Francisco Saavedra | 6-0-0 | 1.000 |
| 1886-87 | Havana | Francisco Saavedra | 10-2-0 | .833 |
| 1887-88 | Club Fé | Antonio Utrera | 12-3-0 | .800 |
| 1888-89 | Havana | Emilio Sabourín | 16-4-1 | .800 |
| 1889-90 | Havana | Emilio Sabourín | 14-3-0 | .824 |
| 1890-91 | Club Fé | Luís Almoina | 12-6-0 | .667 |
| 1891-92 | Havana | Emilio Sabourín | 13-7-0 | .650 |
| 1892-93 | Matanzas | Luís Almoina | 14-9-0 | .609 |
| 1893-94 | Almendares | Ramón Gutiérrez | 17-7-1 | .708 |
| 1894-95 | SEASON NOT COMPLETED (WAR OF INDEPENDENCE) | | | |
| 1895-96 | SEASON CANCELLED (WAR OF INDEPENDENCE) | | | |
| 1896-97 | SEASON CANCELLED (WAR OF INDEPENDENCE) | | | |
| 1897-98 | SEASON NOT COMPLETED (WAR OF INDEPENDENCE) | | | |
| 1898-99 | Havanista | Alberto Azoy | 9-3-0 | .750 |
| 1900 | San Francisco | Patrocinio Silverio | 17-10-2 | .630 |
| 1901 | Havana | Alberto Azoy | 16-3-1 | .842 |
| 1902 | Havana | Alberto Azoy | 17-0-2 | 1.000 |
| 1903 | Havana | Alberto Azoy | 21-13-0 | .618 |
| 1904 | Havana | Alberto Azoy | 16-4-0 | .800 |
| 1905 | Almendares | Abel Linares | 19-11-2 | .633 |
| 1906 | Club Fé | Alberto Azoy | 15-9-0 | .625 |
| 1907 | Almendares | Eugenio Santa Cruz | 17-13-1 | .567 |
| 1908 | Almendares | Juan Sánchez | 37-8-1 | .822 |
| 1908-1909 | Havana | Luis Someillan | 29-13-1 | .690 |
| 1910 | Almendares | Juan Sánchez | 13-3-1 | .812 |
| 1910-1911 | Almendares | Juan Sánchez | 21-6-3 | .714 |
| 1912 | Havana | Eduardo Laborde | 22-12-1 | .647 |
| 1913 | Club Fé | Agustín Molina | 21-11-0 | .656 |
| 1913-1914 | Almendares | Eugenio Santa Cruz | 22-11-2 | .667 |
| 1914-1915 | Havana | **Mike González** | 23-11-0 | .676 |
| 1915-1916 | Almendares | Alfredo Cabrera | 30-12-3 | .714 |
| 1917 | Orientales | **Armando Marsans** | 8-6-1 | .571 |
| 1918-1919 | Havana | **Mike González** | 29-19-0 | .604 |
| 1919-1920 | Almendares | **Adolfo Luque** | 22-5-2 | .815 |
| 1920-1921 | Havana | **Mike González** | 23-10-5 | .676 |
| 1921 | Havana | **Mike González** | 4-1-0 | .800 |
| 1922-1923 | Marianao | **Baldomero Acosta** | 35-19-1 | .648 |
| 1923-1924 | Santa Clara | Augustín Molina | 36-11-1 | .766 |
| 1924-25 | Almendares | José Rodríguez | 33-16-1 | .660 |
| 1925-26 | Almendares | José Rodríguez | 34-13-2 | .723 |
| 1926-27 | Havana | **Mike González** | 20-11-0 | .645 |
| 1927-28 | Havana | **Mike González** | 24-13-0 | 649 |
| 1928-29 | Havana | **Mike González** | 43-12-1 | .782 |

| 1929-30 | Cienfuegos | Pelayo Chacón | 33-19-2 | .635 |
| 1930-31 | SEASON NOT COMPLETED | | | |
| 1931-32 | Almendares | José Rodríguez | 21-9-4 | .700 |
| 1932-33 | Almendares (Tie) | **Adolfo Luque** | 13-9-0 | .591 |
| | Havana (Tie) | **Mike González** | 13-9-0 | .591 |
| 1933-34 | NO OFFICIAL SEASON | | | |
| 1934-35 | Almendares | **Adolfo Luque** | 18-9-1 | .667 |
| 1935-36 | Santa Clara | Martín Dihigo | 34-14-1 | .708 |
| 1936-37 | Marianao | Martín Dihigo | 36-30-3 | .545 |
| 1937-38 | Santa Clara | Lazaro Sálazar | 44-18-4 | .710 |
| 1938-39 | Santa Clara | Lazaro Sálazar | 34-20-2 | .630 |
| 1939-40 | Almendares | **Adolfo Luque** | 28-23-1 | .549 |
| 1940-41 | Havana | **Mike González** | 30-19-5 | .633 |
| 1941-42 | Almendares | **Adolfo Luque** | 28-20-3 | .583 |
| 1942-43 | Almendares | **Adolfo Luque** | 25-19-4 | .568 |
| 1943-44 | Havana | **Mike González** | 32-16-0 | .667 |
| 1944-45 | Almendares | Reinaldo Cordeiro | 32-16-6 | .667 |
| 1945-46 | Cienfuegos | **Adolfo Luque** | 38-23-4 | .617 |
| 1946-47 | Almendares | **Adolfo Luque** | 42-24-4 | .636 |
| 1947-48 | Havana | **Mike González** | 39-33-9 | .542 |
| 1948-49 | Almendares | **Fermín Guerra** | 47-25-0 | .553 |
| 1949-50 | Almendares | **Fermín Guerra** | 38-34-4 | .528 |
| 1950-51 | Havana | **Mike González** | 40-32-1 | .556 |
| 1951-52 | Havana | **Mike González** | 41-30-1 | .577 |
| 1952-53 | Havana | **Mike González** | 43-29-1 | .597 |
| 1953-54 | Almendares | **Bobby Bragan#** | 44-28-1 | .611 |
| 1954-55 | Almendares | **Bobby Bragan#** | 44-25-2 | .638 |
| 1955-56 | Cienfuegos | Oscar Rodríguez | 40-29-0 | .580 |
| 1956-57 | Marianao | Napoleón Reyes | 40-28-0 | .588 |
| 1957-58 | Marianao | Napoleón Reyes | 43-32-0 | .597 |
| 1958-59 | Almendares | Oscar Rodríguez | 46-26-0 | .639 |
| 1959-60 | Cienfuegos | Antonio Castaño | 48-24-0 | .667 |
| 1960-61 | Cienfuegos | Antonio Castaño | 35-31-0 | .530 |

## INDIVIDUAL CUBAN LEAGUE BATTING LEADERS

1922 and 1931 seasons were shortened and uncompleted

| Year | Batting Average Leader | Home Runs Leader | Base Hits Leader | Runs Scored |
|---|---|---|---|---|
| 1878-79 | No Official Record | No Official Record | No Official Record | No Official Record |
| 1879-80 | No Official Record | No Official Record | No Official Record | No Official Record |
| 1880-81 | NO OFFICIAL SEASON | | | |
| 1881-82 | SEASON NOT COMPLETED (DISPUTE BETWEEN HAVANA AND CLUB FÉ) | | | |
| 1882-83 | No Official Record | No Official Record | No Official Record | No Official Record |
| 1883-84 | NO OFFICIAL SEASON | | | |
| 1884-85 | Pablo Ronquilla (.350) | No Official Record | No Official Record | No Official Record |
| 1885-86 | Wenceslao Gálvez (.345) | No Official Record | Three Tied (10) | No Official Record |
| 1886-87 | Ricardo Martínez (.439) | None Hit | Ricardo Martínez (18) | No Official Record |
| 1887-88 | Antonio García (.448) | None Hit | Antonio García (26) | No Official Record |
| 1888-89 | Francisco Salabarría (.305) | None Hit | Francisco Hernández (24) | No Official Record |
| 1889-90 | Antonio García (.364) | Antonio García (1) | Antonio García (24) | No Official Record |
| 1890-91 | Alfredo Crespo (.375) | Antonio García (1) | Francisco Hernández (23) | No Official Record |
| 1891-92 | Antonio García (.362) | Alfredo Arcaño (3) | Francisco Hernández (34) | No Official Record |
| 1892-93 | Antonio García (.385) | Antonio García (2) | Valentín González (36) | No Official Record |
| 1893-94 | Miguel Prats (.394) | Alfredo Arcaño (2) | Miguel Prats (41) | No Official Record |
| 1894-95 | Alfredo Arcaño (.430) | Valentín González (3) | Valentín González (32) | No Official Record |
| 1895-96 | SEASON CANCELLED (WAR OF INDEPENDENCE) | | | |
| 1896-97 | SEASON CANCELLED (WAR OF INDEPENDENCE) | | | |
| 1897-98 | Valentín González (.394) | Season Not Completed | Season Not Completed | |

| 1898-99 | Valentín González (.414) | No Official Record | Valentín González (12) | No Official Record |
|---|---|---|---|---|
| 1900 | Esteban Prats (.333) | No Official Record | Luís Padrón (31) | No Official Record |
| 1901 | Julian Castillo (.454) | No Official Record | Julián Castillo (30) | No Official Record |
| 1902 | Luís Padrón (.463) | Luís Padrón (2) | Valentín González (24) | No Official Record |
| 1903 | Julián Castillo (.330) | Julián Castillo (2) | Julián Castillo (37) | No Official Record |
| 1904 | Regino García (.397) | Valentín González (2) | Regino García (31) | No Official Record |
| 1905 | Regino García (.305) | No Official Record | Valentín González (32) | No Official Record |
| 1906 | Regino García (.304) | No Official Record | Regino García (28) | No Official Record |
| 1907 | Regino García (.324) | No Official Record | Regino García (36) | No Official Record |
| 1908 | Emilio Palomino (.350) | Luís Padrón (3) | Preston Hill (60) | Preston Hill (53) |
| 1908-09 | Julián Castillo (.315) | No Official Record | Julián Castillo (46) | No Official Record |
| 1910 | Julián Castillo (.408) | Rogelio Valdés (1) | Julián Castillo (20) | Strike González (18) |
| 1910-11 | Preston Hill (.365) | No Official Record | Preston Hill (35) | Armando Marsans (22) |
| 1912 | Emilio Palomino (.440) | Julián Castillo (5) | Grant Johnson (43) | Carlos Morán (32) |
| 1913 | Armando Marsans (.400) | Julián Castillo (1) | Spotwood Poles (55) | Spotwood Poles (40) |
| 1913-14 | Manuel Villa (.351) | No Official Record | Manuel Villa (46) | Armando Marsans (28) |
| 1914-15 | Cristóbal Torriente (.387) | No Official Record | Cristóbal Torriente (48) | Cristóbal Torrieinte (33) |
| 1915-16 | Eustaquio Pedroso (.413) | No Official Record | Cristóbal Torriente (56) | Cristóbal Torriente (41) |
| 1917 | Adolfo Luque (.355) | No Official Record | José Fernández 16) | Miguel González (9) |
| 1918-19 | Manuel Cueto (.344) | No Official Record | Miguel González (52) | Baldomero Acosta (30) |
| 1919-20 | Cristóbal Torriente (.360) | No Official Record | Bernardo Baró (37) | Bernardo Baró (21) |
| 1920-21 | Pelayo Chacón (.344) | No Official Record | Pelayo Chacón (32) | Cristóbal Torriente (19) |
| 1921-22 | Bienvenido Jiménez (.619) | Manuel Cueto (1) | Bienvenido Jiménez (13) | Bienvenido Jiménez (7) |
| 1922-23 | Bernardo Baró (.401) | Cristóbal Torriente (4) | Cristóbal Torriente (61) | Cristóbal Torriente (37) |
| 1923-24 | Oliver Marcell (.393) | Bienvenido Jiménez (4) | Dobie Moore (71) | Oscar Charleston (59) |
| 1924-25 | Alejandro Oms (.393) | Mayarí Montalvo (5) | Pop Lloyd (73) | Valentín Dreke (45) |
| 1925-26 | Johnny Wilson (.430) | Johnny Wilson (3) | Johnny Wilson (64) | Valentín Dreke (37) |
| 1926-27 | Manuel Cueto (.398) | José Hernández (4) | Manuel Cueto (41) | Paito Herrera (24) |
| 1927-28 | Johnny Wilson (.424) | Oscar Charleston (5) | Martín Dihigo (54) | Johnny Wilson (36) |
| 1928-29 | Alejandro Oms (.432) | James "Papa" Bell (5) | Alejandro Oms (76) | James "Papa" Bell (44) |
| 1929-30 | Alejandro Oms (.389) | Mule Suttles (7) | Chino Smith (67) | James "Papa" Bell (52) |
| 1930-31 | Oscar Charleston (.373) | Ernest Smith (1) | Dick Lundy (19) | Oscar Charleston (12) |
| 1931-32 | Ramón Couto (.400) | Alejandro Oms (3) | Alejandro Oms (44) | Alejandro Oms (28) |
| 1932-33 | Mike González (.432) | Bobby Estallela (3) | José Abreu, Lázaro Sálazar (30) | José Abreu (17) |
| 1933-34 | NO OFFICIAL SEASON | | | |
| 1934-35 | Lázaro Sálazar (.407) | Eleven Tied (1) | Cando López (36) | Cando López (18) |
| 1935-36 | Martín Dihigo (.358) | Jacinto Roque, Willie Wells (5) | Martín Dihigo (63) | Martín Dihigo (42) |
| 1936-37 | Harry Williams (.339) | Bobby Estallela (5) | Clyde Spearman (84) | Lázaro Sálazar (47) |
| 1937-38 | Sammy Bankhead (.366) | Three Tied (4) | Sammy Bankhead (89) | Sammy Bankhead (47) |
| 1938-39 | Antonio Castaño (.371) | Josh Gibson (11) | Santos Amaro (78) | Josh Gibson (50) |
| 1939-40 | Antonio Castaño (.340) | Mule Suttles (4) | Sammy Bankhead (67) | Sammy Bankhead (41) |
| 1940-41 | Lazaro Sálazar (.316) | Alejandro Crespo (3) | Helio Mirabal (59) | Pedro Pagés (37) |
| 1941-42 | Silvio García (.351) | Silvio García (4) | Silvio García (69) | Silvio García (24) |
| 1942-43 | Alejandro Crespo (.337) | Roberto Ortiz (2) | Alejandro Crespo (63) | Pollo Rodríguez (31) |
| 1943-44 | Roberto Ortíz (.337) | Saguita Hernández (3) | Roberto Ortíz (64) | Roberto Ortíz (41) |
| 1944-45 | Claro Duany (.340) | Claro Duany (3) | Santos Amaro (59) | Four Tied (29) |
| 1945-46 | Lloyd Davenport (.332) | Dick Sisler (9) | Alejandro Crespo (72) | Roland Gladu (41) |
| 1946-47 | Lou Klein (.330) | Roberto Ortiz (11) | Andrés Fleitas (83) | Avelino Cañizares (47) |
| 1947-48 | Harry Kimbro (.346) | Jesús Díaz (7) | Harry Kimbro (104) | Sam Jethroe (53) |
| 1948-49 | Alejandro Crespo (.326) | Monte Irvin (10) | Hank Thompson (85) | Hank Thompson (60) |
| 1949-50 | Pedro Formental (.336) | Roberto Ortiz (15) | Pedro Formental (99) | Pedro Formental (51) |
| 1950-51 | Silvio García (.347) | Four Tied (8) | Lorenzo Cabrera (88) | Orestes Miñoso (54) |
| 1951-52 | Bert Haas (.323) | Pedro Formental, Jim Basso (9) | Johnny Jorgensen (85) | Pedro Formental (47) |
| 1952-53 | Sandy Amorós (.373) | Lou Klein (16) | Paul Smith (93) | Orestes Miñoso (67) |
| 1953-54 | Rocky Nelson (.352) | Earl Rapp, Rafael Noble (10) | Forrest Jacobs (94) | Forrest Jacobs (58) |

| 1954-55 | Angel Scull (.370) | Rocky Nelson (13) | Bob Boyd (90) | Rocky Nelson (60) |
| 1955-56 | Forrest Jacobs (.321) | Ultus Alvarez (10) | Forrest Jacobs (91) | Orestes Miñoso (47) |
| 1956-57 | Orestes Miñoso (.312) | Archie Wilson (11) | Archie Wilson (76) | Solly Drake (52) |
| 1957-58 | Milton Smith (.320) | Four Tied (9) | Tony Taylor (83) | Milton Smith (46) |
| 1958-59 | Tony Taylor (.303) | Jim Baxes (9) | Tony Taylor (88) | Rocky Nelson (37) |
| 1959-60 | Tony González (.310) | Panchón Herrera (15) | Román Mejías (79) | Marv Breeding (41) |
| 1960-61 | Cookie Rojas (.322) | Julio Bécquer (15) | Cookie Rojas (85) | Tony González (42) |

## INDIVIDUAL CUBAN LEAGUE PITCHING LEADERS

1922 and 1931 seasons were shortened and uncompleted

| Year | Winning Percentage | Pitching Victories | Games Pitched | Complete Games |
|---|---|---|---|---|
| 1878-79 | No Official Record | No Official Record | No Official Record | No Official Record |
| 1879-80 | No Official Record | No Official Record | No Official Records | No Official Record |
| 1880-81 | NO OFFICIAL SEASON | | | |
| 1881-82 | SEASON NOT COMPLETED (DISPUTE BETWEEN HAVANA AND CLUB FÉ) | | | |
| 1882-83 | No Official Record | No Official Record | No Official Record | No Official Record |
| 1883-84 | NO OFFICIAL SEASON | | | |
| 1884-85 | NO OFFICIAL SEASON | No Official Record | No Official Record | No Official Record |
| 1885-86 | Adolfo Luján (5-0 1.000) | Adolfo Luján (5) | Adolfo Luján (5) | Adolfo Luján (5) |
| 1886-87 | Adolfo Luján (5-0 1.000) | Carlos Maciá (7) | Carlos Maciá (9) | Carlos Maciá (9) |
| 1887-88 | Cisco Hernández (10-2 .833) | Adolfo Luján (11) | Adolfo Luján (15) | Adolfo Luján (15) |
| 1888-89 | Adolfo Luján (10-3 .769) | Adolfo Luján (10) | Enrique Rojas (20) | Enrique Rojas (18) |
| 1889-90 | Miguel Prats (11-2 .846) | Miguel Prats (11) | José Pastoriza (14) | José Pastoriza (14) |
| 1890-91 | Miguel Prats (9-4 .692) | José Pastoriza (10) | José Pastoriza (15) | José Castañer (12) |
| 1891-92 | Emilio Hernández (4-1 .800) | Miguel Prats (9) | José Pastoriza (17) | José Pastoriza (15) |
| 1892-93 | Cisco Hernández (4-1 .800) | Enrique García (6) | Three Tied (12) | Miguel Prats (8) |
| 1893-94 | José Pastoriza (16-7 .695) | José Pastoriza (16) | José Pastoriza (23) | José Pastoriza (18) |
| 1894-95 | Enrique García (12-4 .750) | Enrique García (12) | Enrique García (17) | Enrique García (15) |
| 1895-96 | SEASON CANCELLED (WAR OF INDEPENDENCE) | | | |
| 1896-97 | SEASON CANCELLED (WAR OF INDEPENDENCE) | | | |
| 1897-98 | SEASON NOT COMPLETED | | | |
| 1898-99 | José Romero (5-2 .714) | José Romero (5) | José Romero (9) | José Romero (7) |
| 1900 | Luís Padrón (13-4 .765) | Luís Padrón (13) | Salvador Rosado (20) | Salvador Rosado (17) |
| 1901 | Carlos Royer (12-3 .800) | Carlos Royer (12) | Carlos Royer (15) | José Muñoz (14) |
| 1902 | Carlos Royer (17-0 1.000) | Carlos Royer (17) | Carlos Royer (17) | Carlos Royer (17) |
| 1903 | Cándido Fontanals (14-6 .700) | Carlos Royer (18) | Carlos Royer (28) | Carlos Royer (28) |
| 1904 | Carlos Royer (13-3 .813) | Carlos Royer (13) | Carlos Royer (16) | Carlos Royer (16) |
| 1905 | Angel D'Mesa (10-4 .714) | Angel D'Mesa (10) | José Muñoz (20) | Luís González (16) |
| 1906 | José Muñoz (8-1 .889) | Luís González (10) | Luís González (19) | Rube Foster (15) |
| 1907 | George Mack (4-2 .667) | Rube Foster (9) | José Muñoz (17) | Julián Pérez (13) |
| 1908 | José Méndez (9-0 1.000) | José Muñoz (13) | José Muñoz (19) | Julián Pérez (13) |
| 1908-09 | José Méndez (15-6 .714) | José Méndez (15) | José Méndez (28) | José Méndez (18) |
| 1910 | José Méndez (7-0 1.000) | José Méndez (7) | Juan Marlotica (9) | Pastor Parera (8) |
| 1910-11 | José Méndez (11-2 .846) | José Méndez (11) | José Méndez (18) | José Méndez (12) |
| 1912 | José Junco (6-1 .857) | Fred Wickware (10) | Cyclone Williams (21) | José Méndez (13) |
| 1913 | Red Redding (7-2 .778) | Eustaquio Pedroso (11) | Eustaquio Pedroso (22) | Eustaquio Pedroso (11) |
| 1913-14 | José Méndez (10-0 1.000) | Pastor Parera (11) | Pastor Parera (21) | Pastor Parera (12) |
| 1914-15 | José Acosta (5-1 .823) | Eustaquio Pedroso (10) | Eustaquio Pedroso (20) | Eustaquio Pedroso (12) |
| 1915-16 | José Acosta (8-3 .727) | Adolfo Luque (12) | Eustaquio Pedroso (21) | Eustaquio Pedroso (12) |
| 1917 | José Acosta (2-1 .667) | Adolfo Luque (4) | Adolfo Luque (9) | Adolfo Luque (6) |
| 1918-19 | José Acosta (16-10 .615) | José Acosta (16) | José Acosta (34) | José Acosta (17) |
| 1919-20 | Emilio Palmero (5-1 .833) | Adolfo Luque (10) | Adolfo Luque (15) | José Acosta (11) |
| 1920-21 | José Hernández (4-1 .800) | José Acosta (6) | José Acosta, Oscar Tuero (13) | Oscar Tuero (8) |
| 1921-22 | Julio LeBlanc (2-0 1.000) | Julio LeBlanc (2) | Emilo Palmero (3) | Oscar Tuero (2) |

| | | | |
|---|---|---|---|
| 1922-23 | Lucas Boadda (10-4 .714) | Adolfo Luque (11) | Adolfo Luque (23) | Adolfo Luque (12) |
| 1923-24 | Bill Holland (10-2 .833) | Bill Holland (10) | Isidro Fabré (20) | Oscar Fuhr (9) |
| 1924-25 | José Acosta (4-1 .800) | Oscar Levis, Bullet Rogan (9) | Oscar Levis, Martín Dihigo (20) | Oscar Levis (12) |
| 1925-26 | César Alvarez (10-2 .833) | César Alvarez (10) | Oscar Levis (15) | César Alvarez (9) |
| 1926-27 | Juan Olmo (3-0 1.000) | Pedro Dibut, Claude Grier (5) | Raúl Alvarez (15) | Raúl Alvarez (7) |
| 1927-28 | Oscar Levis (7-2 .778) | Oscar Levis (7) | Willie Powell (18) | Willie Foster (8) |
| 1928-29 | Adolfo Luque (9-2 .818) | Adolfo Luque, Cliff Bell (9) | Charles Williams (19) | Campanita Bell (11) |
| 1929-30 | Yoyo Díaz (13-3 .813) | Yoyo Díaz (13) | Campanita Bell (23) | Yoyo Díaz (11) |
| 1930-31 | Martín Dihigo (2-0 1.000) | Claude Jonnard (5) | Claude Jonnard (7) | Claude Jonnard (4) |
| 1931-32 | Juan Eckelson (5-1 .833) | Rodolfo Fernández (8) | Luís Tiant (19) | Rodolfo Fernández (9) |
| 1932-33 | Jesús Lorenzo (3-0 1.000) | Jesús Miralles (6) | Jesús Miralles (14) | Jesús Miralles (6) |
| 1933-34 | NO OFFICIAL SEASON | | | |
| 1934-35 | Lazaro Sálazar (6-1 .857) | Lázaro Sálazar, Dolf Luque (6) | Gilberto Torres (13) | Tomás de la Cruz (7) |
| 1935-36 | Martín Dihigo (11-2 .846) | Martín Dihigo (11) | Tomás de la Cruz (23) | Martín Dihigo (13) |
| 1936-37 | Raymond Brown (21-4 .840) | Raymond Brown (21) | Martín Dihigo (30) | Raymond Brown (23) |
| 1937-38 | Raymond Brown (12-5 .706) | Raymond Brown (12) | Bob Griffith (24) | Raymond Brown (14) |
| 1938-39 | Martín Dihigo (14-2 .857) | Martín Dihigo (14) | Alejandro Carrasquel (26) | Raymond Brown (16) |
| 1939-40 | Rodofo Fernández (7-4 .636) | Barney Morris (13) | Tomás de la Cruz (31) | Barney Morris (15) |
| 1940-41 | Gilberto Torres (10-3 .769) | Vidal López (12) | Gilberto Torres (27) | Vidal López (16) |
| 1941-42 | Agapito Mayor (6-2 .750) | Ramón Bragaña (9) | Ramón Bragaña (21) | Ramón Bragaña (11) |
| 1942-43 | Cocaína García (10-3 .769) | Cocaína García (10) | Adrián Zabala (22) | Adrián Zabala (14) |
| 1943-44 | Martín Dihigo (8-1 .889) | Santiago Ullrich (12) | Coty Leal (26) | Tomás de la Cruz (10) |
| 1944-45 | Oliverio Ortíz (10-4 .714) | Oliverio Ortíz (10) | Luís Tiant (29) | Cocaína García (9) |
| 1945-46 | Adrián Zabala (9-3 .750) | Natilla Jiménez (13) | Natilla Jiménez (32) | Three Tied (9) |
| 1946-47 | Cocaína García (10-3 .769) | Adrián Zabala (11) | Sandy Consuegra (31) | Adrián Zabala (14) |
| 1947-48 | Conrado Marrero (12-2 .857) | Conrado Marrero (12) | Steve Gerkin (33) | Alex Patterson (18) |
| 1948-49 | Octavio Rubert (8-1 .889) | Dave Barnhill (13) | Max Surkont (31) | Dave Barnhill (13) |
| 1949-50 | Octavio Rubert (5-1 .833) | Thomas Fine (16) | Thomas Fine (35) | Al Gerheauser (11) |
| 1950-51 | Vicente López (7-3 .700) | Conrado Marrero (11) | Red Barrett (32) | Hoyt Wilhelm (10) |
| 1951-52 | Joe Black (15-6 .714) | Joe Black (15) | Thomas Fine (30) | Red Barrett (12) |
| 1952-53 | Bob Alexander (10-3 .769) | Mario Picone, Al Gettel (13) | Hal Erickson (33) | Al Gettel (13) |
| 1953-54 | Cliff Fannin (13-4 .765) | Dick Littlefield (13) | Joe Coleman (44) | Al Sima (12) |
| 1954-55 | Joe Hatten (13-5 .722) | Joe Hatten, Ed Roebuck (13) | Jim Melton (38) | Ed Roebuck (12) |
| 1955-56 | Pedro Ramos (13-5 .722) | Pedro Ramos (13) | Ben Wade (38) | Wilmer Mizell (13) |
| 1956-57 | Camilo Pascual (15-5 .750) | Camilo Pascual (15) | Joe Hatten (33) | Camilo Pascual (16) |
| 1957-58 | Billy O'Dell (7-2 .778) | Dick Brodowski, Bob Shaw (14) | Orlando Peña (37) | Bob Shaw (12) |
| 1958-59 | Orlando Peña (15-5 .750) | Orlando Peña (15) | René Guitiérrez (45) | Orlando Peña (15) |
| 1959-60 | Camilo Pascual (15-5 .750) | Camilo Pascual (15) | Manuel Montejo (40) | Camilo Pascual (13) |
| 1960-61 | Pedro Ramos (16-7 .696) | Pedro Ramos (16) | Manuel Montejo (36) | Pedro Ramos (17) |

## PRE-CASTRO CUBAN PROFESSIONAL BASEBALL RECORDS AND MILESTONES

### CUBAN INDIVIDUAL BATTING RECORDS

| | |
|---|---|
| Single-Season Batting Average | Bienvenido Jiménez, .619 (1921, Short Season) |
| Single-Season Batting Average | Julian Castillo, .454 (1901, 100 or more At-Bats) |
| Most Batting Titles Won | Antonio García, 4 (1887-88, 1889-90, 1891-92, 1892-93) |
| | Julián Castillo, 4 (1901, 1903, 1908-09, 1910) |
| | Regino García, 4 (1904, 1905, 1906, 1907) |
| Most Consecutive Batting Titles | Regino García, 4 (1904, 1905, 1906, 1907) |
| Most Seasons Batting .300 | Manuel Cueto (11) and Alejandro Oms (11) |
| Consecutive .300 Seasons | Alejandro Oms, 8 (1922-23 thru 1929-30) |
| Most RBIs in a Season | Pedro Formental, 57 (1952-53) |
| | Rocky Nelson, 57 (1954-55) |
| Most RBIs in Single Game | Walt Moryn, 8 (October 14, 1952) |

| | |
|---|---|
| Most Career RBIs | Alejandro Crespo (362) and Pedro Formental (362) |
| Most Seasons as RBI Leader | Leonard Pearson, 3 (1946-47, 1948-49, 1949-50) |
| Most Runs Scored in a Season | Orestes Miñoso, 67 (1952-53) |
| Most Runs Scored in Game | Amado Ibáñez, 6 (January 10, 1954) |
| Most Career Runs Scored | Pedro Formental, 431 (1942-43 thru 1954-55) |
| Most Seasons as Runs Leader | Cristóbal Torriente, 4 (1915, 1916, 1921, 1923) |
| Most Base Hits in a Season | Harry Kimbro, 104 (1947-48) |
| Most Base Hits in Game | Alejandro Oms, 6 (December 30, 1928) |
| | Antonio Castaño, 6 (December 25, 1938) |
| | Lloyd Davenport, 6 (January 17, 1946) |
| | Amado Ibáñez, 6 (January 10, 1954) |
| Most Career Base Hits | Silvio García, 891 (1931-32 thru 1953-54) |
| Most Seasons as Hits Leader | Valentín González, 5 (1893, 1895, 1899, 1902, 1905) |
| Longest Hitting Streak | Alejandro Oms, 30 Games (October 31 to December 24, 1928) |
| Most Home Runs in Game | James "Papa" Bell, 3 (January 1, 1929) |
| | Dick Sisler, 3 (January 24, 1946) |
| Most Career Home Runs | Pedro Formental, 54 (Lefthanded), 1942-43 thru 1954-55 |
| | Roberto Ortíz, 51 (Righthanded), 1939-40 thru 1954-55 |
| Most Home Runs in a Season | Lou Klein, 16 (1952-53) |

## CUBAN INDIVIDUAL PITCHING RECORDS

| | |
|---|---|
| Seasons as Pitching Champion | José Méndez, 5 (1908, 1909, 1910, 1911, 1914) |
| | José Acosta, 5 (1915, 1916, 1917, 1919, 1925) |
| Most Games Won in Season | Carlos Royer, 21 (1903), Raymond Brown, 21 (1936-37) |
| Consecutive Wins in Season | Carlos Royer, 17 (1902) |
| Most Consecutive Wins | Carlos Royer, 20 (1902-1903) |
| Most Career Victories | Martín Dihigo, 105 (1922-23 thru 1946-47) |
| Consecutive Relief Wins | Thomas Fine, 9 (1949-50) |
| Most Career Complete Games | Martín Dihigo, 120 (1922-23 thru 1946-47) |
| Consecutive Complete Games | Carlos Royer, 69 (1901-1904) (Career Record) |
| | Carlos Royer, 33 (1903) (Season Record, with Playoffs) |
| Most Games Pitched (Career) | Adrián Zabala, 331 (1935-36 thru 1954-55) |
| Most Games Pitched (Season) | Joe Coleman, 44 (1953-54) |
| Most Shutouts (Career) | Adrián Zabala, 83 (1935-36 thru 1954-55) |
| Most Shutouts (Season) | Enrique Rosas, 14 (1888-89) |
| Most Seasons Shutout Leader | Luís Tiant, 5 (1932, 1936, 1937, 1940, 1941) |
| Most Strikeouts (Season) | Carlos Royer, 181 (1903, including playoffs) |
| Most Walks Allowed (Season) | Robert Darnell, 107 (1953-54) |
| Most Hits Allowed (Season) | Al Sima, 209 (1953-54) |
| Most Runs Allowed (Season) | Carlos Royer, 128 (1903) |
| Most Strikeouts (Game) | George McCullar, 21 (November 23, 1879) |
| Strikeouts (Modern Game) | Dave Barnhill, 15 (15 innings), January 10, 1948 |
| Consecutive Strikeouts | Adolfo Luque, 7 (February 17, 1923) |

### Cuban Unassisted Triple Play

| Player | Date | Teams |
|---|---|---|
| Baldomero Acosta | December 2, 1918 | Havana versus Almendares |

### Cuban No-Hit Games Pitched

| Pitcher | Date | Score |
|---|---|---|
| Carlos Maciá | February 13, 1887 | Almendares 38, Carmelita 0 |
| Eugenio de Rosas | July 14, 1889 | Progreso 8, Cárdenas 0 |
| Oscar Levis | October 11, 1924 | Havana 1, Almendares 0 |
| Raymond "Jabao" Brown | November 7, 1936 | Santa Clara 7, Havana 0 |
| Manuel "Cocaína" García | December 11, 1943 | Havana 5, Marianao 0 |
| Tomás de la Cruz | January 3, 1945 | Almendares 7, Havana 0 |
| Rogelio "Limonar" Martínez | February 6, 1950 | Marianao 6, Almendares 0 |
| Tony Díaz | November 23, 1957 | Cienfuegos 2, Havana 0 |

# CASTRO-ERA (AMATEUR) CUBAN LEAGUE STATISTICS

## CUBAN BASEBALL FEDERATION RECORDS AND STATISTICS (1962-98)

### NATIONAL SERIES TEAM CHAMPIONSHIP AND INDIVIDUAL BATTING LEADERS IN CASTRO-ERA CUBAN LEAGUE

#### NATIONAL SERIES CHAMPIONSHIPS (PROVINCIAL)

| Years | Teams (Records) | Managers | Individual Batting Champions |
|-------|-----------------|----------|------------------------------|
| 1962 | Occidentales (18-9) | Fermín Guerra | Erwin Walter, Occidentales (.367) |
| 1963 | Industriales (16-14) | Ramón Carneado | Raul González, Occidentales (.348) |
| 1964 | Industriales (22-13) | Ramón Carneado | Pedro Chávez, Occidentales (.333) |
| 1965 | Industriales (25-14) | Ramón Carneado | Urbano González, Industriales (.359) |
| 1966 | Industriales (40-25) | Ramón Carneado | Miguel Cuevas, Granjeros (.325) |
| 1967 | Orientales (36-29) | Roberto Ledo | Pedro Cháves, Industriales (.318) |
| 1968 | Habana (74-25) | Juan Gómez | José Pérez, Azucareros (.328) |
| 1969 | Azucareros (69-30) | Servio Borges | Wilfredo Sánchez, Henequeneros (.354) |
| 1970 | Henequeneros (50-16) | Miguel Dominguez | Wilfredo Sánchez, Henequeneros (.351) |
| 1971 | Azucareros (49-16) | Servio Borges | Rigoberto Rosique, Henequeneros (.352) |
| 1972 | Azucareros (52-14) | Servio Borges | Elpidio Mancebo, Mineros (.327) |
| 1973 | Industriales (53-25) | Pedro Chávez | Eusebio Cruz, Camaguey (.341) |
| 1974 | Habana (52-26) | Jorge Trigoura | Rigoberto Rosique, Henequeneros (.347) |
| 1975 | Agricultores (24-15) | Orlando Leroux | Fermín Laffita, Cafetaleros (.396) |
| 1976 | Ganaderos (29-9) | Carlos Gómez | Wilfredo Sánchez, Citricultores (.365) |
| 1977 | Citricultores (26-12) | Juan Bregio | Eulogio Osorio, Agricultores (.359) |
| 1978 | Vegueros (36-14) | José Pineda | Fernando Sánchez, Henequeneros (.394) |
| 1979 | Sancti Spíritus (39-12) | Cándido Andrade | Wilfredo Sánchez, Citricultores (.377) |
| 1980 | Santiago de Cuba (35-16) | Manuel Miyar | Rodolfo Puente, Metropolitanos (.394) |
| 1981 | Vegueros (36-15) | José Pineda | Amando Zamora, Villa Clara (.394) |
| 1982 | Vegueros (36-15) | Jorge Fuentes | Fernando Hernández, Vegueros (.376) |
| 1983 | Villa Clara (41-8) | Eduardo Martín | Juan Hernández, Forestales (.367) |
| 1984 | Citricultores (52-23) | Tomás Soto | Wilfredo Sánchez, Citricultores (.385) |
| 1985 | Vegueros (57-18) | Jorge Fuentes | Omar Linares, Vegueros (.409) |
| 1986 | Industriales (37-11) (6-0)* | Pedro Chávez | Omar Linares, Vegueros (.426) |
| 1987 | Vegueros (34-13) (5-1) | Jorge Fuentes | Javier Méndez, Industriales (.408) |
| 1988 | Vegueros (39-9) (5-1) | Jorge Fuentes | Pedro José Rodríguez, Habana (.446) |
| 1989 | Santiago de Cuba (29-19) (5-1) | Higinio Vélez | Juan Bravo, Industriales (.414) |
| 1990 | Henequeneros (37-11) (4-2) | Gerardo Junco | Omar Linares, Vegueros (.442) |
| 1991 | Henequeneros (33-15) (6-1) | Gerardo Junco | Lázaro Madera, Vegueros (.400) |
| 1992 | Industriales (36-12) (7-1) | Jorge Trigoura | Omar Linares, Vegueros (.442) |
| 1993 | Villa Clara (42-23) (8-3) | Pedro Jova | Omar Linares, Pinar del Río (.446) |
| 1994 | Villa Clara (43-22) (8-5) | Pedro Jova | Lourdes Gourriel, Sancti Spíritus (.395) |
| 1995 | Villa Clara (44-18) (8-2) | Pedro Jova | Amado Zamora, Villa Clara (.395) |
| 1996 | Villa Clara (48-17) | Pedro Jova | Luís Ulacia, Camaguey (.421) |
| 1997 | Pinar del Río (50-15) (8-2) | Jorge Fuentes | José Estrada, Matanzas (.391) |
| 1998 | Pinar del Río (56-34) | Alfonso Urquíola | Roberquis Videaux, Guantánamo (.393) |

*Playoff between Western and Eastern Division winners to determine champion after 1986 (Postseason record in parentheses)

## NATIONAL SERIES CHAMPIONSHIPS (PROVINCIAL)

| Years | Home Runs Leader | Base Hits Leader | ERA Leader (Innings) |
|-------|------------------|------------------|----------------------|
| 1962 | Rolando Valdés, Orientsales (3) | Urbano González, Occidentales (40) | Antonio Rubio (1.39) (45.1) |
| 1963 | Rolando Valdés, Orientales (5) | Fidel Linares, Occidentales (36) | Modesto Verdura (1.58) (79.2) |
| 1964 | Jorge Trigoura, Industriales (3) | Miguel Cuevas, Orientales (44) | Orlando Rubio (0.63) (57.1) |
| 1965 | Miguel Cuevas, Granjeros (5) | Lino Betancourt, Industriales (56) | Maximiliano Reyes (1.57) (63.0) |
| 1966 | Lino Betancourt, Henequeneros (9) | Urbano González, Industriales (76) | Alfredo Street (1.09) (74.1) |
| 1967 | Erwin Walter, Centrales (7) | Pedro Chávez, Industriales (78) | Ihosvani Gallegos (0.80) (67.2) |
| 1968 | Felipe Sarduy, Granjeros (13) | Eulogio Osorio, Habana (129) | Braudilio Vinent (1.03) (122.1) |
| 1969 | Agustín Marquetti, Habana (19) | Wilfredo Sánchez, Henequeneros (140) | Roberto Valdés (1.03) (192.0) |
| 1970 | Raul Reyes, Industriales (10) | Wilfredo Sánchez, Henequeneros (98) | Rolando Castillo (0.60) (74.2) |
| 1971 | Miguel Cuevas, Granjeros (10) | Elpidio Mancebo, Mineros (77) | Manuel Hurtado (0.67) (107.2) |
| 1972 | Agustín Marquetti, Industriales (11) | Wilfredo Sánchez, Henequeneros (90) | Ihosvani Gallegos (0.37) (72.1) |
| 1973 | Armando Capiró, Habana (22) | Armando Capiró, Habana (95) | Braudilio Vinent (0.85) (191.2) |
| 1974 | Antonio Muñoz, Azucareros (19) | Lázaro Cabrera, Pinar del Río (97) | Juan Pérez (1.13) (151.1) |
| 1975 | Fernando Sánchez, Henequeneros (6) | Eulogio Osorio, Agricultores (58) | Walfrido Ruíz (0.61) (87.2) |
| 1976 | Antonio Muñoz, Azucareros (13) | Wilfredo Sánchez, Citricultores (62) | Omar Carrero (0.46) (78.0) |
| 1977 | Pedro José Rodríguez, Cienfuegos (9) | Armando Capiró, Metropolitanos (52) | Isidro Pérez (0.90) (60.1) |
| 1978 | Pedro José Rodríguez, Cienfuegos (13) | Julián Villar, Industriales (72) | José Riveira (0.82) (55.0) |
| 1979 | Pedro José Rodríguez, Cienfuegos (19) | Wilfredo Sánchez, Citricultores (80) | Nivaldo Pérez (0.90) (73.2) |
| 1980 | Luís Casanova, Vegueros (18) | Lourdes Gourriel, Sancti Spíritus (77) | José Sánchez (0.76) (83.1) |
| 1981 | Agustín Lescaille, Guantánamo (15) | Pablo Pérez, Isla de la Juventud (76) | Rogelio García (1.31) (116.2) |
| 1982 | Lázaro Junco, Citricultores (17) | Fernando Hernández, Vegueros (76) | Julio Romero (1.45) (112.0) |
| 1983 | Lázaro Junco, Citricultores (15) | Oscar Rodríguez, Guantánamo (71) | José Riveira (0.63) (57.0) |
| 1984 | Lázaro Junco, Citricultores (20) | Lázaro Vargas, Industriales (102) | Manuel Alvarez (1.17) (92.1) |
| 1985 | Lázaro Junco, Citricultores (24) | Amado Zamora, Villa Clara (115) | Andres Luís (1.67) (135.0) |
| 1986 | Reynaldo Fernández, Camaguey (18) | Lázaro Vargas, Industriales (75) | Jorge Luís Valdés (1.56) (115.1) |
| 1987 | Orestes Kindelán, Santiago (17) | Luís Alvarez Estrada, Las Tunas (66) | René Arocha (1.31) (113.0) |
| 1988 | Lázaro Junco, Henequeneros (25) | Pedro Luís Rodríguez, Habana (87) | Rogelio García (2.21) (81.1) |
| 1989 | Orestes Kindelán, Santiago (24) | Luís Alberto Guerra, Vegueros (78) | Lázaro Valle (1.93) (70.0) |
| 1990 | Ermidelio Urrutia, Las Tunas (20) | José Estrada, Henequeneros (77) | Jorge Fumero (1.44) (62.1) |
| 1991 | Lázaro Junco, Henequeneros (17) | Eddy Rojas, Villa Clara (66) | José Ibar (1.73) (78.0) |
| 1992 | Romelio Martínez, Habana (19) | Luís González, Habana (71) | Osvaldo Fernández (1.19) (113) |
| 1993 | Lázaro Junco, Matanzas (27) | Remberto Rosell, Cienfuegos (100) | Jorge Pérez (1.74) (108.1) |
| 1994 | Lázaro Junco, Matanzas (21) | Pedro Luís Rodríguez, Habana (100) | Osvaldo Fernández (1.62) (105) |
| 1995 | Miguel Cáldes, Camaguey (20) | Alex Ramos, Isla de la Juventud (100) | Rolando Arrojo (1.88) (86.0) |
| 1996 | Ariel Benavides, Guantánamo (25) | Jorge Safrán, Metropolitanos (106) | Jorge Fumero (1.94) (65.0) |
| 1997 | Julio Fernández, Matanzas (15) | José Estrada, Matanzas (104) | Pedro Luís Lazo (1.15) (109.1) |
| 1998 | Oscar Machado, Villa Clara (24) | Roger Poll, Ciego de Avila (125) | José Ibar (1.51) (196.1) |

# SELECT SERIES TEAM CHAMPIONSHIPS (SUPER-PROVINCIAL)

| Years | Champion | Record | Manager | |
|---|---|---|---|---|
| 1975 | Orientales | 33-21 .612 | José Carrillo | |
| 1976 | Habana | 53-25 .679 | Roberto Ledo | |
| 1977 | Camagueyanos | 36-18 .667 | Carlos Gómez | |
| 1978 | Las Villas | 35-25 .583 | Eduardo Martín | |
| 1979 | Pinar del Río | 40-20 .667 | José Pineda | |
| 1980 | Pinar del Río | 39-20 .661 | José Pineda | |
| 1981 | Orientales | 38-21 .644 | Carlos Martí | |
| 1982 | Pinar del Río | 35-22 .614 | Jorge Fuentes | |
| 1983 | Las Villas | 42-18 .700 | Eduardo Martín | |
| 1984 | Pinar del Río | 28-15 .651 | Jorge Fuentes | |
| 1985 | Las Villas | 26-19 .578 | Eduardo Martín | |
| 1986 | Serranos | 41-22 .651 | Fernando Reynaldo | |
| 1987 | Serranos | 42-21 .667 | Higinio Vélez | |
| 1988 | Pinar del Río | 40-23 .635 | Jorge Fuentes | |
| 1989 | Las Villas | 45-18 .714 | Amando Triana | |
| 1990 | Ciudad Habana | 46-17 .730 | Servio Borges | |
| 1991 | Pinar del Río | 41-22 .651 | Jorge Fuentes | |
| 1992 | Serranos | 4-3 .750 | Higinio Vélez | (Championship by playoff) |
| 1993 | Orientales | 4-2 .667 | Fernande Reynaldo | (Championship by playoff) |
| 1994 | Occidentales | 27-18 .600 | Jorge Fuentes | |

# INDIVIDUAL CAREER LEADERS IN CASTRO'S CUBA
# (BASED ON SELECT SERIES AND NATIONAL SERIES) (1962-98)

| Career Individual Batting Records | | Career Individual Pitching Records | |
|---|---|---|---|
| National Series | Antonio Muñoz (24) | National Series | Braudilio Vinent (20) |
| Games | Fernando Sánchez (1994) | Games | Jorge Luís Valdés (514) |
| Innings | Sergio Quesada (16,702.1) | Games Started | Jorge Luís Valdés (412) |
| At Bats | Antonio Muñoz (8377) | Complete Games | Braudilio Vinent (265) |
| Runs | Omar Linares (1390) | Relief Apprearances | Euclides Rojas (342) |
| Hits | Fernando Sánchez (2215) | Wins | Jorge Luís Valdéz (234) |
| | Wilfredo Sánchez (2174) | | Braudilio Vinent (221) |
| Batting Average | Omar Linares (.371) | Losses | Braudilio Vinent (167) |
| Doubles | Antonio Muñoz (355) | Winning Percentage | Orlando Hernández (.728) |
| Triples | Evencer Godínez Soria (81) | Shutouts | Braudilio Vinent (63) |
| HRs | Orestes Kindelán (430) | Saves | Euclides Rojas (90) |
| Total Bases | Antonio Muñoz (3569) | Innings Pitched | Braudilio Vinent (3259.2) |
| Slugging | Omar Linares (.661) | Strikeouts | Rogelio García (2499) |
| Steals | Victor Mesa (588) | Bases on Balls | Rogelio García (1077) |
| RBI | Antonio Muñoz (1407) | ERA | José Huelga (1.50) |
| Sacrifice Bunts | Giraldo González (125) | Runs Allowed | Jorge Luís Valdés (1332) |
| Sacrifice Flies | Victor Mesa (76) | Wild Pitches | Jorge Luís Valdés (189) |

## (ACTIVE CUBAN BIG-LEAGUE PLAYERS APPEAR IN BOLDFACE)

| Name | Debut | Position | Debut Team | Big-League Seasons |
|------|-------|----------|------------|---------------------|
| Enrique Esteban Bellán | 1871 | Infielder | Troy Haymakers | 1871-73 (3) |
| Armando Marsans | 1911 | Outfielder | Cincinnati Reds | 1911-18 (8) |
| Rafael Almeida | 1911 | Outfielder | Cincinnati Reds | 1911-13 (3) |
| Mike (Miguel) González | 1912 | Catcher | Boston Braves | 1912, 1914-29,1931-32 (19) |
| Mérito (Baldomero) Acosta | 1913 | Outfielder | Washington Senators | 1913-16, 1918 (5) |
| Jack (Jacinto) Calvo | 1913 | Outfielder | Washington Senators | 1913, 1920 (2) |
| Angel "Pete" Aragón | 1914 | Infielder | New York Yankees | 1914, 1916-17 (3) |
| Adolfo Luque | 1914 | Pitcher | Boston Braves | 1914-15 (1918-35) (20) |
| Manolo (Manuel) Cueto | 1914 | Outfielder | Cincinnati Reds | 1914, 1917-19 (4) |
| Emilio Palmero | 1915 | Pitcher | New York Giants | 1915-16, 1921, 1926-28 (5) |
| Joseito Rodríguez | 1916 | Infielder | New York Giants | 1916-18 (3) |
| Eusebio González | 1918 | Shortstop | Boston Red Sox | 1918 (1) |
| Oscar Tuero | 1918 | Pitcher | St. Louis Cardinals | 1918-20 (3) |
| José Acosta | 1920 | Pitcher | Washington Senators | 1920-22 (3) |
| Ricardo Torres | 1920 | Catcher | Washington Senators | 1920-22 (3) |
| Pedro Dibut | 1924 | Pitcher | Cincinnati Reds | 1924-25 (2) |
| Ramón (Mike) Herrera | 1925 | Infielder | Boston Red Sox | 1925-26 (2) |
| Oscar Estrada | 1929 | Pitcher | St. Louis Browns | 1929 (1) |
| Roberto "Tarzán" Estalella | 1935 | Outfielder | Washington Senators | 1935-36, 1939, 1941-45 (8) |
| Mike (Fermín) Guerra | 1937 | Catcher | Washington Senators | 1937, 1944-51 (9) |
| Rene Monteagudo | 1938 | Pitcher | Washington Senators | 1938, 1940, 1945 (3) |
| Gilberto Torres | 1940 | Infielder | Washington Senators | 1940, 1944-46 (4) |
| Jack (Angel) Aragón | 1941 | Pinch Runner | New York Giants | 1941 (1) |
| Roberto Ortíz | 1941 | Outfielder | Washington Senators | 1941-44, 1949-50 (6) |
| Sal (Chico) Hernández | 1942 | Catcher | Chicago Cubs | 1942-43 (2) |
| Mosquito Ordeñana | 1943 | Shortstop | Pittsburgh Pirates | 1943 (1) |
| Nap (Napoleón) Reyes | 1943 | Infielder | New York Giants | 1943-45, 1950 (4) |
| Tomás (Tommy) de la Cruz | 1944 | Pitcher | Cincinnati Reds | 1944 (1) |
| Preston (Pedro) Gómez | 1944 | Infielder | Washington Senators | 1944 (1) |
| Baby (Oliverio) Ortíz | 1944 | Pitcher | Washington Senators | 1944 (1) |
| Luís Suárez | 1944 | Third Base | Washington Senators | 1944 (1) |
| Santiago (Carlos) Ullrich | 1944 | Pitcher | Washington Senators | 1944-45 (2) |
| Roy (Rogelio) Valdés | 1944 | Pinch Hitter | Washington Senators | 1944 (1) |
| Jorge (Poncho) Comellas | 1945 | Pitcher | Chicago Cubs | 1945 (1) |
| Sid (Isidoro) León | 1945 | Pitcher | Philadelphia Phillies | 1945 (1) |
| Armando Roche | 1945 | Pitcher | Washington Senators | 1945 (1) |
| Adrián Zabala | 1945 | Pitcher | New York Giants | 1945, 1949 (2) |
| José Zardón | 1945 | Outfielder | Washington Senators | 1945 (1) |
| Reggie (Regino) Otero | 1945 | First Base | Chicago Cubs | 1945 (1) |
| Angel Fleitas | 1948 | Shortstop | Washington Senators | 1948 (1) |
| Moín (Ramon) García | 1948 | Pitcher | Washington Senators | 1948 (1) |
| Enrique (Julio) González | 1949 | Pitcher | Washington Senators | 1949 (1) |
| Minnie (Orestes) Miñoso | 1949 | Outfielder | Cleveland Indians | 1949, 1951-64, 1976 (17) |

| | | | | |
|---|---|---|---|---|
| Witto (Luís) Aloma | 1950 | Pitcher | Chicago White Sox | 1950-53 (4) |
| Sandy (Sandalio) Consuegra | 1950 | Pitcher | Washington Senators | 1950-57 (8) |
| Connie (Conrado) Marrero | 1950 | Pitcher | Washington Senators | 1950-54 (5) |
| Limonar (Rogelio) Martínez | 1950 | Pitcher | Washington Senators | 1950 (1) |
| Julio Moreno | 1950 | Pitcher | Washington Senators | 1950-53 (4) |
| Carlos Pascual | 1950 | Pitcher | Washington Senators | 1950 (1) |
| Cisco (Francisco) Campos | 1951 | Outfielder | Washington Senators | 1951-53 (3) |
| Willie (Guillermo) Miranda | 1951 | Shortstop | Washington Senators | 1951-59 (9) |
| Ray (Rafael) Noble | 1951 | Catcher | New York Giants | 1951-53 (3) |
| Sandy (Edmundo) Amorós | 1952 | Outfielder | Brooklyn Dodgers | 1952, 1954-57, 1959-60 (7) |
| Mike (Miguel) Fornieles | 1952 | Pitcher | Washington Senators | 1952-63 (12) |
| Héctor Rodríguez | 1952 | Third Base | Chicago White Sox | 1952 (1) |
| Raul Sánchez | 1952 | Pitcher | Washington Senators | 1952, 1957, 1960 (3) |
| Carlos Paula | 1954 | Outfielder | Washington Senators | 1954-56 (3) |
| Camilio Pascual | 1954 | Pitcher | Washington Senators | 1954-71 (18) |
| Vicente Amor | 1955 | Pitcher | Chicago Cubs | 1955, 1957 (2) |
| Julio Becquer | 1955 | First Base | Washington Senators | 1955, 1957-61, 1963 (7) |
| Juan Delís | 1955 | Third Base | Washington Senators | 1955 (1) |
| Lino Donoso | 1955 | Pitcher | Pittsburgh Pirates | 1955-56 (2) |
| Wenceslao González | 1955 | Pitcher | Washington Senators | 1955 (1) |
| Román Mejías | 1955 | Outfielder | Pittsburgh Pirates | 1955, 1957-64 (9) |
| Pedro (Pete) Ramos | 1955 | Pitcher | Washington Senators | 1955-70 (16) |
| José (Joe) Valdivielso | 1955 | Shortstop | Washington Senators | 1955-56, 1959-61 (5) |
| Humberto (Chico) Fernández | 1956 | Shortstop | Brooklyn Dodgers | 1956-63 (8) |
| Evelio Hernández | 1956 | Pitcher | Washington Senators | 1956-57 (2) |
| Cholly (Lazaro) Naranjo | 1956 | Pitcher | Pittsburgh Pirates | 1956 (1) |
| Rene Valdéz | 1957 | Pitcher | Brooklyn Dodgers | 1957 (1) |
| Ossie (Oswaldo) Alvarez | 1958 | Infielder | Washington Senators | 1958-59 (2) |
| Pancho (Juan) Herrera | 1958 | First Base | Philadelphia Phillies | 1958, 1960-61 (3) |
| Dan (Daniel) Morejón | 1958 | Outfielder | Cincinnati Reds | 1958 (1) |
| Orlando Peña | 1958 | Pitcher | Cincinnati Reds | 1958-75 (18) |
| Freddy Rodríguez | 1958 | Pitcher | Chicago Cubs | 1958-59 (2) |
| Tony (Antonio) Taylor | 1958 | Infielder | Chicago Cubs | 1958-76 (19) |
| Rudy (Rodolfo) Arias | 1959 | Pitcher | Chicago White Sox | 1959 (1) |
| Mike (Miguel) Cuéllar | 1959 | Pitcher | Cincinnati Reds | 1959, 1964-77 (15) |
| Zoilo (Zorro) Versalles | 1959 | Shortstop | Washington Senators | 1959-71 (13) |
| Borrego (Rogelio) Alvarez | 1960 | First Base | Cincinnati Reds | 1960, 1962 (2) |
| Joe (Joaquin) Azcue | 1960 | Infielder | Cincinnati Reds | 1960, 1962-70, 1972 (11) |
| Ed (Eduardo) Bauta | 1960 | Pitcher | St. Louis Cardinals | 1960-64 (5) |
| Leo (Leonardo) Cárdenas | 1960 | Infielder | Cincinnati Reds | 1960-75 (16) |
| Mike (Miguel) de la Hoz | 1960 | Infielder | Cleveland Indians | 1960-67, 1969 (9) |
| Tony (Antonio) González | 1960 | Infielder | Cincinnati Reds | 1960-71 (12) |
| Héctor Maestri | 1960 | Pitcher | Washington Senators | 1960-61 (2) |
| Leo (Leopoldo) Posada | 1960 | Outfielder | Kansas City Athletics | 1960-62 (3) |
| Berto (Dagoberto) Cueto | 1961 | Pitcher | Minnesota Twins | 1961 (1) |
| Manny (Manuel) Montejo | 1961 | Pitcher | Detroit Tigers | 1961 (1) |
| Héctor (Rodolfo) Martínez | 1962 | Outfielder | Kansas City Athletics | 1962-63 (2) |
| Marty (Orlando) Martínez | 1962 | Infielder | Minnesota Twins | 1962, 1967-72 (7) |

| | | | | |
|---|---|---|---|---|
| Orlando McFarlane | 1962 | Catcher | Pittsburgh Pirates | 1962, 1964, 1966-68 (5) |
| Tony (Pedro) Oliva | 1962 | Outfielder | Minnesota Twins | 1962-76 (15) |
| Cookie (Octavio) Rojas | 1962 | Infielder | Cincinnati Reds | 1962-77 (16) |
| Diego Seguí | 1962 | Pitcher | Kansas City Athletics | 1962-77 (16) |
| José Tartabull | 1962 | Outfielder | Kansas City Athletics | 1962-70 (9) |
| José Cardenal | 1963 | Infielder | San Francisco Giants | 1963-80 (18) |
| Marcelino López | 1963 | Pitcher | Philadelphia Phillies | 1963, 1965-67, 1969-72 (8) |
| Tony (Gabriel) Martínez | 1963 | Infielder | Cleveland Indians | 1963-66 (4) |
| Aurelio Monteagudo | 1963 | Pitcher | Kansas City Athletics | 1963-67, 1970, 1973 (7) |
| Bert Campaneris | 1964 | Shortstop | Kansas City Athletics | 1964-83 (20) |
| Tany (Atanasio) Pérez | 1964 | Infielder | Cincinnati Reds | 1964-86 (23) |
| Chico Ruiz | 1964 | Infielder | Cincinnati Reds | 1964-71 (8) |
| Luís Tiant, Jr. | 1964 | Pitcher | Cleveland Indians | 1964-82 (19) |
| Paul (Paulino) Casanova | 1965 | Catcher | Washington Senators | 1965-74 (10) |
| Tito (Rigoberto) Fuentes | 1965 | Outfielder | San Francisco Giants | 1965-67, 1969-78 (13) |
| Jackie (Jacinto) Hernández | 1965 | Shortstop | California Angels | 1965-73 (9) |
| Sandy (Hilario) Valdespino | 1965 | Outfielder | Minnesota Twins | 1965-71 (7) |
| José Ramón López | 1966 | Pitcher | California Angels | 1966 (1) |
| Minnie (Minervino) Rojas | 1966 | Pitcher | California Angels | 1966-68 (3) |
| Hank (Enrique) Izquierdo | 1967 | Catcher | Minnesota Twins | 1967 (1) |
| George (Jorge) Lauzerique | 1967 | Pitcher | Kansas City Athletics | 1967-70 (4) |
| José Arcia | 1968 | Infielder | Chicago Cubs | 1968-70 (3) |
| Chico (Lorenzo) Fernández | 1968 | Infielder | Baltimore Orioles | 1968 (1) |
| José Martínez | 1969 | Infielder | Pittsburgh Pirates | 1969-70 (2) |
| Minnie Mendoza | 1970 | Infielder | Minnesota Twins | 1970 (1) |
| Oscar Zamora | 1974 | Pitcher | Chicago Cubs | 1974-76, 1978 (4) |
| Orlando González | 1976 | First Base | Cleveland Indians | 1976, 1978, 1980 (3) |
| Bobby (Roberto) Ramos | 1978 | Catcher | Montreal Expos | 1978, 1980-84 (6) |
| Leo (Leonard) Sutherland | 1980 | Outfielder | Chicago White Sox | 1980, 1981 (2) |
| Bárbaro Garbey | 1984 | Outfielder | Detroit Tigers | 1984-85, 1988 (3) |
| **José Canseco** | **1985** | **Outfielder** | **Oakland Athletics** | **1985-98 (14)** |
| **Rafael Palmeiro** | **1986** | **First Base** | **Chicago Cubs** | **1986-98 (13)** |
| Orestes Destrade | 1987 | First Base | New York Yankees | 1987-88, 1993 (3) |
| Nelson Santovenia | 1987 | Catcher | Montreal Expos | 1987-93 (7) |
| Israel Sánchez | 1988 | Pitcher | Kansas City Royals | 1988, 1990 (2) |
| **Tony (Emilio) Fossas** | **1988** | **Pitcher** | **Texas Rangers** | **1988-98 (11)** |
| Ozzie Canseco | 1990 | Outfielder | Oakland Athletics | 1990, 1992 (2) |
| Tony Menéndez | 1992 | Pitcher | Cincinnati Reds | 1992 (1) |
| **Rene Arocha** | **1993** | **Pitcher** | **St. Louis Cardinals** | **1993-97 (5)** |
| **Ariel Prieto** | **1995** | **Pitcher** | **Oakland Athletics** | **1995-98 (4)** |
| **Osvaldo Fernández** | **1996** | **Pitcher** | **San Francisco Giants** | **1996-98 (3)** |
| **Rey Ordoñez** | **1996** | **Shortstop** | **New York Mets** | **1996-98 (3)** |
| **Livan Hernández** | **1996** | **Pitcher** | **Florida Marlins** | **1996-98 (3)** |
| **Elieser (Eli) Marrero** | **1997** | **Catcher** | **St. Louis Cardinals** | **1997-98 (2)** |
| **Rolando Arrojo** | **1998** | **Pitcher** | **Tampa Bay Devil Rays** | **1998 (1)** |
| **Orlando Hernández** | **1998** | **Pitcher** | **New York Yankees** | **1998 (1)** |
| **Vladimir Nuñez** | **1998** | **Pitcher** | **Arizona Diamondbacks** | **1998 (1)** |

# CUBAN BASEBALL HALL OF FAME, HAVANA

## (PLAYERS, FOUNDERS, OFFICIALS SELECTED BEFORE 1962)

1939  Luís Bustamente, José de la Caridad Méndez, Antonio Márquez Garcia, Gervasio "Strike" González, Armando Marsans, Rafael Almeida, Valentín González, Cristóbal Torriente, Adolfo Luján, Carlos Royer
1940  Alfredo Arcaño, José Muñoz
1941  Emilio Sabourín, Regino García
1942  Agustín Molina, Alfredo "El Pájaro" Cabrera
1943  Luís Padrón, Eliodoro Hidalgo, Julián Castillo
1944  Carlos Maciá, Alejandro Oms
1945  Ramón Calzadilla, Carlos Morán, José "Juan" Pastoriza, Valentín Dreke, Bernardo Baró
1946  Wenceslao Gálvez, Ricardo Caballero, Rogelio Valdés, Arturo Valdés, Francisco Poyo
1948  Juan Antiga, Antonio Mesa, Tomás Romañach, Jacinto Calvo, Rafael Hernández, Nemesio Guillot
1949  Eduardo Machado, Julio López, Pelayo Chacón, Gonzalo Sánchez, Manuel Villa
1950  Eugenio Jiménez, Eustaquio Gutiérrez, Rafael Figarola, Manuel Cueto, Ricardo Martínez
1951  Martín Dihigo, José Maria Teuma, Alfredo Arango, Bienvenido Jiménez, José Rodríguez
1953  Moisés Quintero, Juan Violá, Carlos Zaldo
1954  Emilio Palmero, Pablo Ronquillo
1955  Baldmero "Mérito" Acosta
1956  Miguel Angel González
1957  Emilio Palomino, Isidro Fabré
1958  Adolfo Luque
1959  Lázaro Salazar, José Acosta
1960  Ramón Bragaña, Armando Cabañas
1961  Oscar Rodríguez, Tomás de la Cruz

## CUBAN BASEBALL BIBLIOGRAPHY

Alonso, Alfredo Santana. *El Inmortal del Béisbol: Martín Dihigo*. Havana: Editorial Cientifico-Técnica, 1998.

Bjarkman, Peter C. *Baseball with a Latin Beat: A History of the Latin American Game*. Jefferson, NC, and London: McFarland & Company Publishers, 1994.

Bjarkman, Peter C. *Baseball and Castro's Revolution*. Jefferson, NC, and London: McFarland & Company Publishers, to appear (2000).

Delgado, Gabino and Severo Nieto. *Béisbol Cubano, 1878-1955: Records and Estadisticas*. Havana: Editorial Lex, 1955. (Spanish text)

González Echevarria, Roberto. *The Pride of Havana: A History of Cuban Baseball*. New York and London: Oxford University Press, 1999.

*Guía Oficial de Béisbol, Cuba 1998*. (*Official Cuban League Baseball Guide*). Havana: Editorial Deportes (INDER), 1998.

*Memoria de los Campeonatos Mundiales de Béisbol Aficionado*. (*Recollections of the World Amateur Baseball Championships*). Havana: Ediciones Deportivas (INDER), 1971.

Muro, Raúl Diez. *Liga de Base Ball Profesional Cubana*. (*Cuban Professional Baseball League Guidebook*). Havana, 1949.

Padura, Leonardo and Raúl Arce. *Estrellas del Béisbol* (*Baseball Stars*). Havana: Editoria Abril, 1989. (Spanish text)

Senzel, Howard. *Baseball and the Cold War: Being a Soliloquy on the Necessity of Baseball in the Life of a Serious Student of Marx and Hegel from Rochester, New York*. New York: Harcourt, Brace Jovanovich, 1977.

Torres, Angel. *La Leyenda del Béisbol Cubano, 1878-1997*. (*The Legend of Cuban Baseball*). Montebello, California, 1996. (Spanish text)

Torres, Angel. *La Historia del Béisbol Cubano, 1878-1976*. (*The Story of Cuban Baseball*). Los Angeles, California, 1976. (Spanish text)